MOZART IN MOTION

MOZART IN MOTION

*His Work
and His World
in Pieces*

PATRICK MACKIE

FARRAR, STRAUS AND GIROUX   NEW YORK

Farrar, Straus and Giroux
120 Broadway, New York 10271

Printed in the United States of America
Originally published in 2021 by Granta Books, Great Britain
Published in the United States by Farrar, Straus and Giroux
First American edition, 2023

Library of Congress Cataloging-in-Publication Data
Names: Mackie, Patrick, 1974– author.
Title: Mozart in motion : his work and his world in pieces / Patrick Mackie.
Description: First American edition. | New York : Farrar, Straus and Giroux, 2023. |
    Includes bibliographical references and index.
Identifiers: LCCN 2023000088 | ISBN 9780374606206 (hardback)
Subjects: LCSH: Mozart, Wolfgang Amadeus, 1756–1791. | Mozart, Wolfgang
    Amadeus, 1756–1791—Criticism and interpretation. | Composers—Austria—
    Biography. | Music—Europe—18th century—History and criticism. |
    LCGFT: Biographies.
Classification: LCC ML410.M9 M33 2023 | DDC 780.92 [B]—dc23/eng/20230103
LC record available at https://lccn.loc.gov/2023000088

www.fsgbooks.com
www.twitter.com/fsgbooks • www.facebook.com/fsgbooks

1 3 5 7 9 10 8 6 4 2

Contents

I

II

III

I

1

In Motion

Don Giovanni

Opening nights of new operas may be the most fraught of all. So many things have to go right. The paint must have dried on the backdrops, the soprano's throat must be clear of infections and the tenor of overly distracting fits of pique. The orchestral players must be confident that their strings or reeds will behave themselves. Enough copies of the score must have gone out, and everyone needs to know which big aria has been cut at the last minute. Large amounts of money hinge on the airy stuff that musical performance comprises. An eerie tension awaits anyone without enough to do; but everyone generally has far too much to do. No one can control how the audience will react, though sometimes in the eighteenth-century sections would be paid to get their reactions right. Mozart's era often left it unclear who was meant to be in charge of this broadly purposeful chaos; the role of the conductor had for one thing not yet attained its later clarity. As the first notes got closer, an entire social world was readying itself to be funnelled into drama and music.

In the autumn of 1787 an impresario called Pasquale Bondini may or may not have felt in control of such a night. He ran the resident opera company at the recently built Nostitz theatre in Prague whose success earlier in the year with a staging of *Le nozze di Figaro* quickly led him and his co-director to commission a new Mozart opera. It seems to have been Mozart who gravitated towards the figure of Don Juan and the old Spanish folk tales about his lascivious career that had already inspired literary and operatic versions across the century. Prague had adored Mozart's rampantly expansive, vertiginously original opera about the rebellious valet Figaro, so it must have struck him as a good place to hit with an even more drastic reinterpretation of his world's cultural possibilities. The composer was a local hero in Prague at a point when he and Vienna were unsure how enthusiastic they remained about each other. Writing the opera for somewhere other than the imperial capital might have seemed a retreat if he had not used it to leap into yet more artistic freedom, and his popularity in Bohemia must have charged the mood and raised the stakes for this first night. In *Don Giovanni*, his fusions of elegance with fieriness speak with almost painful directness of an artistic desire both to summarize his culture and to move it onwards.

Mozart would have been vibrantly hard to pin down on this first night, a small and indistinct man caught up in a blur of needs and actions, hardly visible once he had taken charge of the music and his dark creation was beginning to unfurl. The opera wheels through eighteenth-century conventions and reference points, but the score could not be more distinctly his, treating them with a copious freedom that renders them luminous. His daily levels of nervous energy must have helped keep him free of any great nervousness on even the biggest musical nights. But lashing excitement among the audience and the orchestra does seem to have marked the launch of *Don Giovanni*, after hitches and delays that cannot have lessened the feeling that something major was coming. The fierce blazonry with which the overture opens declares the opera's high stakes. Nervous tension is on the agenda for anyone listening. Something new was in motion within the opera, but its innovations are cloaked and refracted by atavism and a sumptuous feel for conventions. Its early audiences were exhilarated and bewildered.

Mozart's new opera finally premiered very late in October; the richly dressed listeners would have met with murky, bumpy streets around the opera house as seven o'clock approached. The imperial governor's own money had built the theatre a handful of years earlier, a space ready for novelty, in a city chafing against decades of indifference or even neglect from its Habsburg rulers in Vienna. A restless underlying resentment and a skittering cultural inventiveness pervaded the Bohemian capital, making it the perfect landing place for such an exuberantly complex opera. Erratic, smoky light would have drifted around an auditorium only barely separated from backstage chaos as the opera's action opened. In Mozart's century an audience did not stop being noisy and sociable just because the performance was under way; it may often have given them something else to talk about. Maybe Mozart felt some burst of control once the thing had started, as he willed the music onwards and coaxed his performers on. But the opera was also now ceasing to be his. At the heights of art power and its loss can join hands.

The opera's shadowy overture throws it into events in which sex, violence, comedy and loss briskly overlap. Giovanni's flight from one of his exploits brings him face to face with Donna Elvira, an abandoned lover who has been on his trail. He abandons her again now and leaves his manservant and sidekick Leporello to deal with her. We may feel momentarily disappointed that Giovanni has left the stage; the opera depends on his charisma and our appalled fascination with him. But the aria that Leporello comes up with is the point at which the opera becomes as fully itself as Giovanni is irreparably himself, as it fuses charm with power and drastic moral truthfulness. It is known as the 'catalogue' aria because it inflicts on Elvira an expansive, brutally playful enumeration of the lovers or victims that Giovanni has left behind. An ambiguous courtly swagger fizzes through Mozart's music as it streams through arch and aching shifts of pace and texture; its artfulness is both dizzying and dizzy as mischief and cruelty embroil it. Comedy and bleakness mix in Leporello's voice, and the nearly sobbing tenderness that seems close whenever he mentions Spain is punctured by the aria's punchline, as he gives the appallingly precise number of one thousand and three for his boss's successes in that famously devout country. Elvira needs to hear who this man is, and even those in the audience familiar with the story need to hear his rapacity rampantly set out. But the awful truth is delivered here in a vein of brisk, outrageous comedy by a waggishly officious manservant. Whose side are these frisky violins on?

The opening of a new opera brought the disparate, spinning social and cultural forces of late eighteenth-century Europe together like no other occasion, and in this aria Mozart satisfies all the motives of pleasure and excitement that took people to the opera while also turning them inside out. Europe was wavering on the brink of the modern world, and Mozart became the key artist of the modern world because his music was so richly fired by so many of the factors and energies at work in this process. Sometimes this Europe was as elegant as its nicest fictions claimed and sometimes it was as violent as its turbulent dreams suggested; the revolution in France whetted the culture's vastest hopes, but using the guillotine became official policy there just a few months after the composer's death. Mozart was the sharpest analyst of this world, and his music lets us listen in to the heartbeat and the brainwaves of modern experience in the throes of its emergence. Extremes of skill and originality are needed to represent a world as teeming and fluctile as his was as richly as he did. Mozart guides us through his restless historical world, and thinking more deeply about the world in which he worked should also change how we hear his music; our ears should open to more of what those beautiful sounds chase after.

The impact of Leporello's aria comes partly from the acute, rueful parallels hidden within it between the seducer's voracity and the hunger for experiences, styles and vistas that powers Mozart's music. Giovanni's manservant runs through a list of countries that have hosted his employer's conquests, and gives us a prancing tour of the social classes and physical types indiscriminately pulled in. Mozart's music is likewise expansively cosmopolitan and dashingly inclusive of influences and registers and possible listeners; sometimes it is all but desperately eager to please. Eighteenth-century music had readied itself for him by making itself the place where the culture could advance its possibilities with the utmost sophistication and ambition, at the same time as wildly enjoying itself. Music moved across boundaries and carried vistas of freedom more profusely even than the ideas of the French *philosophes* or the English novel's cult of passionate sentiment. Mozart drew deeply on the craze for Italian styles of vocal music that had poured across Europe as the era's most ardent cultural movement. Rapturous fandom and often rancorous controversy greeted such music across the culture, as it was carried far beyond Italy, and taken on or revised by musicians and singers from any number of centres. It enchanted popular audiences and the most backward courts and the most ambitious intellectual circles; the prominence of women singers and of castratos made it a sphere in which singular versions of individuality could make their dazzling voices heard. The liquid hedonism of this music, its technical bravura and its sophistication of outlook had taken it to the heart of cultural life in staunchly monarchical Lisbon and heatedly bourgeois Amsterdam, and up into the unlikely cultural revolution imposed by Catherine the Great in Russia.

The most ambitious surges of musical form were electrically joined to the biggest social and political questions. At the same time Mozart's need to sell himself, the headiness with which he worked and his position as both a composer and a performer make his music sharply porous to how he lived or what he thought or suffered. Mozart's music processes and swivels between any number of needs and reference points and agendas, keeping new compositional ideas or influences spinning alongside professional exigencies and ethical or personal dilemmas or interests, and larger historical forces and trends. His endless capacity for polish and finesse allowed him an endless imaginative multifariousness, and the result is that his music comes to us bearing dazzling questions. How does one thrive in a world full of change? How can people pursue new flavours of liberty while remaining generous and faithful? Can we combine high aristocratic tastes with commitments to democratic openness? We can find in an aria an account of how to move from lament to possibilities of personal change, in a chamber work ways of reconciling intellectual density with pleasure and panache, and in an orchestral piece recognition of our need for both pluralism and coherence. At the core of Mozart's work is the attempt to reckon with the coming of the modern world, and the point of modernity is that it will be full of questions, about itself and everything that it contains or touches. A modern world breaks from its past and wants to know where that will leave it, or take it. New visions of culture based on innovation and change were taking shape all around him. In fact he was shaping them more deeply and playfully than anyone, because music was both the highest promise of happiness that his world gave to itself and the finest disguise that its more radical inclinations ever found.

Mozart was pulled between historical worlds, suspended between a deep but sceptical attachment to the patchwork of courts and hierarchies that made up the Europe into which he emerged, and deep intimations of the versions of freedom and selfhood and power that were on their way. Sometimes these intimations were euphoric and sometimes they were troubled. Mozart was deeply conventional yet driven to extremes of originality. He was highly ambitious but profligate with money and with his creative brilliance; he was a joker who was also capable of deep solemnity and severe moral earnestness. If we want to know how to live amid historical suspense, or how to be simultaneously serious and light-hearted in response to the dilemmas of our lives, Mozart's music wants to show us. He could seem bewilderingly irresponsible himself, but his music became intricately answerable to opaque historical pressures, and to the pathos of human aspiration and disrepair. Mozart's world was up for grabs, debating everything from optics to grain trade regulations and the moral status of luxury. Rococo pleasure gardens and masked balls pulled towards one vision of modernity while reformist zeal and the beginnings of modern political science pulled towards another, and revolutionary conspiracies and the massive expansion of state power towards yet others. Unflinching excitement about the new suffuses Mozart's music, but it also longs for inclusiveness and coherence. Mozart was in on modernity at the point of its emergence, and he tells us not just about the world that he worked in but about how we have kept wavering since, and how we live now. One question is how much we now really want a world that could again be up for grabs.

The success with which the composer's music expressed its world has had paradoxical, disabling effects on how we listen to it. Mozart remains so culturally central that it can be hard to hear how volatile, strange, wilful or precarious his work can be. The sheer number of attitudes towards the modern world's swerving approach is one reason for the inexhaustibility of his music. But the trickier or darker aspects of his vision can end up being elided or skipped. His music loves the marketplace, relishing its vibrancy and willingness to give pleasure. The deep humanitarian pathos with which his work is riven involves not just moral protests against inequality and injustice, however, but surges of rebellious political desire. His music meditates on a world in which diverse visions janglingly coexist, but it also loves clearing the air for serene vistas of its own. It brims with the suggestion that another sort of modernity was once possible, one less vehement and crushing, one more plural and flexible. We often claim to despise the modern world that we have ended up in. Living without our contempt for our world can itself seem hard to imagine.

Listening to music is a strange act, and Mozart's music is an education fit for a world in motion and the selves in motion within it. The first night of *Don Giovanni* summarized his talent for swallowing his world whole. In one of many stories about his life as the opera emerged and flourished in Prague, Mozart's wife keeps him awake through the night before it opens, so that he can finish composing the overture. In another he jumps out and grapples with one of the glamorous singers in the middle of a rehearsal, in order to get her to scream with terror as her character should. In the background wanders Giacomo Casanova himself, towards the end of his career as an important intellectual and an epochal libertine, who at the time frequented similar circles in the city to the composer. He may well have attended this first performance, and he may have discussed with Mozart the dark story that the opera reconstrues, and its resonances for a society unsure of its moorings. Stories like these are clues to how much this opera mattered, and how much it took on. Mozart pours the culture's energies and wishes into a vision of the modern soul as endlessly on the run, ravaged by his own urges and powers. Giovanni's manservant tells his abandoned lover truths that she both needs to know and hates, and the music moves through riffs and cascades and bleakly sweet dips of momentum which assert a tough and dazzling argument about how complex pleasure is becoming. The catalogue aria is a painstakingly offhand endgame for eighteenth-century music and all its elaborately charged versions of fun and charm and passion. But this means firing up its own new and acute versions.

We cannot decide whether our own late modern world is too fluid or too stifling, too changeable or too relentless or too inert. Incessant change itself ends up feeling stifling, and it is not even clear whether this is a tragedy or a comedy or a farce. Mozart loved mixing the tragic with the comic and cogency with levity and despair with grace, and he knew that some of the most powerful responses to a creative work are fuelled by how much contradiction or multiplicity it contains. The vim and the comedy of the catalogue aria are as exhilarating as its picture of a continent with its values upended by one man's extravagant libido. But exhilaration is mixed here with cruelty, as the aria wheels through territories and categories with a spirit of violent flexibility drawn from Giovanni. Its expansiveness starts to feel grotesque, and so do the combinations of coolness and glee with which this odd manservant runs through the shadowy, crushing facts. The suaveness of the music leaves us nowhere to stand. Finally, the flighty, brutal mockery astir in the aria feels close to reaching out of the opera and turning on us. Are we inside or outside the world shown to us? We do not know whether to be fascinated or repulsed. The music is in motion and so is the opera's moral world; we listen in inexorable motion too.

2

A Beautiful Revenge

Piano Sonata in A minor

In Mozart's early twenties, he went to try his chances in the grand, enticing and difficult metropolis of Paris. He arrived in the spring of 1778 convinced of his unique powers, and hopeful that the city would provide a more fertile field for them than the spate of minor courts that he had recently been trying to impress. The young man must have cut a strange figure amid the fashionable power-brokers and high-speed gossips who thronged the city's musical circles. He was small with an odd mixture of dumpiness and eagerness to please. His preternatural intelligence and his feel for other people's characters could make him inordinately charming, but also push him into fits of high-handed provocation or zany humour. The snazziness with which he liked to dress may not have convinced the suave city's arbiters, and he was travelling with his mother, a fairly dowdy middle-aged lady from provincial Austria. Paris was in many ways the capital of the whole of Europe at this point, the place that defined the trends for the entire culture. It appeared the perfect place for a young composer who was beginning to grasp the largeness of his own ambition. But there were ways in which it was utterly wrong for him.

Who did Mozart think that he was in 1778 in Paris? He must have oscillated between feeling like a masterful virtuoso on tour and simply a young man in need of a job. To others he may have seemed sometimes a sort of tourist drinking in the grand city's culture, and at other times some odd combination of high emissary and needy refugee from Salzburg or the wider Habsburg sphere. All of these things and more were true of him. Extreme creativity can make life weirder and harder for its bearer precisely because it multiplies so many possibilities; someone like Mozart can find himself inventing obstacles that talents of lesser reach do not even envisage. His extreme talent made him both inordinately suited to his world and a constant anomaly within it. He could please anyone and create a welcome for himself anywhere, but could also be bristlingly proud or pedagogically assertive, or merely disdainful. Was Mozart in 1778 still meant to be a dazzling novelty playing cards of brio and impudence, or was he becoming one solid professional among others, whose track record may not always have seemed to explain his high sense of his own status and ambition? Someone so talented can be addicted to pleasing others and to disregarding or even jettisoning them too.

As the 1770s moved him towards Paris, Mozart had run through plenty of the obvious options. He had tried pushing his way up the ladder of service at his native Salzburg court, but had also tried pushing his music onto the agendas of more glamorous centres of culture within the larger German-speaking world, including the emerging powerhouse of Munich and the grand Habsburg capital of Vienna. He had dipped in and out of the maelstrom of possibilities thrown up by the Italian opera world. The milieux of Italian opera were relentlessly glamorous and enticing, but also fraught with hype and cliques, fragile deals and evaporating hopes. Court careers tended to be dourly attritional and at the same time hostage to political turbulence. The smoothly administered wealth and the cultural haughtiness of Paris might provide a more solid stage. But maybe the largest terror confronting Mozart was the thought that none of the available forums was big enough to satisfy his talents, to meet their continual demands for vast approval and extravagant new challenges. It is partly this terror that makes him so modern. A modern artist is someone in constant touch with insolidity, in all its sometimes grinding permanence. Mozart was finding that the harder he pushed his talent and the more questions he asked of it, the harder it became to know where his life was heading. He kept asking more of his talent, and more kept coming from it. Aspects of his life might have been easier if he had been able to find its limits, to determine once and for all what to do with it. Instead, the brilliance that was his foundation also removed the ground beneath him. A certain wheeling anger is built into much artistic greatness.

During the six months or so immediately leading up to his arrival in Paris, Mozart had been travelling with his mother among various small courts and musical centres of southern Germany, as he tried to figure out how to leave behind his backwater family base in Salzburg. His life on the road had become a peculiar mixture of scratching out an almost hand-to-mouth existence and enjoying luxurious access to the highest circles of politics and culture. A letter to his father Leopold describes a typical venture in February 1778 to play for the Princess of Nassau-Weilburg at Kirchheimbolanden. The trip meant flattering courtly treatment including an 'elegant, covered four-seater' in which to travel. But the tale deflates as he does 'not receive more than seven louis d'or' in the end. Reading his letters, we encounter someone addicted to the dazzling first impressions that he can keep making on processions of audiences and grandees, but who cannot relish the grind of enduring commitments. In Munich he considered developing a series of German operas, while in Augsburg he got caught up in a particularly messy set of conflicting concert arrangements. In Mannheim he thought the vocal forces deficient, but wrote a mass there nonetheless.

Nothing came to much fruition amid lengthy and gyrating sequences of negotiations, rumours of contracts, changes of address, campaigns of heady, often slightly resentful charm and ingratiation, and numerous brilliant private concerts. Great stretches of his letters praise musicians like the flutist Johann Baptist Wendling and the oboist Friedrich Ramm to his father, before he loses interest in them and reports instead that the former is irreligious and the latter 'is a good person but a libertine'. He was travelling and working for the first time away from Leopold's daily prodding and pushiness, and in Mannheim he had fallen in love for the first time too. Mozart thought for a time that the beautiful young soprano Aloysia Weber returned his heady feelings, but the prospect did not endure. She was on his mind throughout his time in Paris though, an alluring and distracting promise of happiness. No version of the future could really settle for the young man while he did not know whether she would feature; it was as hard for him to admit that she might not want to be part of his life as it was to know how his plans should include her if she did.

Mozart was playing a double game with his reputation throughout this period. He needed to project an image of himself as a solid, lauded figure in his Austrian world in order to seem like someone to be reckoned with in these new milieux. At the same time he wanted to be flexible and open to offers. He enjoyed dissimulation and rhetoric, but that may not have lessened the strain of such a double image. The building in which he and his mother initially lodged after their arrival in Paris was too cramped for the composer to work in, the staircase too narrow for a keyboard to go up. In Joseph Legros the composer was acquainted with the organizer of the city's most prestigious series of public concerts, and he traipsed daily to his grandly bustling house. Hanging around in the glare of the cultural establishment must have both elevated the composer and hemmed him in, and soon enough he and Legros fell out. But even then he went regularly to the house to spend time with his friend the tenor Anton Raaff who was also a personable link back to Mannheim amid all this Parisian strife. Meanwhile his mother was daily left on her own after what had already been months of travel and cheap, ratchety accommodations. She was lonely and fretful, and only began to feel her way towards a more expansive take on the possibilities of the great city after a couple of months, at which point she promptly became seriously ill. She had been missing her husband and her daughter and their Salzburg friends for months; she had kept hearing in letters how much the family dog missed her.

Paris was an odd mixture of golden apple and last resort for the young man. He had wavered for months as to whether to go there at all. The city opened up all sorts of grand vistas, but he knew all along how snobbish and complacent its whirls of polish and politeness could be. Its glitziness was set up to be impenetrable as well as irresistible. Paris had been nourishing its sense of eminence at least since the reign of Louis XIV a century or so earlier, and earning it with the feats of talk and culture that filled its halls and apartments. Intellectual elites everywhere relied on French, and a scrupulous version of the language was compulsory in the political life of courts across the continent, but there have often been anxious or even paralysing aspects of the city's pride in its own cultural indispensability. Yet the great city was as uncertain as Mozart in which of many directions its resources should be pushed. The grandiose rituals of the French monarchy still loomed large, but the court's removal to Versailles a few generations earlier had imbued the city with a sense of vacancy, handing it a freedom that it could not yet grasp. Paris was no longer even fully the centre of French politics even while it sought ever more pushily to define culture for the whole continent. The salon and its values of discussion and taste formed one simmering response to these dilemmas, offering whirlpools of freedom but too little real power and influence.

The dynamic and vastly wealthy city was also dingy, crowded and unfriendly; the composer was thrown into a city with two faces. It was huge but packed tight with narrow streets and volatile crowds, a long way still from the urbane City of Light that boulevards and street lamps would grind it into during the nineteenth century. Big talents flowed into the city from all around and Europe's cultural attention was obsessed by it, but its shiny heights of lifestyle and talk were found behind doors that were mainly very much closed. Mozart's letters home to Salzburg complain with wry astonishment about the filth, turbulence and inconvenience encountered as he plied his skills across the city's bitter and brutally expensive expanse. Walking everywhere is impossible because 'the dirt in Paris is beyond all description', but taking cabs is too expensive when no one will pay him properly for anything, and 'it is terrible how fast a thaler disappears around here' anyhow. His letters from across that summer compile a litany of invectives against a place more dreadful than his father can imagine.

All the age's drives of modernity and reaction were epitomized there and wrestled on its streets and within its institutions and salons. To someone of Mozart's generation and outlook, the enlightenment movement defined the city's culture. It was in Paris around the middle of the century that the era most fully succeeded in giving dazzling, and spirallingly complex, social and institutional life to its bright cults of free reason and critical scrutiny. But the further anyone penetrated into Paris, the more the roles of its intellectuals and *philosophes* could seem cranky, unsure and diffuse. Paris was no longer simply the acme of etiquette or gravitas; it was also pioneering a future in which such definitions would shake. The enlightenment movement wanted to stay irreverent while attracting reverence. By the end of the 1770s its lions were in any case ageing, and mired in odd fusions of disappointment and smugness. The future that they had wanted had had plenty of time to fail to arrive. The lengthy, aimless reign of Louis XV had ended just a few years before the composer's arrival, but his ill-fated son neither blew radical new life into the royal mystique nor reframed its possibilities with any determination. The new Louis XVI had the sort of tinkering, reclusive personality that could only further distance the monarchy from a metropolis that loved controversy and splashiness, but he could never transmute that distance into anything like awe. So the enlightenment lacked both vibrant official acceptance and whatever grand monarchic enmity might have renewed its fires. A cultural glut crammed with satire and dispute filled a city whose politics had largely been emptied in favour of now largely rundown projects of national glory. Lampoons, slander and caricature filled its slews of pamphlets and cartoons, as if corrosive accusation was mistaking itself for the culture of richly critical dissent that had been promised. The city that largely invented modern intellectual life was slamming up against its drawbacks and blind spots.

One reason why this mattered to Mozart is how vitally, and controversially, music had been at the heart of enlightenment culture in Paris. Admirers of the febrile melodic ardours of the vocal styles linked to Naples clashed with those who wanted a more sober aesthetic of reform to carry the day. The names of the composers Piccinni and Gluck were the banners under which these tendencies vaunted themselves most noisily, but the largest meanings were also in play as the enlightenment's hedonistic levity and its corrective strands undertook proxy skirmishes. The city's intellectual atmosphere was drenched with the questions and pleasures that Mozart knew in his bones; in fact he knew both these composers personally at different points. Further, the young man could not have been thrown more acutely into the fractiousness of the late enlightenment than through the household where he ended up living. Mozart's father had needed persuading to let the young man go off without him, and Leopold now placed great hopes in an old friend of the family called Friedrich Melchior Grimm, a grand Parisian intellectual and arbiter. Leopold liked finding ways to exert remote control over his son; in one letter well before Mozart's arrival in Paris, his father warns him of the specific sort of slipperiness to be expected from the city's paving stones. While Grimm was still something of a man on the make over a decade previously when he first became friends with Leopold, he was in his pomp by the time of the young composer's arrival; in 1775 he had been made a baron. Mozart called on him unsuccessfully on the day after arriving in Paris late in March, and on the following day succeeded. A few months later he ended up taking up lodgings in Grimm's house, as his Parisian venture resolutely failed to gain focus.

Alliance with Grimm was a succulent prospect. He came from southern Germany and had made it to Paris in his twenties around the midpoint of the century. He made his best marks as a radical intellectual journalist, guiding the whole continent's views of the city's cultural frontiers by means of his editorship of the prestigious *Correspondance littéraire*. But his other roles as a busily ranging diplomatic and political advisor had gradually come to define him, as he dispensed highbrow counsel to paying customers and smoothed his world's cosmopolitan networks. As Grimm rose in prestige, his friends increasingly found him pompous, brittle and truculent. The soulful and subversive young thinker took to hoarding influence, titles and finery; his passionate friendship with the writer and encyclopaedist Denis Diderot would finally collapse not long after the young composer's erratic months in his ambit. Mozart's putative guide to the city had become over the years a living summary of the paradoxes of enlightenment Paris, someone whose combination of hauteur, genuine brilliance and needy social mobility fitted an era lurching between hierarchical conformism and a yearning for new energies. Archness and waspishness had always given Grimm pep, but had been soured by the endless controversies swirling in his circles, while his love of white face powder was a notorious absurdity even in a city crammed with vanity. Mozart must have been curious about the household that he ran alongside his acknowledged mistress, the intellectually voracious and famously charming Louise d'Épinay, and to begin with seems to have found the great man stimulating and impressive. But the excitement of these circles had become hectic and embattled over the years, and the older man's self-importance became stultifying to the brilliant young sojourner buzzing with large but inchoate intentions. By the end of his stay Mozart is calling the household 'smug and dumb' in a letter to his father, a defiant blast of a verdict for Leopold to swallow.

In return Grimm would have been justified in finding Mozart a mystifying or even troubling prospect. The composer complained about much over these months, and his behaviour was often either prickly or nonchalant. But Grimm was loyal to the young man's intense talent, at a time when Mozart's plans were baffling and mutable. Mozart was fortunate to be faced in Grimm with someone who saw musical form as charged with deep meaning and ramifications. He was a positive zealot of the Italophile faction within the city's musical disputes, to the extent that Mozart's final disillusionment with him announces itself in a letter where he harrumphs that he is as good as Grimm's darling Piccinni, despite being 'only a German'. Paris was also confronting the composer with a much less nourishing vision of what musical appreciation could become, in the pedantic whims and conventions of the fashionable upper-class life to which it was often a merely decorative appendage. In a letter to the composer's father, the great Parisian allows Leopold to think that it is the depth of his son's talent that is holding him back 'in a country where so many mediocre and even detestable musicians have made immense fortunes'. Mozart's letters back home fill with invective against the pampered and presumptuous salon audiences and patrons that he was being urged from all directions to cultivate. Music had a double life within this culture, at once the carrier of its brightest energies and the prisoner of its most slyly lethargic constrictions. It was this doubleness that Grimm represented to

Mozart, as he educated this odd young man in the spirit of the age, and badgered him to cultivate fashions and connections.

Mozart composed little during these fraught months. His Parisian life was suspended between everything and nothing, in a sharpened version of the dilemmas that generally beset the period's musicians, whose vocations could put them among their culture's more brilliant stars or its more dispensable servants. He was at the sumptuous heart of the grandest version of itself that European culture could muster, and yet knew how happily the metropolis could spit him out. It is no wonder that his moods gyrated and his plans remained diffuse, to the consternation of both Grimm and Leopold. His mother's presence was a constant, awkward reminder of versions of identity that he wished to leave behind, but may also have helped him to avoid fitting in to these smart French circles too sleekly. One of the oddest patterns of Mozart's career is the way in which starry success and disreputable failure were interlaced. We can imagine him in Paris contemplating writing or sitting at the keyboard in a mood of something like fierce patience, unwilling to commit himself to any of the versions of music or life that his world seemed to be offering. Paris may have been the most agglomerative of the great eighteenth-century musical centres, but its absorbency did not emerge out of any spirit of quiet mutual respect. Rather, it argued endlessly about the culture's many styles and directions and weighed them anxiously. Mozart's head must have thronged with other composers' music, and with the snippy remarks and grand theories and rippling disputes that they provoked in all directions. He needed a form of music that would both belong to its world and tear away from it, one that would be fully pleasing but utterly intransigent too. His K310 piano sonata in A minor is the breakthrough work that these months produced, and in it he sounds nearly imperious in his grasp of his uniqueness, but also desperately honest about the uncertainty and storminess that it is opening up.

In the piece's three vehemently inventive movements, we seem to hear a merely brilliant talent cracking open so that a more caustic, restless and expansive idea of his art can be released. Among other things, the sonata amounts to a nimbly strident analysis of the frustrations of late enlightenment culture and of the artist's place in it. Mozart's music opened doors for him all over Paris, but even worse than the incomprehension or dismissiveness that it found behind some was the emptiness of so much of whatever praise greeted him elsewhere. In one letter he mocks the Parisians who still go on about what a prodigy he is, how 'inconcevable' and 'étonnant' his playing is, but in the end give him nothing. 'Adieu' is what they always end up saying. Leopold and Grimm both seem to have thought that he should keep touring around the homes and salons of the city's upper classes as a sort of door-to-door salesman of his own brilliance, but Mozart increasingly feels that he is 'living among brutes and beasts' as far as musical taste is concerned. Spirits of anger and revenge lurk within the vexation that all this wrought for the composer; in one letter he imagines writing an opera that will finally teach the French to appreciate him, and describes the 'veritable fire' that the thought inspires and how his 'hands and feet tremble with impatience'. No such opera was ever written. But the A minor sonata fills itself with these livid emotions and drives, and charges itself with making sense of them too.

Sometimes the Parisian atmosphere of ambition and rivalry wholly embittered him, and he saw himself surrounded by conspiracies of rejection and plotted against by 'enemies'. On one particularly absurd occasion, Mozart got himself inside the salon in the Faubourg Saint-Germain of the influential Duchesse de Chabot, but appears not to have realized that he was expected simply to provide pleasant background music for her drawing group. Already suffering from 'headache and boredom' and with fingers 'numb from cold' in a room whose windows were stubbornly open to the Parisian spring, he describes himself as having 'to play to the chairs, table and walls' while the grand lady and her gang of gentlemen continue inexorably drawing, seated in a large circle. The room has not even got a fireplace, and at one point Mozart suggests that he be shown to one that has; the duchess graciously acknowledges that he is right and does nothing. Nothing came of the access to the even headier Duchesse de Bourbon that the whole venture was meant to elicit.

Madame de Chabot was married to a scion of the Rohan family, one of the grandest and most storied of the clans whose embroilment in old ideas of France was so deep that they had found it hard to adapt to the new world of Bourbon centralization, let alone to whatever further versions of modernity were gathering. Daily life for a brilliant outsider meant a constant flow of encounters that were all the more disorientating, and bruising, because of the layers of nicety and mystique encrusting their hierarchies and humiliations. Etiquette was a martial art in this world, and Mozart would have heard so many compliments that led nowhere that their swelling phrases must have started to sound less encouraging than sarcastic. Salons were filled with fine talkers whose conversational skills could be as stifling as they were impressive, while doors opened and closed for yet more guests whose plush attire made them seem both grand and interchangeable. Swarming quietly around these scenes would have been little crowds of coachmen, valets and chambermaids, whose impassiveness may not often have seemed meant to reassure. Friendliness or solicitude from servants may have seemed even more unreassuring to anyone afraid of finally belonging in their midst. The duchess's husband eventually turned up, and he listened to Mozart's playing more attentively than she did. He was an admired veteran of the Seven Years' War during which the Prussian king Frederick the Great had given mid-century Europe a preview of the modern models of sovereignty and militarism that were coming, and in which Grimm too had been involved as the secretary to a general. The febrile, uneasy hedonism of Mozart's Europe was shadowed throughout by both the sense of fragility instilled by that war and the lassitude incurred by the peace that followed.

His A minor sonata never breaks wholesale from the salon's elegant sound-world, but fuses it with a spiralling protest at the limitations of that setting, and with a sort of mordant poignancy. No one could ever really mistake it for background music; instead what we can hear in the piece's relentless inwardness and edginess is a certain beautiful revenge on these circles, a revenge that Mozart could have imagined serving up hot in their drawing rooms as they listened. Playing alone at the keyboard was the heart of what he had to offer on these occasions, and his drastic powers as a keyboard soloist had always driven his renown; but in the sonata the player's solitude becomes itself a source of drama and a subject of inquiry. During the wandering months that brought him to Paris, Mozart's letters often seem to strain to submerge whatever uncertainties he must have been feeling, but there is no doubting the surges of conviction and ballast whenever solo keyboard music becomes a topic. Always he could be plugged in to the deep sources of his artistry and his self-image by the feeling of his fingers as they struck or stroked or danced upon a keyboard. The A minor sonata has a headlong, sharply etched moodiness that seems designed to lock its musical vision down to the barebones fact of a player's isolation at a keyboard, but also to show how much that state can contain. Beauty would end up meaning for Mozart something all but diametrically opposed to the spirit of revenge. But maybe it had to learn to coexist with such dark factors first.

Mozart had in fact been concentrating more and more on solo keyboard music during the year or so leading up to this sonata, as if in preparation for its psychic breakthrough. He does not depart even here from the basic conventions of the three-movement structure that he had already explored and polished in the set of six keyboard sonatas that now run from K279 to K284 in his works. The numbering system was introduced by a nineteenth-century scientist called Ludwig von Köchel, a musical enthusiast who recoiled from the classificatory chaos in which the composer's oeuvre remained. Right from the terse and distinctly unmelodic propulsiveness that initiates its opening allegro, it is clear that this sonata means to turn those conventions to its own singular, choppy purposes. In particular the opening passages feature textures whose levels of intricacy are designed to be slowly worked out over the course of a complex musical argument, rather than to yield the easy pleasures of melodic lightness or even mere technical flamboyance. The player's hands must both work hard to keep these textures alive. We meet in this movement an almost ruggedly abrupt version of the way in which Mozart's feeling for arcs of long-range organization allows him to explore local effects that are unpredictable or mercurial or downright gnomic. The allegro twists through harmonic ideas at a rate that would be unthinkable if its overall structure was not so secure. But this means in turn that there is something biting and severe about the coherence that structure here brings. The rhythmic agitation and the fretful expressive density pull away from any thought of mere diversion. A growling, crackling pushiness invests the bass registers that goes far beyond what the period normally asked the left hand to deliver.

If this music asks to be heard as a sort of portrait of the artist as a restlessly brilliant young man, in the two following movements not even this image remains static. The slow movement that comes next is one of the first to feature the fusion of extreme starkness with an equal extreme of melodic sweetness that would become the uncanny hallmark of Mozart's finest adagios and andantes. Contrasts of texture or harmony had been so veeringly dominant in the opening allegro that now it becomes the contrast between the two movements that counts. The grind of textures in the allegro yields to a different world, and a pristine melodic intensity takes control. Instead of the quickfire crush of rhythms and harmonies, the notes create space around themselves. Bright emphasis is thrown as a result on the expressive weight within a melodic line that might otherwise be merely pleasant, as if the real stakes of emotional heft that can underpin cantabile pleasure are suddenly pulled to the surface. After the first movement's wiry constrictions, a roomy beauty opens up that is no less tense in the finesse that it demands from the techniques or sensibilities of those faced with it. In case anyone has missed the point, a whisperingly turbulent development passage then opens up as if from deep within the melody.

Let us imagine what it would have meant for someone in the Paris of the late 1770s to be faced with this music. The effect must have been both gripping and disorientating; it can seem at once almost confrontationally solid in its sense of formal sureness and at the same time recklessly fluid and mutable. It seems telling that the sonata did not manage to find a publisher. A solo piece like this would not have been meant for public performance, but for playing at smaller gatherings in drawing rooms or salons. But this music is unsure who it wants to let listen; it both seems to insist on the most absorbed engagement and to dart away from even the most intimate audience. By contrast the one real hit that Mozart achieved during these Parisian months was with his K297 symphony in D, a piece designed with fulsome meticulousness to please a large public audience, and which duly became a success when one of the city's prestigious Concert Spirituel events included it. Plushly scored and trimmed to exploit the snazziest vogues in 1770s orchestral style, the symphony has come to sound a little stuck in the sumptuousness of its gestures, while the A minor sonata mines all the forces of resentment or disdain that were left in the wake of such accommodations. The sonata's fierce joke is then how resonantly it cries out for deeper acts of attention than the ambiance of cultivated appreciation within exclusive gatherings can mainly have suggested, as drinks kept flowing and the background filled with smart chatter. It broods relentlessly on exactly how far it does and does not belong to this world, to these listeners, to their very powers of listening.

The sonata's presto finale is where it comes closest to running or sliding entirely away from anything that its audiences can have expected, closest to releasing itself into a spirit of questioning errancy far deeper than the formulas of scepticism that the enlightenment prided itself on. Paris was full of palates so jaded that it must have seemed doubtful whether they could count anything as new. But this movement sounds determined to show that real expressive innovation is not just going to titillate connoisseurs of boredom but will throw them off balance. Its textures are less clotted and more tumbling and prolific, and indeed it has the feeling of a sort of *perpetuum mobile*, as if the array of different attitudes towards music and experience to which Mozart is now exposed can afford him no single place to stand. The assumption of a finale movement is that its thematic bases should feel disposed right from the outset to produce a resolute and logical conclusion. In many cases even for Mozart this means that final movements employ fairly simple, sometimes even simplistic, musical ideas. But in this presto by contrast, movement piles onto itself or seems to hurry itself away from any conclusion that is not provisional and abrupt, and anxious. Of course the movement must eventually conclude, and it does so with an almost juddering briskness, since no other exit is possible from its sheer kinetic charge. It is one of Mozart's shorter finales, but its brevity intensifies the feeling that psychic tension here finds no culminating point of release. The music can only answer its own agitation by plunging into it as deeply as it can, and then abruptly cutting itself off.

The sonata as a whole is stridently original and expressive. But the brusque twists of its opening allegro are not far from some of the busiest advances in contemporary German music, while the slow movement has an Italian melodiousness which keeps pulling its plangency back into recognizable spheres of lyricism and sweetness. It is the originality of the finale that could hardly be more stark, and wayward. Mozart's desire to impress this world and his disappointment or even rage at it become layered together, and the sonata's last sounds are full of both harmonic richness and a nearly explosive curtness. We can hear in them Mozart's almost tortuously mixed feelings as he played for the ears of Paris, as the notes resound with one last burst of expressive flamboyance, at the same time as they propel the piece to a hasty conclusion that will allow their composer to move onwards and beyond it. Paris was a city lost between worlds itself, no longer capable of the optimistic gleam of the enlightenment at its highest, but unable to reach back with any confidence towards the old splendour of the monarchy or towards the aristocratic or military elites to which the latter was ever more tenuously allied. Mozart's sonata fuses a wildly disappointed pathos with a stubborn sense of possibility.

Two epochal deaths coincided with these decisive Parisian months for Mozart, as he attained new fragility and new power. One of the sourest episodes brought by the hothouse ambiance of enlightened Paris had been the collapse of the friendship between Grimm and Jean-Jacques Rousseau, whose rampantly inventive but also often rampantly truculent intellectual output across diverse genres comprised both an ongoing zenith of the enlightenment movement, and a mountainous rebuke to its urbane faith in culture and progress. The friendship between the two men had begun around 1750 as a faintly idyllic rapport during Rousseau's heyday in the metropolis and was consecrated in their shared love of playing keyboard music, but it soon spilt itself out in deep fits of offence and recrimination. During the 1770s Rousseau had come back to live in Paris, a strange mixture of celebrity intellectual and impoverished pariah; he had to work hand to mouth as a music copyist because the endless originality of his ideas had combined with his stubbornly tricky character to make his circumstances harshly straitened. Rousseau's intellectual life had been wholly bound up with his musical passions, and the quest for origins that powered his inquiries drove him to an all but frenzied partisanship for Italian vocal styles above all rivals. In Paris during the 1750s his pungency as a critic of the city's preferred alternatives brought the players at the Opéra to burn him in effigy. He never resumed contact with Grimm's circle of enlightened high society during this later stint in the capital, but we can assume that his legend preoccupied his erstwhile intimate. His example probably reared up when Grimm was faced with someone as brilliant, as odd and as sometimes obstreperously wilful as Mozart. Hearing of Rousseau's angry disillusionment with Grimm and his world may in turn have stimulated and reassured the young composer. Rousseau's almost grotesque brilliance had carried him like Mozart to the heart of enlightenment circles, but his harshly volatile character was ill-suited to their tense subtleties. One account records how captivating he could be while in the flow of talking, but says that he left a dismal impression behind. By the end of the century he would have an ambivalent revenge on this Parisian world, as his ideas fuelled the course of the revolution in France which both consummated and despatched that world and its attempts to be radical.

Rousseau finally left Paris during May, a few weeks after the composer's arrival, to live in the guest house of a friendly marquis in the nearby countryside. Early in July he died after years of failing health, though rumours rapidly spread that he had killed himself. During that same summer Mozart's sojourn in the metropolis also coincided with a spate of speculation around what was seeming certain to be the final illness of Voltaire, the writer who had since the 1720s personified intellectual glamour at its most acrobatically critical. Rousseau had represented the tumult and pathos of the eighteenth-century intellect, but Voltaire had kept alive the dream of a winningly worldly intellectual life in which elegance burnished revolt. Now he had returned from a long and ambiguous exile to die in Paris, and a special feverishness imbued the reports of some deathbed reconciliation on his normally at best sardonic part with the church and its stratospheric dogmas. All the stridently eager cultural aplomb that had marked the early years of the Parisian enlightenment was funnelled into the gossip surrounding these two deaths. Did figures like Voltaire and Rousseau really represent the future of the culture, or a past glory that had failed to change anything enough, or alien excitements by which the great city had consented to be stimulated or merely amused in passing? Mozart was on hand to inherit aspects of both their projects; his powers of osmosis were incalculable, and often enough involuntary too. The A minor sonata's breakthrough is to suggest a version of modern culture capable of declaring its bleakest losses and uncertainties even while it maintains the most radiant surfaces.

In a letter home Mozart records Voltaire's death in tones of swatting disdain towards this enlightenment icon which say much about the composer's mood in the capital. Maybe it is to please Leopold that he says that the great but controversial intellectual has died 'like a dog', or maybe it is out of a gathering dislike for the Parisian circles around him, but some flickering anxiety as to the fate of artistic or critical perspectives in the surrounding world may have been involved too. The other death that he had to report on during these months was his mother's. She had replaced her husband at Mozart's side in his travels partly as a way of testing how far family guidance was becoming an irrelevance or an impediment to their son. But she was far less able than the paterfamilias might have been to find her own reasons for being in the glamorous but opaque French capital. Mozart's mother was an appealing, substantial character, a subtle and fun woman who was not overwhelmed by her formidable and bizarre family. But Paris was a place of congestion and stench and furious pace and addled agendas; it was no place for a thoughtful but mild provincial Austrian lady who was increasingly alienated from her dazzling son's disappointments and efforts. Years of wrangling with the musical life had no doubt weighed heavily, and her health seems to have faded fast once some metropolitan bug or fever got hold of her. She had originally wanted her son to travel on to Paris alone, while she returned to Salzburg. Leopold and her daughter had been worrying about her health during the previous winter. She died in July 1778 amid the dust of the urban summer, around the time when this sonata was emerging.

We should not try too hard to sketch direct connections between his mother's death and this music; Mozart's creativity is too mercurial and obscure, too wayward. But her labile morale and failing health during their time in Paris stemmed from many of the same factors that enter into the sonata one way or another, and that are redescribed and transmuted in it. Listeners have often heard a lament for his mother in the slow movement, and it is easy to see why. But the larger point is the bitter hymn to the inevitability of artistic solitude that the whole piece amounts to. Mozart's music had for years been opening up kaleidoscopes of pleasure and power for himself and innumerable others. It must have been a volatile fate even when it kept working, maybe no less than when hints of stalemate or derailment showed through. The A minor sonata is such a pivot because it shows him turning determinedly towards volatility and emptiness. He wanted the world that he had at his fingertips to be a real world, filled with both transience and harshness.

Mozart would never lose his capacity for twisting the losses and impasses of personal life and civilizational history alike into forms of creative radiance. Perhaps nothing like this could emerge in someone's life without bringing certain qualities of coolness or even ruthlessness in its undertow. His letters back to Salzburg about his mother's illness and death are sincere in their grief, but they are also weirdly artful as they arrange what happened into narrative. Losing his mother meant also breaking psychically with his father, whether that prospect seemed a necessity or a sort of bleak promise. He seems to have ended up writing a letter home detailing his one great

Parisian success with the symphony in D while her corpse lay nearby in the rooms that they had been sharing. The idea seems to have been to lessen the shock of her death by first sending at least one letter describing the seriousness of her illness as if its outcome is still in doubt. But the letter soon turns from such 'mournful thoughts' to describing the 'great applause' and 'the shouts of *Da capo*' inspired by the symphony, and the ice cream that he ate at the Palais Royale afterwards, and then indeed wheels on to such other topics as how 'Voltaire has kicked the bucket' or how it continues to be 'very difficult to find a good libretto'. It is hard to know whether to call all this generous or ruthless; the ruthlessness within his own brilliance was something that his music would learn to transmute. Maybe the shock of his mother's death came not so much from the pain of her loss as from the fact that it had happened just as he was bracing himself for the seriousness and solitude that his creative identity would bring. Hereafter a side of him would be alone with his art, pressed up with it against the losses and promises of a modern world.

3

Leopold Mozart's Grandly Talented Son

Violin Concerto in A

Leopold Mozart travelled from Salzburg to Vienna in the painfully cold February of 1785 to stay with his son and daughter-in-law in the new, plush and very expensive apartment that they were renting. Father and son would never meet again after the weeks that they then spent together, and the depth of trust and involvement in their correspondence would diminish until Leopold's death a couple of years later. It had been dwindling since at least as far back as Mozart's marriage a couple of years earlier, though their letters would always feature revivals of trust and tenderness and mutual insight, and of their often caustically shared humour. In one way this trip sealed how much had ended in the relationship between the two, showing Leopold the success that Mozart had built for himself since breaking loose from his father's immersive guidance. Mozart's new apartment was at the top end of the market in a city where property had been booming; it was lavishly decorated and had enough spacious rooms to accommodate not just the composer's musical requirements but also his beloved billiards table. Leopold's reports to his daughter are ambivalent towards what must have seemed his son's giddily high lifestyle. Yet all this was a consummation of what Mozart's father had worked for painstakingly himself.

Not long after Leopold's arrival, Mozart was joined by his dear friend Joseph Haydn for an evening of music that included a run-through of three of the six string quartets that he had dedicated to the older composer. The two of them took a string part each in the quartets, so that half the music that evening was being played by two men who were in the midst of transforming Europe's musical culture. Haydn's terse roughness of character informed all the affectionate esteem in which he was held by Mozart and innumerable others; his personal charm and the charm of his music alike combined the sleekest skill with a love of hard contrasts and an explosive directness. It would not have seemed flattery or hype when he made a large declaration to his friend's father during the evening. Weighing his words carefully enough to make what might have seemed hyperbole sound splendidly sober, he told Leopold that his son was the greatest composer known to him in person or by name in the world. On the next evening Leopold attended the grand public concert at which Mozart unwrapped a new piano concerto. At the state-of-the-art concert hall by his son's apartment, he found himself greeted by high society's most elevated members, and heard the emperor offer a loud ovation to his son. Not even the most rigorous father could fail to be impressed.

Mozart's life pivoted on his decision in 1781 to break away from Salzburg and to settle in Vienna. The decision was long in the making, and seeing it through was drawn out and fraught. If it made him what he became, it was also a move that drew deeply on forces and ruptures in the world around him; the largest creativity is always both anomalous and representative. He would find in Vienna that freedom brings its own constraints, and his music is often about the need for freedom to invent its own versions of structure. But Salzburg had long provided an education in ambivalence for the young composer. Probably there was no single moment when he decided that staying there forever was not an option, and over much of at least the late 1770s he may still have contemplated maintaining a base there even if he wanted his field of operations to be as wide as possible. Mozart and his father returned in March 1773 from Italy, at the end of their last great journey together in search of work and acclaim for the young maestro. Salzburg then claimed him for slabs of the middle part of the decade that were only relieved by odd trips to Munich and Vienna, ahead of the major embarkation in the summer of 1777 that would lead him to France without Leopold. His father's ambitions for him were vital to how widely

Mozart's plans and aspirations roved across musical Europe. But it was a double rupture when he did finally break away from Salzburg. It took him away from his father's towering ambit as well as from a form of employment that stifled and disheartened him, at a court and in a milieu that he had psychically broken with years earlier.

Mozart's talent so thoroughly shaped him that his music becomes more than just its product. It offers itself to be heard as an interpretation of what it means to have such gifts, an account of what being exorbitantly talented feels like or amounts to. Gifts in fairy tales and fables often bring dark results, and so too a gift on such a scale in the psyche will be trailed by shadows and wounds. Someone whose gifts so sharply involve display cannot fail to feel like a monster at times, a freak whose talent has torn him out of his world but brought nowhere else to stand, except in the glare of other people's hopes and demands. Failure may become unthinkable but this can make success either paralysing or addictive. Displaying the grand talent can bring moods of utter absorption capable of effacing the world, and this may not help that world feel solid or nourishing, or make its responses seem trustworthy. The responses of audiences are never exactly right, either not rapturous enough or rapturous in ways that do not feel entirely real or apt. Seeing others strive so hard for what comes so easily makes success seem flimsy and pointless, or the talent itself seem empty or capricious in the lavishness of what it bestows. Seeing others rewarded for distinctly lesser achievements is also not the easiest thing. No achievement feels really solid; another is always meant to be on its way. Day by day many more potential masterpieces may seem to be lost or forgone than the ones that actually reach creation. If such talent conveys sway and potency, it can also bring neediness and insecurity. Mozart's zest for communication came partly from his brilliance and partly from needing to find exits from its impasses.

Mozart's extreme talent made him an ideal son for Leopold. It also pulled him away from the paternal orbit. His deepest rebellion against his father lay, not so much in the various decisions that he made contrary to Leopold's judgement, but in how exorbitantly he in the end surpassed his capacity to imagine what artistic success and power could be. Mozart never ceased wanting to be a good son. But it is as if he had to expand the meaning of that phrase, pulling away from mere dutifulness or loyalty, finding instead a virtuosically different set of talents and prisms for what being a son means. Mozart was a virtuoso of filiation and development in his personal life and his musical structures alike. Having a genius as a son is possibly only bearable if he is also a sort of genius at being a son, someone capable of processing his own roles as a son with the boundlessly flexible combinations of skill and care and panache that Mozart had at his disposal. It is normally wise of the father to fall short of genius himself. Was Leopold lovingly devoted to developing his son's talent or recklessly determined to exploit its every juice? Mozart's biographers seem split on the question, but he appears dazzlingly unconcerned. His life more widely was driven along by his own and others' often frantic needs to make the most of his gifts, but he seems relentlessly uncurious as to their nature. In letters he can by turns deflect his father with wit or manipulate him with sentimentality, or confront him with stunning bursts of honesty or waspishness. But his main answer to him was to write pieces that would both meet and overspill anything that Leopold could expect. Likewise, his music sets out innumerable ways of inheriting and metabolizing the stuff of his culture. It proliferates stylistic fathers at a rate that can seem both giddy and gruelling. Was this because he wanted ever more fathers, or because the one that he had was too much already?

Leopold wanted his son to be the best composer around at doing the sorts of things that everyone else did. Yet all that they did together to cultivate Mozart's powers fed their rampant singularity. In Milan in January 1773 Mozart unleashed the exhilarating coloratura repetitions of the single word 'alleluia' in the celebrated K165 'Exsultate' motet that he wrote for the great castrato Venanzio Rauzzini, and the glimmering, swooping plasticity of its syllables can serve as the last word on the phases of his life when some uneasy but often blazing synchronicity between these factors was possible. The whole motet exudes a drastic ebullience, but it is in this last of its three short movements that it exults in its own artistic prowess with the fiercest giddiness. As the word spins and glides and shines, the music starts to feel like a test of its resilience and of the resilience of the world, a way of probing the word and the world alike for whether they can withstand and join in with the capacities of talent when it is so brilliantly extended. It turns out that they really can; a certain febrile volatility nearly overruns the syllables as they repeat and repeat, but each time they are also stabilized by gaining a new expressive shape. Not even Mozart ever came up again with music that feels so breathtakingly unique, yet so nearly anonymous too. In fact this motet can seem to mark the end of an era within the sweep of Italian music. Rauzzini is sometimes taken as the last of the great castratos, and perhaps the very particular practices behind his voice's brilliance struck odd affinities with the composer's own intense relationship to his own talent and to musical pleasures. A great castrato voice was something made at an unignorable price, after all, and a great castrato was someone whose talent had defined his life with fierce completeness. The lungs of star castratos like Caffarelli and Farinelli had powered the triumph of Italian singing styles across Europe over the bulk of the century, and the fading of their era was leaving vast gaps in the soundscape by the time of Mozart's major operas.

A lot was changing more widely in the culture's basic ideas about talent, and what artistic creation really means. The eighteenth century often liked to think that it was neoclassical, though the variants within the trend could include both Pope's extravagantly dainty riffing on epic in *The Rape Of The Lock* and Lessing's stony meditation on violence and time in his famous essay on the 'Laocoön' sculpture. But the energy of these projects was instilled with a restlessness that the classical past would at least as much stoke as palliate; the American and French revolutions were suffused with ancient political models, and figures like Rousseau and the pungently capricious Italian painter Tiepolo and the rigorously eccentric English poet and artist William Blake used visionary revisions of past culture to charge their different sorts of blaring originality. One fashion in Italian painting was for pictures whose fulsome homages to the classical world cast it in the form of ruins. Pushing its way into German literary culture in particular was the fateful idea of artistic genius. An era feeling exhilarated and threatened by prospects of breaking from history was always going to be drawn to forms of creative life that broke away and innovated and convulsed. Mozart's life had thrown raptures of acclaim at him that went far beyond what basic ideas of talent and aesthetic craft would suggest. If artistry just meant following precepts and doing a good job for someone, how had his own created such force fields of exultant assent, and why did he feel capable of achievements larger even than these audiences could grasp?

An electrically receptive teenager in a wealthy, nodal city like Milan was well placed to enjoy being dazzlingly talented. Mozart's talent was too big for its world, but hearing someone like Rauzzini singing his music must have made the world feel capable of expanding to fit him, of being forced by his artistry to overrun its current shapes. The question was how to stay in touch with his own best possibilities and the world's headiest vistas when back in Salzburg. Mozart's works are fascinated by rules and conventions and will squeeze them for all the nutrients that they contain. But this also means pressing them to their limits, and he often cannot resist traversing these limits once he has found them out. Daily life back in Salzburg in the middle of the 1770s bubbled with pressures and vexations, but one of the most telling struggles for a major creative imagination as it develops is with the temptations of ease and structure that the place poured staidly out. Disdain and nonchalance are vastly useful tools if they are joined with an awareness that they can both turn noxious.

A paradoxical fate awaited the little city set among the more placid and appealing stretches of western Austria, close enough to the mountains for its topography to be piquant but not over-shadowed by anything too grandly Alpine. Its proud, lucrative status as the home town of maybe the greatest and most beloved cultural figure of the era has had to contend with how much he seems to have disliked almost everything about it. The parochial steadiness that bored Mozart may well also have helped him develop briskly and lavishly. As he moved towards turning twenty in 1776 his daily sense of provincial confinement there cannot have failed to fuel his avidity for the world beyond it. But it must also sometimes have provided him with buffers that helped him to experiment with that avidity so richly. Salzburg was big enough to have a busy musical culture with skilful players and appreciative listeners, but small enough for Mozart to be thrown plenty of its opportunities and for his sense of importance to be nourished. It was small enough too for the young composer to have got to know most of whatever grandees or otherwise well-connected figures passed through. The little city presented him with a manageable microcosm of Europe's musical culture that sat at a nice point of geographical balance between the visions of that culture that Italy, Germany and France often competitively pushed; its architecture mixed Italian with more northern pulls in some of the same ways as his music. One professor at the Benedictine University was an early explainer to a broad public of the science of electricity with its innovations and surprises. But few would be surprised if someone wanted to leave Salzburg, and anyone trying chances elsewhere could expect that not much would move on there in the meantime. It may have been the perfect place for a talent large enough to dwarf it to emerge in.

It is too easy now to think that the courtly, hierarchical Europe of such a place was simply doomed. We should not underestimate how much resilience and flexibility hid within the frantically polished serenity of somewhere like Salzburg in the century's middle decades. No one could have known better than Mozart how deeply confident that courtly world was of its own survival and importance, and indeed how many confident prospects of change it already considered itself to harbour. Salzburg's political arrangements were distinctive in ways that let it slip nimbly through the period's dynastic ructions. Its ruling prince was elected as an archbishop by and from a special body of canons attached to the cathedral, and the ancient eminence of the archiepiscopal see gave him prestige and room to manoeuvre once he was in the job. The principality was grand enough to be a vivid centre of politics and culture, but too small to get tempted into large and destructive or even merely demanding political projects. Salzburg's ruler at the time of Mozart's departure was a toweringly grand count called Hieronymus von Colloredo whose connections at the Habsburg court in Vienna helped his elevation in 1772 from among, and by, the archiepiscopal canons. Becoming Salzburg's ruler was more like being elected Pope than succeeding to a dynastic monarchy, and the process this time was convoluted and prolonged. The haughty, sardonic count was not a popular choice with the residents. He is now remembered primarily as Mozart's disliked employer, the antagonist of an annoying minor functionary who just happened to be the greatest figure of the age. But Archbishop Colloredo was a substantial and talented man, a fine administrator who was also committed to at least some establishment version of enlightenment thought. In his study hung a portrait of Voltaire, whose death Mozart would meet with tones of such exultant vilification.

Leopold's intentions for his son were shifting by the middle of the 1770s from the simple aim of building a reputation while making a ton of money towards more inventive plans. He was beginning to think further into the future, perhaps because he wanted as much as possible to be decided while his influence still prevailed. Mozart's brilliance was a glitzy novelty, and novelty does not endure. The temptation is to try to keep thinking of new things to do with it, but the problem then may only replicate itself. Bemusing quantities of courts and musical centres spread across the heart of the continent from Milan to Mannheim and beyond, and many of them became targets. All this meant that the time that Mozart did spend in Salzburg and the music that he wrote for the place were riddled with a fretful preoccupation with other vistas. Often it must have been hard to believe that the professional hierarchy there was worth climbing at all; the reward for his delayed return from Paris at the end of the decade was for his days to be crammed with the responsibilities of a court organist.

Salzburg loaded the young composer with tasks and occasions that were onerous without being challenging, and the odd, glazed leisureliness that seems to have hung around the city would have seemed torpid to someone who wanted to be elsewhere. The role of the church in ruling the place may have helped it seem primly apolitical, but seems not to have charged life with any radically pious atmosphere. The city's blandness had a sort of managerial perfection around the time when Mozart turned twenty. Its demands on him could be copious, but they were not the right demands, so they grated on his intense sense of mischief and his shimmering ambition. Mozart's days could wander past in a merely nice daze of social calls and hobbies and garden walks, all of them dotted with routines of musical and church life that mixed the bad sides of rigour and lassitude. He was a keen member of a shooting club and especially keen on the ribald or obscene illustrations that jollied up the targets. At the same time the hazily intense orderliness of Salzburg life allowed the young composer amounts of psychic leeway that play out in the almost aggressive aloofness and chutzpah of some of his music from this phase. The smooth, dashing sense of fun that runs through his more sociable instrumental music of this period can sometimes feel paradoxically intense in its insistence on nonchalance, and flavours of insolence get mixed into the basic eagerness. His willingness to please Salzburg audiences must have needed to refresh itself with insolence in order to survive. Salzburg's atmosphere was one of a hard-won idyll and a scrupulously policed enclave, and this period must have revealed much to Mozart about the frenzies contained within idylls and the high stakes involved in playfulness.

He would never give up on light refinement and sumptuous froth and witty sweetness; the odd imperturbability of his music is joined to these qualities. Structural rigour and twisting multifariousness again and again combine in Mozart's works in ways that must take their bearings from the layering across so many of the small courts around his Europe of provincial torpor with scintillating cosmopolitanism. The *Sturm und Drang* movement in literature was turning storm and stress into the formula whereby cultural centres in the German-speaking world announced their restlessness. Tourists and dignitaries and entrepreneurs criss-crossed this European era, along with travelling musicians and theatrical companies, and Salzburg was an amiable and porous node on their circuits. Salesmen, charmers and charlatans of all sorts tried their chances at the innumerable small centres of power and wealth that were looking out for new trends and tricks; it is hard to tell where in all this showbusiness began and ended. The comfortable house to which the Mozarts moved during the 1770s was well positioned for attending the new theatre installed under the new archbishop's auspices. The city's general cultural energy does seem to have picked up around the time of Colloredo's accession, but his relative disregard of music stopped this from being much good to the Mozarts. Watching his son's talent swing open within the city's confines must have been about as complex an experience for Leopold as actually undergoing it all was for the composer. But Leopold's ideal became for Mozart to end up as some sort of imperial court composer, and staying in favour in their home town seems to have struck him as an indispensable aid to such a prospect. Mozart's sense of his routes into the future cannot have been simplified by how much the crucial person anchoring him in Salzburg chafed against the place himself, against its mixtures of authoritarianism and hedonism and sleepiness.

As Salzburg soured for him towards the end of his teenage years, Mozart composed mainly in 1775 a series of violin concertos. To himself even more than to others, he must have seemed both a consummate insider in the place and someone already far outside it. In these concertos we hear precisely the psychic and artistic work required to sustain such a double attitude, to remain the masterful denizen of a little cultural domain while also straining dazzlingly to reach beyond it. One clue to the concertos is the slipperiness of his official role at this point. He held a title of 'concert-master' that is impressive enough but also rather vague; Leopold teasingly chided his son at least once with the suggestion that his big title did not necessarily make him anything more than a fiddler. The divisions of labour in the classical orchestra did not really settle until the nineteenth century, so being concert-master did not yet mean exactly the role of first violin and leader of the orchestra that it came to suggest. Musical life at the Salzburg court was a fairly unruly affair even by contemporary standards, and who was in charge on any given occasion seems to have varied. Yet the title cannot have been intended just to boost the young composer's ego, and it suggests that he would have had some role in guiding the daily musical life of the orchestra, and maybe the task of ushering it as a lead violinist through whatever passed for rehearsals. All this would have crystallized the ways in which he both did and did not belong to the musical community that he worked in. His youth and his father's presence and his travels and commissions elsewhere and indeed the basic fact that he was writing ambitious music for them must have coloured his relationship to his often hard-bitten colleagues. Duties like these would have both hugely stimulated and hugely annoyed a brilliant, pushy young man considering how to develop his art. His colleagues were conceivably both stimulated and annoyed in return.

Mozart's powers threw him into the centre of this musical scene and tore him out of and beyond it. So what we hear in the swish and bright plasticity of the orchestral workings of these concertos is a point-by-point negotiation between a talent flexing its possibilities and the recognition that it must stay comprehensible, engrossing and fun. In them the solo violin is not a dramatic protagonist or a spotlit vehicle for technical display, but a sort of mobile pivot point that opens up styles and expressive options, and lets the overall fluency map itself as clearly as it can at every stage. It is both inside and outside the orchestra in ways that reflect Mozart's own wavering condition. Getting this genre to analogize his own situation so finely was also a way of grappling with aspects of what his father meant to him. Leopold's own reputation revolved around his expertise precisely as a violin teacher; his tract on playing the instrument ended up perhaps the century's most influential work on the subject. Composing a number of such concertos in quick succession flung Mozart deep into his father's zone of prowess. The rushes of creativity that run through them suggest that finding himself there was heady.

If we wanted to sketch some alternative future in which the young composer stayed in Salzburg, and developed in ways that did not burst its banks, we could start from these concertos. Their ebullience tells us for one thing how richly musical style in the middle of the century thronged with possibility even amid Salzburg's constraints. Musicologists have been kept busy identifying the types of folk music that they relate or allude to, or some particular French courtly rhythms that a passage suddenly dances to. But if all this quick-fire cosmopolitanism shows how far Salzburg could stretch, it also suggests a composer reckoning with the sheer variety of directions that his career and his music could end up taking. So the eclecticism of the concertos contains two possible futures sleekly superimposed on each other. In one Mozart carries on pleasing Salzburg with agile syntheses of the culture's musical trends; in the other the concertos turn out to have been packed with a restlessness beyond the little city's compass. The mercurial adroitness with which the pieces are charged, as they slip and flow between ideas and styles, is as desperate as it is delightful. Mozart is trying to be at least two people simultaneously, so he has to move fast and with a sort of flighty smoothness. He described his own success in playing one of them to an audience at a monastery a couple of years later, during the travels that culminated in Paris, as a matter of getting it to flow like oil.

The layered aims of these concertos can be pursued so successfully in parallel partly because the violin concerto was itself in transition over the second half of the century. Its extravagant openness to feats of technical display had been crucial in the seventeenth century, as the violin rose from its origins in taverns and street music to take its place at the pinnacle of baroque style. During the nineteenth century likewise, grand romantic concertos would all but relentlessly mine the instrument's virtuosic possibilities. But Mozart's five concertos move around in a space that seems to have somehow become fleetingly available between these two very different but equally soaring sets of peaks. Concertos composed before and after his go for different sorts of compounds of sonic mass and fiery showmanship, but Mozart is more taken with the instrument's sheer flexibility, because it is what lets him get styles and themes to flow into one another in these pieces in such a spirit of shimmering cosmopolitan comprehensiveness. Technical bravura might have been an obvious or even lurid fit to the dilemmas of a brilliant young man pulling at the bit of his locale. After all, the virtuoso fits in perfectly with his world precisely by doing what no one else there can. But Mozart's way of relating to his world here is more agile and multiple. He pushes himself artistically without breaking from the talents and tastes around him, doing so through an extravagant fertility at the level of compositional artifice instead. A new sort of mastery of phrase length and phrasal construction on his part is crucial, because it means that the concertos can be filled with elements that combine balance with nimble sorts of momentum. Crucial too is the sense of singing style whereby their frequently swerving musical courses keep such smoothness and evenness.

The fifth and last of the group is the concerto in A, and in its opening allegro the composer throws drastic and sly new emphasis onto these issues of creative selfhood and the mutable world that it both does and does not belong to. Mozart does so at the moment of maximum impact when the solo part enters. The orchestra has set up thematic blocks for the movement to base itself on, but instead of taking them up or pushing them forwards with responses or reinterpretations, the violin wants to pause for thought. It spins away from the surrounding sounds and rhythms, and departs into a sonorous little adagio passage of its own devising. A few hushed strings do immediately join it, drawn away from the structural work set up so far into a more ruminative and fluctile present tense in which the piece's creative meaning is up for grabs. The music steps back into an intimate space where it can ponder its options; it is as if the meditative intensity of the compositional process itself wants to surface for a moment. Composing and performing music are typically symbiotic or at least interwebbed, but the former can often seem subsumed by performance. It is where music is meant to end up after all, and in Mozart's century its drives and privileges often overran whatever had been composed all but wholesale. Maybe he wanted music for once to point the other way, briefly.

In this passage what we hear is a musical epitome of the most propitious aspects of this Salzburg period. We hear the violin construct an idyllic little enclave for itself in which it can ruminate on what it wants to become, and renew strenuousness by way of a momentary looseness. The mood soon spins out again into the impetus and texture of a normal concerto allegro; the solo violin takes off into yet another new melody of imperious lyrical freshness, and the orchestra's initial forcefulness resumes. But the rest of the concerto, across the lissome second-movement adagio and the closing minuet's swagger and flightiness, is inhabited too by at least a memory of this moment of reflective openness. So the sense of fertility and profuseness that defines its final movement is underpinned by what this small displaced adagio suggested about the concerto's sensibility. Elegant minuet idioms intersect with far more bracing folk music rhythms in a sort of polystylistic collage; a constant sense of rethinking is part of what Mozart now wanted musical form to be able to convey. The gently faltering rhythm of the concerto's very last phrase wittily but defiantly returns us to the hesitancy of the soloist's original entrance. A certain playfully halting reflectiveness has been defining this music all along, and we are not to forget it. Mozart is sometimes at his most impressive when he disdains to stun us; in moments like these he invites us almost conspiratorially into the complex open-endedness of musical construction. He may have taken the solo part himself when the concertos were first performed, but it is more likely that it fell to Antonio Brunetti, who was becoming the court's leading violinist. We can be confident that Brunetti did play them and also that he did not take to this final concerto, or at least thought its adagio movement excessively studied; he requested a replacement which Mozart unfussily provided. Perhaps he wanted a more virtuosically charged stage on which to show his chops, though the new adagio is no great move in that direction.

In his letter to Colloredo from the summer of 1777 the young composer asks his boss officially for permission to undertake the journey that culminated in Paris, and treats the archbishop to a conceivably unwelcome little homily on his duty to develop his gifts. 'The Gospel teaches us to take advantage of our talent', as he writes with a high mixture of sententiousness and verve. The archbishop allows the point with dripping sarcasm in his reply acceding to the request; maybe they both now knew that a break between them was inevitable sooner or later. Extreme creativity is always about the future. The dynamism of Mozart's music and its feel for multiple lines of development and slow–burn structural effects stem from this orientation and convey it; so does its feel for loss and transience. Modern experience is transient to its bones, and the multifariousness of art has been a vital way of knowing and coping with this condition, if also often enough a way of exacerbating it. Mozart was constantly dashing between projects that led down different routes, and soliciting or entertaining prospects from different directions. At any given point he can seem both settled and restless, or both well rewarded and broke, or both popular and neglected. He composed in a state of something like endless potentiality, and the arrows of time that he creates in his music are more compelling and ample than any arc that we can try to get his biography to fit. The fundamental arc of Mozart's career and basic facts like the fluctuations of his finances have stayed open to interpretation partly because he was endlessly oriented towards future prospects, changes or projects on the way or in the making which often themselves altered or evaporated. In this little passage of withdrawal and fluctuation at its opening, his last ever violin concerto shows his music wanting to step back from and to size up and to open out its relationship with its world. It is like hearing the future pause for thought inside the present.

4

Victoire Jenamy

'Jeunehomme' Concerto

Around the beginning of 1777 a young woman probably passed through Salzburg on her way to Paris from Vienna who was definitely not called Jeunehomme. Her name was in fact Victoire Jenamy, and the great K271 keyboard concerto in E flat that Mozart seems to have given her to play should have immortalized it. Mozart's characteristically eccentric transcription turned her surname into 'Jenomy', however, and scholarship somehow managed to amplify the glitch until it was 'Jeunehomme' that she had become. Earnest and brilliant sleuthing has since been required to put this right. No doubt the mislabelling was especially sticky because the French words for 'young man' are heard in it; Mozart wrote the concerto around the time of his twenty-first birthday. Record labels and concert promoters would always be keen to keep such a resonant nickname.

But the actual facts are resonant too. Victoire Jenamy was the daughter of a renowned ballet choreographer called Jean-Georges Noverre and she had followed her father from France to Vienna when he was lured there in 1767 by the Habsburg court. She was a few years older than Mozart, and her new surname came from her marriage to a wealthy Viennese merchant. Noverre's was a career almost restless enough to rival that of the young composer, and he and his daughter formed a close friendship with Mozart. We have evidence of her playing to public acclaim in Vienna during these years. But our sense of her artistry at the keyboard rests on the suggestive likelihood that Mozart wrote this dazzling concerto for her, a work that is a shimmering and tough leap deep into new artistic terrain. No one can be certain that he did not just hand over to her a piece that he had already been working on, but he was not regularly concerned with the keyboard concerto at this point, and in any case he would then have tended to remodel the piece for an important recipient like Jenamy. Mozart did not tend to identify works by the names of others unless the links were fairly direct.

The concerto can seem electrically insistent evidence that Mozart more than warmed to Jenamy, at least as a musician. She would also have been a vector for him, a way of reaching out from his home town exiled far from the centres of progressive culture, and of claiming allegiance to the wider circles embodied in her father. Noverre had just moved on again to work back in Paris, at the behest of none other than Marie Antoinette, whose Habsburg origins helped make her the great man's great ally in that difficult capital of culture. Jenamy in all likelihood stopped off in Salzburg while on her way there to join him. But the misnamed concerto that is likely to have been composed then may have been written by Mozart as a profuse way of restating his own identity to Noverre, a boldly expansive calling card sent to him by way of his daughter.

Noverre was far more than just some talented choreographer doing the European rounds. He was a revolutionary figure whose contribution to his art was on the scale of the great twentieth-century choreographer George Balanchine. The moment of the Jenamy concerto found him at a decisive point in his progress. Paris had many great cultural claims, but maybe the most important at the time was its status as the capital of dance. Dance had been central for at least a century to the French court's rhythms of ritual and display; the Sun King himself had been an excellent and rather vain dancer. But over his early career Noverre had developed his attitudes of innovation and reform at various points of remove from the Parisian centre of grand gravity, at lesser centres of dance like Lyon and Strasbourg, and amid the exuberance of London's commercial theatre scene in the age of Garrick. By the 1770s Noverre had already published his epochal treatise on the art of dance, the *Lettres sur la danse et sur les ballets*, and his aim seems to have been to mesh together Garrick's bravura psychological naturalism with the insistence on mimetic rigour and moral truth by which figures like

Diderot had tried to reorient enlightenment aesthetics in France. We can assume that he felt like a sort of exile from the great city which believed that it alone determined the ideals of the art, and that his attitudes thus gained penetration and trenchancy.

Paris was now calling on Noverre however, and it was its young Austrian queen who had sought to pull him in. Mozart would have been right to feel lightning bolts of affinity and identification with the older man's struggle for an aesthetic merger of fluidity with rigour. Noverre thought that the official style of Parisian dance was hardening into habits of mannered courtly sclerosis and recapitulatory flim flam, and he wanted instead an art pared down to the musculature of human existence. He wanted to throw down the world of masks and perukes and mechanical displays of courtly graciousness, and to recentre dance instead on an almost minimalist vision of realistic narrative action. The pithiest accuracy of observation and expression was meant to guide it, and he sought its lines of attack in the gestural intensity of everyday actions and in the range within ordinary movement, rather than aspiring to the easy hauteur of ordained taste or technical panache. The allure of this vision may have grown for Mozart as he chafed at Salzburg's courtly decorum. He then seems to have dispatched in Noverre's direction this guided missile of a concerto, itself concerned with throwing down all routine and inertia, at just the moment when the choreographer had been invited to the city where his work had hitherto remained alien. Now Noverre became master of ballet at the very opera house to which the continent looked to define the art of dance. Heard within the ambit of this moment of Noverre's ascent, Mozart's concerto reveals all its revolutionary litheness.

It starts with a gesture whose originality is both gleeful and stark. The orchestra's opening phrase is a brief and sonorously conventional fanfare that is immediately, astonishingly, answered with an antic impudence by the solo instrument itself. No one would have seen this coming; the soloist's first entry should wait until the orchestra has fully unwound some opening themes. But the keyboard cannot wait to intervene, as if music itself suddenly cannot wait to show what it can become. Mozart never again used this flaring trick;

maybe it shocked even him. Momentarily it feels like the breaking of a contract, as Mozart pushes the soloist so trenchantly to the fore that it pulls his own artistic sovereignty into the sharpest focus. The further twist is the speed with which the solo part then straightaway recedes, leaving the orchestra to resume its original momentum, before it then interrupts this exposition again with a fabulously surprising and ruminative trill just before what would have been its decisive conclusion. The opening gesture turns out not to have come from some wilful virtuoso clamouring to be heard or to dictate artistic terms, but to set loose a dynamic and complex recalibration. If the keyboard's entrance throws its part into solo emphasis, its withdrawal unnervingly frees up the orchestra to have its own say too. The soloist responds with ever more mobile and multicoloured passages, and throughout the opening movement and beyond the rhythms of different instrumental parts slide and interlock with drastic freedom, as if time itself had set out in search of new bearings. Music seems to surprise itself with its own freedom as this allegro opens, but then seems determined to figure out what it really wants to do with it.

By pulling the soloist with such taut briskness into the music at this early point, Mozart's concerto pushes the bodily reality of the player forwards with new force and clarity. The soloist's flesh is cast into the fray with a sort of rich suddenness that can remind us of Noverre's vision of dance, an art that after all centres on pressing out meanings from the flesh of its performers. Noverre sought direct, feelingful access to the bodily lives that dancers bring to their roles, and Mozart's breaking of the soloist loose from the concerto's normal litanies carries a comparable charge. Decorum is eviscerated, whether in its baroque guise of an overall rhythmic pattern guiding exchanges between orchestra and soloists, or in the galant version of a decorative interchange between accompaniment and melody. In its place come action and narrative and restlessness; the soloist's entrance is both vividly suggestive and rigorously cogent, and throws the player deep into the shifting decisions about dynamism and articulation that became central to Mozart's music. The piece's andantino middle movement is his first concerto movement

written in a minor key, and it does indeed suggest that he discovered in the very flow of composing it how he wanted his most
passionate music to sound. Expressive directness was one of
Noverre's ideals, but the sweltering intensity of this slow movement
becomes all but unassimilable. If the concerto is partly a manifesto
for a new expressive force in music, it does not hold back on how
far it may go. Maybe the classical style had romanticism straining
within it all along.

Its rondo finale then pivots on a passage that both reverses the
concerto's opening gesture and restates its liberating headiness. The
rondo starts with a presto section full of a rushing, rugged dynamism
which makes brilliant demands of the very muscles of the soloist's
fingers. Orchestra and keyboard throw phrases to and off each other
with wit and vigour, and textural density; we assume that the
movement will reach closure by pursuing this hurtling rhythmic
momentum rather than by complexity of structure or grand harmonic
twists. But suddenly the soloist draws back from the breathless fray
and seems to take a deep breath, while finding a new and dramatically slower theme to pitch the music next into a delicately stately
minuet that no one is expecting. A surprise can double when it
comes with an outburst, not of noise, but of quietness and restraint.
By taking such a densely prestigious dance form as the minuet and
stirring it with such force into a presto finale, the composer may
have found a way to send a fabulously specific greeting to the great
choreographer in France. The minuet had been adopted with fierce
insistence by courtly styles of dance, and absorbed into the most
ambitious versions of instrumental music, while retaining deep
links to its popular and even rustic origins. An implied history of
all the eighteenth century's wiry ambiguities dances through the
minuet movements in Haydn's symphonies. Mozart's writing here
conjures up the minuet's repertoire of bodily states with a sort
of delicate ruggedness. Suave, lisping courtliness on one hand
and hearty populism on the other were the dance's two terrains, and
Mozart's passage is full of darting suggestions of both these worlds.
Finally its force and its poignancy come from combining this
allusive treatment of minuet form with the lilting simplicity of

melodic line which the composer could floatingly borrow at will from the world of vocal music. We end up with a minuet that is at once crammed with the dramatic physical life that the concerto's opening stressed, and injected with cantabile style and its singing linearity. Bristling polystylistic brio combines with a certain enchanted poise.

Its sheer stylistic headiness should tell us how high the stakes were for Mozart in this concerto. He was more or less in psychic flight from his daily life in Salzburg by this point, and may have latched on to Noverre as a way of trying to set up a sort of ideal listener in the distance. The composer was in need of new fathers now that he was psychically ready to leave Salzburg, the family home and the archbishop behind. The same year would launch him on the ill-fated journey around Europe which would lead to his mother's death in Paris and his dissatisfied and unsatisfactory return. Salzburg was not a happy city in 1777 at all, as the still relatively new Archbishop Colloredo continued to inflict reforms on a place that he seems to have seen far less as some untainted idyll than a forlorn bastion of backwardness, in need of being both gripped and shaken up. Administrative chaos had pervaded the city's finances and its musical life alike when he took the job on. He was a deeply clever man and impressively determined to bring change, but Colloredo's prickly, mordant character was never likely to win over the adherents of Salzburg's long-standing ethos of backslapping and camaraderie. His agenda was doubly tricky for the Mozart family, since they had always thought of themselves as on the enlightened and cosmopolitan edge of their home town's social and cultural rhythms, and the cause of modernization was now identified with a figure for whom they had no more sympathy than their neighbours did. Mozart's music in the period building up to this breakthrough concerto is full of church sonatas and society music, rather than the grand and demanding commissions that he coveted. In their absence he was in danger of treating the latter of those genres particularly with hectic levels of ambition and technical vim. The K250 serenade that he wrote for the Haffner family is electrically expansive. Not long before the probable composition of the Jenamy concerto, he scored his K286 so-called *Notturno* for no fewer than four distinct bands to play in complex, teeming concatenation.

Mozart asserts himself with stark force as the concerto begins, and then steps back as if listening to what music really wants to be. He is an aspiring young man in tepid Salzburg as he writes, and he is also the master of all that he surveys, while trying to show his culture that it needs to be inclusive and harmonious and constructive if it is to thrive. As he composes or plays, his hands teem with possibilities brought by artistic strength, but they are also full of restraint and charm. Maybe Salzburg never really thought that it could keep him, but parts of him must have thrived on some sense that there he was at once contained and irrepressible. We might wonder too what the great Noverre could really have thought of this concerto in which the young composer did not just winningly refer to but deeply rethought the choreographer's own world of dance. Mozart's music generally is both sweepingly its own and infinitely open to other people's inputs. The Jenamy concerto can be rapt in its assertion of artistic identity at the same time as it seems to have been so densely and admiringly spurred by others. One of the things that his keyboard concertos are movingly about is their own openness to being played and remade by others. If this condition of openness seems obvious, it is one that virtuoso piano concertos over the nineteenth century would subject to exorbitant pressure, by interposing such exaggerated technical demands between themselves and ordinary players. But the restlessly gregarious concern with other minds that courses through Mozart's operas fertilizes much of the rest of his work too, and indeed often coloured his lifestyle. The composer and Jenamy and her father coincided in Paris later in the decade during Mozart's sojourn close to the opaque heart of French culture, but the ballet that he and the choreographer collaborated on helped him about as much as its title of *Les petits riens* prophesied. Links were quicksilver among such denizens of the cutting edge of creative Europe. Mozart had seemed unsure during the build-up to his Parisian venture what sort of a connection Noverre could be, but he was soon reporting proudly that he could have lunch with him daily.

Noverre may or may not have had the slightest suspicion at any point that this uncanny young man could end up overshadowing him, and seems to have been largely baffled by Mozart in the meantime. The great choreographer liked explicating his own greatness, and the fact that his work began to stall more generally around this time meant that the many remaining years of his life were often spent in making hectoring restatements of his importance and of the ingratitude of a world which he had shown the one true future of dance. His big appointment in Paris became mired in infighting and controversy and the city's increasing cultural deadlock well before the revolutionary events of a decade or so later. Marie Antoinette was not in the long run a secure source of patronage. Although his circumstances were reduced and his sense of personal prestige must have taken many knocks during the following decades, Noverre seems to have been wrong if he really worried that his ideas were being neglected. Dance historians think that it was more that they took on lives of their own. By the time of his death in 1810 his achievements had been so fully absorbed into Europe's churning culture that few seem to have cared much about him as an actual individual any longer. His name could be forgotten because his afterlife was so immense.

In art it is possible to be impatient and patient simultaneously; in fact great art relies on being so. Mozart shows himself in this concerto in the act of turning impatience into a form of patience. The concerto could not be clearer about the rushes of impetuousness and vitality fuelling it, but the impetus that it takes from these forces is in the end directed towards a very clearly meticulous and expansive act of artistic construction. Salzburg in the second half of the 1770s became a grindingly ideal education for the composer in both patience and impatience. As visitors and dignitaries and fellow musicians and travelling troupes went on passing through, the ways in which it was plugged into the world's grand currents may only have exacerbated the extent of its removal. Their leaving must often have seemed to take away more than their coming had given. It was the sort of place where the constant arguing in musical circles could seem to be for high stakes until the worlds towering in the distance were recalled. The young composer's violin concertos from a couple of years earlier are drenched with Salzburg even as they open up horizons well beyond it. But there is something almost terrifying about its irrelevance to the new keyboard concerto. The piece eviscerates the cosy winter pleasantries surrounding Mozart as he writes it. His father constantly complained about Salzburg, but it is easy to feel that in his case querulousness and restlessness were ways of belonging to the place. His son was good at creating new fathers for himself out of men like Noverre, and maybe he sometimes got all the more out of the process when it was tenuous and quickly relinquished.

5

The Lowly Viola

Sinfonia concertante in E flat

In Salzburg at the wintry start of 1779 Mozart's return was impatiently awaited by a father whose own life had irreparably changed during the previous months. On the day of the young composer's departure with his mother more than a year earlier on the journey that took them to Paris, Leopold sat alone after saying his farewells, but then suddenly realized that he had not given his son a paternal blessing. He rushed to try to send it after them before they disappeared, but it was too late already. He mordantly called himself a 'widower' as they travelled without him, and the full force of his wife's eventual demise must have been hard to grasp until Mozart returned without her; the absoluteness of her loss came home with him. The next question was whether Leopold was still a father, at least according to the model of fatherhood as a mixture of high vocation and hard labour that he had tried to maintain at a distance as Mozart wandered and delayed across Europe. Leopold was not in the habit of changing. He was an opinionated and highly emotional man, and the whole meaning of his life was rolled into his devotion to two things. One was his son's talent, and the other was the violin. His views on the violin did not just echo loudly in and around the Mozart household, but had made him an authority across musical Europe. Doubtless this could be annoying for his son. But it is characteristic of Mozart that he could both absorb and circumvent potential impasses, could find ways around them that also turned them into fuel for creative growth. The keyboard was always there for him as a stronghold. But around this time he seems to have found in the viola a way of both processing and exiting his mixed feelings about the violin.

A musical instrument is not just a little slab of matter cut and trained so that it turns the movements with which it is wielded into waves of sound. It is the embodiment of a set of feelings about the world that are so richly specified in each case as to amount to something like a set of proposals about what a body can be, about how it can move and how or why it might seek expression, and hence about what a person is and about the world in which people find themselves making music. So a composer deeply exploring writing for the clarinet is living in a different landscape or a different body from one immersed in the trombone or the xylophone; sudden access to this or that instrument's possibilities may resemble breathing some new variety of air. Mozart seems to have experienced this towards the end of the 1770s with the viola, and the crucial resulting piece shows how densely his grasp of its powers was embroiled with its closeness to the violin and its differences from it. The lushly exciting K364 *Sinfonia concertante* in E flat is the signal instrumental work of Mozart's final period before his move to Vienna and is a sort of double concerto for violin and viola, but with an orchestral part so rich itself that it disputes ideas of accompaniment.

By the middle of the 1780s the composer's favoured instrument when playing alongside Haydn with their Vienna quartet group was the viola. He probably took to it during the latter part of the 1770s however, during his later years in Salzburg on either side of the adventure that took him to Paris, and he certainly seems to have started around then to drift away from his father's strictures regarding the violin. The rise of the violin to its slightly haughty pre-eminence among string instruments was largely complete when Leopold became its spokesman. A partly humorous love for the lowly or overlooked may have aided the viola's appeal to Mozart. It has always been unfashionable, and jokes about it remain sources of baffling hilarity in orchestral circles. While it may not be intrinsically funny that the viola is not the violin, it does often seem to glance enviously at it. Its development had been driven by the desire to provide a lower harmonic counterpart to the violin that could still be played with roughly the same freedom as its lighter, friskier relation. Viola-makers have always sought to furnish it with as large and reverberant a sound box as possible while still allowing the instrument to be played in the same way as the violin, lifted up into manoeuvrable position on the player's shoulder level. So this is the viola's existential dilemma; it wants to be as sonorous as a cello but as agile as a violin, and wants to live up in the air while making sounds better suited to ground level. Mozart's interest may have been coloured by the ways in which the instrument hangs between two worlds.

The violin was meanwhile the exemplary instrument of the eighteenth-century court, because it brought melodic excitement and glittery display. Its tonal brightness combines with its easy manipulability to make it capable of singing its way above the orchestra, and of any number of virtuosic tricks once it is up there too. As concerto fever slid up from Italy across musical Europe during the first half of the century, the violin was the crucial instrument. Without it, the massive, intricate baroque styles of those decades would not have been so limber or liquid. Its qualities were also pivotal around the middle of the century, as those styles more and more loosened up, slimmed down and became flightier. The danger soon enough was that the instrument's soaring sound and its flexibility of expression were becoming predictable, unmotivated or meagre. Leopold wanted to cajole his son into becoming as much a virtuoso on it as he was on the keyboard, but the *Sinfonia concertante* suggests that it was more than just filial rebelliousness pulling Mozart towards a rather critical, angular perspective on the thing's airy powers. We may wonder how much his father was driven by some desire to keep Mozart's excellence from wholly outrunning the areas that he could control.

During the later 1770s the violin would have been at the heart of Mozart's duties with the Salzburg court orchestra. As he wrestled with the mediocrity of institutional musical life there and the humdrum standards of the players, and the general levels of distraction and querulousness that must often have prevailed, the violin would typically have been the vehicle for all these rankling involvements. The instrument was embedded not just in his father's exuberant pedagogical drives, but in all the demands and constraints that merged for Mozart with his home town's small streets and limitless sense of decorum. Its sound must have seemed soaked with the whole little world of the court band and its routines of organization and rehearsal, the chores of picking pieces that it could be trusted to play and of keeping an eye on which players were drinking too much and of getting them to tune their instruments and to keep the right tempos. After his months of partly awful, partly exhilarating travel, it must have been hard to know whether he wanted to remember or to forget the vastly expanded possibilities for orchestral musicianship that Paris and Mannheim had especially shown off. The dynamic slaloms and the unisonal discipline that orchestral playing was capable of in those two centres amounted to a thrilling break with a model of musical life structured around a meagre opposition between general mediocrity and individualistic virtuosity. A brilliant solo violinist was what Mozart did not want to be. He wanted comprehensiveness, a vision of music that would not subside into the surrounding insipidity, but without taking the easy routes of showy virtuosity in order to stake its claims.

The composer had managed to spend so little of his young life there that he must sometimes have been tempted to think himself not from Salzburg at all. But leaving and going back may confirm a place's claim on someone more surely than staying put would. The more Mozart had resented the idea of returning, the more starkly he knew that he did have to do so. Daily life on his return must have been full of conversations with friends, relations and officials in which questions of why he was back and for how long and why he had not found a starrier berth elsewhere may have been sometimes asked and sometimes left driftingly unstated. But there were no clear answers. Doubtless some thought that musical Europe had been insufficiently impressed. But little out there had entirely impressed Mozart; no better place could claim his full allegiance. The *Sinfonia concertante* is an intricate sonic map of these factors, one calibrated to show how well he knew the largest musical currents, and to prove that he was responding to them at levels of depth and inventiveness that were richly his own. His run of violin concertos from the middle of the decade had been his major attempt, during his previous stint in Salzburg, to synthesize his ambitions with the place. Without them the *Sinfonia concertante* could not exist, but adding the extra solo instrument of the viola acts as a sort of diagrammatic marker of much that he had amassed in the meantime, and of all that he now wanted to add to music. The lovely, impulsive liquidity of the earlier concertos shows how the violin's soloistic tunefulness could lure even Mozart towards a merely arbitrary or merely fluent brilliance. By contrast, the viola's fascination for a composer comes from its place in the thick of the world of orchestral sound, a place that it cannot sing or cut or blare its way out of.

Mozart wrote the piece after he had been back in Salzburg for at least a few months. It may have been longer; it may have felt like longer. Relishing and extending and investigating the viola meant engaging with the basic machinery of making music. It sounds from the piece as if he played the viola more and more around the time when he composed it. The instrument has a greater physical heft than the violin that pulls the body wielding it down and away from the dancing heights of melody, and into a larger and more even landscape of sound. Choosing the double or multi-instrument concerto as a genre was itself an expansive gesture, one that showed the composer feeding and sharpening his sense of ambition. The genre was a sort of modish updating of the old baroque form of the concerto grosso whose ways of weaving together soloistic and orchestral styles of playing had been fashionable themselves much earlier in the century, and then superseded by the coming of the symphony. But the symphony could not exhaust the styles and techniques that it helped foment, and the prestige of the new genre was particularly high in places like Paris and Mannheim which were rife with orchestral splendours. Mozart had a few goes at it around this stage, and the surviving results range from the dashing and vociferous K365 concerto for two keyboards to the inconsequential K299 flute and harp concerto, written for a father and daughter pairing of aristocratic amateurs towards whom the composer developed resentments that the piece's all but aggressive insipidity hints at. Writing such a concerto for the violin and the viola was nicely calibrated to his ambiguous position back in Salzburg; if the piece gestured towards more advanced horizons, pairing these specific instruments was not too great a stretch in itself for the place's tastes and resources. Plenty of his listeners and his fellow musicians there could have been expected to grasp at least parts of its dialogue with the earlier violin concertos, parts of the panache with which it extends what they achieved while breaking from them into a new expressive reach.

Right from the start the *Sinfonia concertante* tilts its meditation on the two instruments towards the more lowly and immersive partner. So even before the solo lines begin, the opening passages feature writing so low in the violins' register that it is almost polemically clear straightaway that they will for once play something more like second fiddle. Mozart had recently been immersed in French musical styles that had long favoured more complex, filled-out versions of the orchestra's middle registers. But the thorough remodelling of sonority that he pursues here is driven by a deep insight into equality itself. Since the violin suffused and slanted the musical world surrounding him in Salzburg, any real recalibration of the relationship between the two instruments had to happen on a terrain pulled hard in the other direction. A certain grainy, thronging bulkiness marks the orchestral sound from this opening onwards, and the lower registers stay vibrant and flexible. Various incidental factors contribute throughout, so that the sound-worlds of the horns and of the oboes are played off against each other with a richness that projects a sort of middle register in between the two. The piece fills itself with sonic bridges and analogies between its vision of the orchestra and the viola soloist, and as a result the solo viola part ends up reinterpreting what soloistic music is meant to be. Far from rising above the orchestra as solo violins tend to do, its colours glint or glare or swim from right within the heart of the sound. It is like watching sunlight work its way through rich clouds.

It is crucial that the solo violin and viola first enter in unison. In fact their sounds emerge only very gradually or even hazily out of the orchestral texture, at the end of an orchestral exposition that has become extended and dramatically exciting. Likewise, it is important that the two instruments are meant to play alongside their orchestral counterparts when they are not soloing. The viola was the right instrument for Mozart to throw himself into now that his life had thrown him back on himself, because its position in a piece of music can seem oddly parallel to that of a composer. The viola binds together an orchestra's various registers, surveying the melodic lines above it and the bass parts or the harmonic textures or the layers of sonority beneath or around it. Violas do their work amid the joints and links of music, its syntax; the instrument's sound may be something like the voice of the constructive element within musical form which composers need to cultivate if they are to make sounds work together at all. Mozart was around halfway through a stretch of about five years during which he did not produce a single concerto for solo keyboard, and this was a long period to be cut off from the forum in which he could most openly address the relationship between his artistry and the surrounding musical world. He was clearly a very accomplished player of both these string instruments. But bringing them together here allows him to create something that investigates and celebrates composing, and the endless scanning and renewing of existence involved for him in composing. The two instruments scan and renew each other.

The sheer physicality of the viola, as an instrument and indeed an object, is part of what makes it the medium in which Mozart can here remake himself. But this is a medium that resists; playing a viola with the bravura technical precision needed here enjoins a level of physical commitment that parallels and embodies the piece's sense of enlarged musical scope. The violin does more often than not trigger the basic thematic material that the two instruments share, as befits the higher register that makes it a naturally plausible vehicle for melody. Mozart's music is always grounded in a realism that is directed not least at what instruments are really capable of and good at. But the violin's melodic aptitudes are reshaped throughout. Its ideas are liable to be taken up and answered in the viola's related but flaringly distinctive tones, and must suit the whole piece's expansive sound-world. In turn the violin picks up on these restatements from the viola, and so learns a different set of ways of being a musical instrument. Its talent for bright melodic invention has to reckon with an orchestra that is discovering what it can do with its own large textures and momentums. Not just the viola but the orchestral parts are recharged by the violin, and learn how to engage with the versions that this changed territory gives to its variously soaring and impish swagger. The two soloists respond to and play off each other in feats of intense listening; receiving sound rather than producing it turns out to centre musical creation.

After the opening movement's flickering richness, the *Sinfonia concertante* gives a different version of expanded physical and psychic commitment by sweeping into a middle movement that is almost wildly plangent. The piece's extrovert artistic confidence is only one side of its vision of selfhood; in this movement especially it knows too the costs and griefs involved in coming to have any identity at all. One reason to keep calling Mozart a classical composer in the widest sense is that his flights and expansions keep arching back towards comprehensiveness and coherence. So in this work every frisson of innovation comes alongside an insistent drive downwards into the solid earth of structure, and every gleam of melody brings broad stretches of orchestral sound in its train. The stability of harmony and overall sound that the *Sinfonia concertante* exudes becomes inseparable in its final presto movement from a ranging giddiness, as if extremes of tenacity and of gliding motion were being made to intersect. Violin and viola lead and mimic and answer and ornament and dance away from each other. Ignition itself is earthed by such music; being inspired may indeed be the easy part of creativity, and the real work and perhaps also the real joy lie instead in turning it into structure and communication and abundance.

Mozart has blocked the violin from its favourite role of virtuosity; he then inundates the whole piece with a more thorough form of creative joy. We can hardly avoid wondering whether Mozart and Leopold might together have been the first soloists, and it is distinctly possible that he composed the piece as something that he could play on the viola alongside his violinist father. By now the composer must have known how much his powers had moved beyond his father's reaches, but that would only have been the starting point of whatever juxtaposition between the pair this music sketches. The viola relates to the violin part with delicacy and robustness; a broad, tender consanguinity prevails. All upstaging is in fact precisely pre-empted, and the piece installs a sort of firm and affirmative tactfulness instead, as the two instruments nudge and nourish each other. If the work must partly have been a way of warding Leopold off, it seems to reassure him that he still has a rich place in his son's life too. Whether or not they played it together, the piece suggests that the highest relationships have values of equality built in.

Mozart's return to Salzburg early in 1779 was hesitant and rueful. He had hedged options and thrown clouds of vagueness on his plans throughout the preceding months of autumn and winter, and his reluctance must have come from having no clear sense of what he had achieved, as well as from having so little enthusiasm for what he was returning to. His life could have seemed to him, or to anyone, a list of failures and impasses. German musical culture at its most advanced had failed to bombard him with offers or commissions, Paris had stayed remorselessly unconquered, and he appeared to remain a merely dazzling young man heading back to his homely home town and its bucolic and upright languor. He had not convinced his father or anyone else that he should be pulling the talented young soprano Aloysia Weber up along with him towards gleamingly successful horizons, and Leopold even seems at times to have held him responsible for his mother's death, miles away from home and at the mercy of French doctors. Salzburg must have felt like a place of privation, maybe even a sort of punishment. But it becomes necessary at times to stop ignoring or explaining away or transcending loss and failure, and to start absorbing and transforming them instead. The composer pours into the *Sinfonia concertante* as much of his situation as possible, the extravagance of his aspirations as well as his most sumptuous sadness, and the metamorphic resilience that both playfulness and beauty impart. Within it he can push deep into the sound of the Salzburg musical world, while projecting his artistic claims out onto the culture's furthest reaches. He can ready himself to break with the little city without ceasing, meanwhile, to be immersed in whatever it still offers. He can be alongside his father without feeling ground down or boxed in. Becoming capable of teaching Leopold was one thing; an even finer achievement was staying able to learn from him.

In 1783 Mozart made his only visit back to Salzburg as a married man, and there he wrote a pair of duos for violin and viola alone. The story that gets told to explain their origin comes from two students of Michael Haydn's, the great Joseph's brother and an important friend and colleague for the Mozarts in Salzburg. We hear that a set of six such duos had been requested from this Salzburg Haydn as part of his court duties, but that getting them done was proving tough. Joseph's reputation was galloping ever faster, but Michael cut a disappointed figure at this point, and alcoholism probably contributed to whatever indisposition held him back from finishing the set. It was a chance for Mozart to exhibit at once his largesse and his creativity, and perhaps to work some small mischief on Colloredo and his court. It is a good moment when our mischief and our benignity concur; it is like getting two different musical instruments to align. Mozart felt affection as well as ambivalent respect for Michael Haydn. His stifled fate in Salzburg must have been vicariously unsettling, a reminder of what could await someone who did not escape. He had even been given some duties once apportioned to the younger man.

According to these two students, Haydn had come up with four of the six duos needed, and Mozart volunteered to supply two of his own and to let them be credited to the older composer. It remains possible that he wrote them in more general response to Haydn's examples; but this would still have meant reopening the murky question of whether he and Salzburg could ever have fitted together. Their economical recapitulation of the *Sinfonia concertante*'s line-up suggests that he wanted to reconnect with that piece's gestures of exploration and grounding. Haydn's writing for the two instruments has a staid melodic tastefulness, but Mozart imports something of the experimental flair that his work for string quartet during the early 1780s was bringing. The viola slides back into the accompanimental roles that Haydn kept it in, but then breaks out into interaction and initiative and wit; the two instruments sometimes probe each other as densely as fencing duellists. Few alert listeners could have failed to notice the different level at which the two Mozart duos operate. But then perhaps Colloredo was more wryly aware of his lapsed employee's tricksiness than posterity has tended to assume, and more wryly regretful of what the city had lost in him.

6

Musical Homelessness

Idomeneo

Idomeneo opens with a solitary woman who stirs herself into an aria of incandescent lament. Her solitude is the first thing that we apprehend in this first of the sequence of great operas that Mozart wrote from his early twenties onwards. Modern productions may populate the stage around her with other characters from the opera, but the stark power with which the music pulls us into the oncoming drama is inseparable from Ilia's aloneness. She is an exiled Trojan princess, and a captive at the hostile court of Crete as the bloody war on her home city reaches its end in wholesale destruction. Her situation is complicated most forcefully by what this opening aria shows to be a fervent and self-lacerating love for the heir to the Cretan throne, whose father's imminent return from the war is set to make her status even more uncertain. The catastrophic shipwreck on his return sets in motion events that bring out all the contours of anomalousness and broken loyalty that define her. *Idomeneo* is an opera of disconcerting and sometimes jarring power, and our first point of identification within all this power is with a figure whose aria inspires both sympathy for her situation and awe at the sheer expressive force yielded by it.

The composer turned twenty-five on the day near the end of January 1781 when *Idomeneo* had its dress rehearsal. It had been more than half a decade since Mozart had seen a new and full-blown opera of his composition reach the stage, and *La finta giardiniera* had still felt like the product of a titanic apprentice, so sure that he is already a master of the available forms that he is all the more lurchingly mystified as to how he wants to advance their possibilities. His vision of what it meant to be an ambitious composer revolved around opera, so this had been a long hiatus, one strewn with stand-alone arias and other related or fragmentary projects that may have allayed some aspects of the frustration and stoked others. Above all, he had been immersed over the intervening years in the swirl of debates about opera with which European culture was both besetting and exciting itself, arguments often conducted with piquant polemical openness among critics and writers which were even more fervent when crammed into the actual lines and textures of music. The sound of *Idomeneo* belongs to someone ready to have his say about what his art is, someone who knows what a large-scale operation this must be. Its orchestration is on a huge scale and expects players of virtuoso standard to be dotted liberally around the pit; it makes huge demands on its chorus and on dancers. As Ilia stands before the audience after the kaleidoscopically expansive overture, but with nothing of her own except her drive for expression and desire to understand herself, she becomes a representative of Mozart's art. Why does music find its voice here in loss and exile? Of course, Ilia's version of those states throngs with desires for connection and belonging.

Mozart had already spent years pouring out his artistry and his intensity of feeling in front of innumerable strangers, in often haphazard and sometimes downright hapless contexts. *Idomeneo* came together as a fairly arbitrary project, and he made it his own only by some sinuous efforts of personal control and artistic will-power. The resulting mixture of grandeur and jerkiness has continued to make it a hard piece to stage. The opera was commissioned by the Munich court to celebrate the 1781 carnival season, and the conventional plot may have been picked with minimal involvement from the composer. The story of Idomeneo's fateful return from Troy was among the repertoire of stock situations that matched the needs of eighteenth-century *opera seria*, or 'serious opera', closely enough to keep suggesting themselves to the mainly less than innovative grandees and administrators in charge of it. All this makes it more remarkable how insistently Mozart took up a driving role in shaping how the narrative would be presented, and even deciding the libretto's details. His librettist Giambattista Varesco remained in

Salzburg when Mozart went to Munich to supervise the rehearsals, and letters whirring with requests for rewrites or news of cuts and changes darted from the composer to his father, who was mediating between the two collaborators. In particular Mozart was obsessed with paring the libretto back and making it swifter. At one point he asks Varesco for cuts that 'should be as drastic as possible'. He seems to have known from very early in the process that the sheer scope of his musical vision would gain from having a tightly defined dramatic object to wreak itself on, and constantly looks for this or that way 'to eliminate another unnecessary segment', as one letter phrases it. By the middle of January 1781 opening night is approaching, and he has made at least one cut himself that Varesco does not need to be told about, since 'in print it will appear just as he wrote it'.

Homelessness would have been in the air at the Munich court that commissioned the opera. It so happens that the whole apparatus of this court, all its personnel and their dependants and all its ramifying appurtenances, and crucially also its orchestra, famously the most advanced and virtuosic to be found, had just been uprooted from highly cultivated Mannheim, and shunted down rather precipitously in Munich. As normal, the blame lay with the sheer array of minor German states and the constantly shuffling pack of intrigues and claims that made up their politics. Mannheim's ruler Karl Theodor had just added the electorate of Bavaria to his titles, and was relocating himself unhappily to its capital. He and his retinue seem to have thought Munich a backwater, and exerted themselves to open it to cosmopolitan winds. Europe throughout the eighteenth century was constantly disrupted by territorial and dynastic disputes that were often minor but ripplingly contagious, and Karl Theodor's early years in his new job were grimly typical. He had needed to set himself up in Munich as quickly as possible to forestall Austrian claims, and his rule girded itself with complex bits of military strong-arming and diplomatic nicety. At one point the neatest solution seemed to be an odd sort of transcontinental land swap with the Habsburgs.

The audience that first heard Ilia's aria was thus full of people who knew what she was singing about and who faced threats of more of it, and they were listening to musicians whose lives were shot through with the same factors. The whole affair was chaotic and unsettling even if its actual military side was only ever fitful; the peace that followed was at best tetchy. Mozart was frequently caught up in such unpredictable shifts and their periodic lurches into outright warfare. Italy was the heartland of music during this period, and it exemplified this world of criss-crossing jurisdictions and hybrid allegiances and chequered, reversing political futures. Across the culture conversations among musicians were drenched with news and rumours about the latest manoeuvres and controversies there and elsewhere. The music that we now call classical carries the sound of a culture restlessly unsure, not just across chequerboard territories like Italy and Germany, whether the future would be on the side of those monolithic slabs of sovereignty called nation states or a gleeful or convulsive cosmopolitanism. Europe was a jostling tapestry in which innumerable small courts or minor potentates wanted reputations for endeavour and wealth and style.

By the middle of the century, cosmopolitanism was working itself deeply into musicians' lives and practices, and musical fashions skipped ever more fluently across and between societies and cultures. Musicians were moving all the time between courts, churches and cities, between opportunities and failures and new horizons. At the same time older versions of their professional lives based on courtly service and fairly oppressive ideas of loyalty were in many quarters budging only slowly. Often the same competitive factors that spurred mobility militated against it, since courts and other centres did not want to lose luminaries to one another. The musicians who moved from Mannheim to Munich demonstrate both sides of these charged vectors, since theirs was a mobility that had been more or less forced on them by their courtly roles. Principal among them was the great music director Christian Cannabich, the best that Mozart had ever seen according to one letter to Leopold; he was instrumental in commissioning *Idomeneo* and in charge of performing it. Having studied in Rome and Stuttgart, Cannabich became versed in the Parisian scene too, so he was well placed to supervise the synthesis of Italian and French musical styles that Mannheim was well located to attempt.

But innumerable centres and traditions flowed into and were fed by the stretching cosmopolitanism that made up music in the eighteenth century. Music was homeless, and its qualities of transfer and reinvention were replete with loss and fracture. Their sensuous dash and their openness to technical streamlining made Italian styles especially contagious. During the second half of the century, the 'concerto grosso' style of the long-dead Arcangelo Corelli enjoyed a vogue in the early industrial boom city of Newcastle, because one of his finest successors Francesco Geminiani, had a favoured pupil in the English composer Charles Avison who was from the region. Saint Petersburg became an unlikely northern hothouse for Neapolitan operatic trends, and during the 1790s the great French memoirist Chateaubriand found the same musical style being sung in the makeshift houses of settlers, as he journeyed through the forests stretching up to Niagara Falls during his own exile.

Celebratory tones can be hard to avoid when describing this cosmopolitan world. At the first performances in Munich the role of Ilia was taken by a famous singer called Dorothea Wendling, whose family typified the brilliant and expansive musical scene for which Mannheim had become famous. Her sister took another of the major roles in this first production of *Idomeneo*, while her husband had become a bulwark of the Mannheim orchestra's magnificently detailed sound; he was a flautist who was also renowned as a virtuoso soloist. The Mannheim authorities had long used music and the often rather frantic extremes of artistic distinction associated with it to boost their small court. Musical life was set up to allow for expansive touring on the part of such a prestigious adornment as Dorothea Wendling, and she also became an important singing teacher. The prevailing internationalism can be gauged by the variousness of the operas that were performed over the years before the court moved to Munich, during its seasons at its summer resort of Schwetzingen; pieces from the Italian and French and German traditions all mingled.

Homelessness and home had particular meanings for Mozart at

the moment of *Idomeneo*. The commission found him in a situation in some ways more difficult even than exile. In fact his return to Salzburg from the protracted, erratic tour that had culminated in Paris had left him a sort of failed exile. Mozart had long known the wandering life of a working musician. But as his extremes of talent and promise had failed to flow automatically into attainment and reward, the grinding relentlessness waiting within all such restlessness had come to the surface. By his mid-twenties he had come to know the darker sides of such destinies, the cruelty of the shifting weather of favour and rejection to which the clouds of jobbing musicians were subject. So too the deepest cut may come on returning to a home that has either changed or, worse, become all the more alienating because it has not changed enough. Having a home can be one of the more corrosive disguises that homelessness assumes. The offer to put on an opera in Munich promised further uprooting but must have been a thrilling relief.

Mozart's letters show how trenchantly he took this juicy commission as a chance to assert and to define himself. *Opera seria* was the house style of Europe's eighteenth-century culture of musical cosmopolitanism and homelessness. Two grand factors had come together in the two hundred years or so during which serious Italian opera had emerged from the peninsula's courtly entertainments to stream across the culture; one was the melismatic aptitude of the language for liquid musical settings, and the other the systematic revival of classical cultural precedents that the Italian renaissance had bequeathed to the baroque. The result was this all-conquering and hectically malleable form whereby highbrow tales from ancient history or myth became conveyor belts for vocal set pieces. Its lineage reaches back at least as far as Claudio Monteverdi's swirlingly sensuous, intellectually dense experiments in Mantua and Venice early in the previous century, but during the first half of the eighteenth century especially it spiralled across Europe's erratic terrain of merchant cities and hybrid jurisdictions and small but disputatious dynasties and alliances. On the other hand by the time of *Idomeneo* this dominance had for decades been audibly straining, eroded from within by the gross material and financial demands that the style's prestige and the resulting rivalries exerted, and buffeted by factors like the rise of its comic counterpart of *opera buffa* in esteem and popularity and in artistic scope. By the beginning of the 1780s Mozart's assertive ambitions could tilt *Idomeneo* into offering an implicit reassessment of the whole world of *seria* values. The genre had thrived on the volatile cultural cosmopolitanism to which he had been dizzyingly exposed, but this volatility was in danger of subsuming it too.

It is striking that the opera's plot concerns precisely a warped, violent process of generational change, as Ilia's beloved prince comes by crooked routes to replace his father on the Cretan throne. The story turns on his determination to go out alone to fight the sea monster inflicted by the circumstances of his father's return, and we may well think of the mixture of dashing exuberance and almost terrifying force with which Mozart himself here takes on the cultural world around him. The craggy, veering amplitude of *Idomeneo* is the sound that the composer makes as he battles to find a form capable of containing as well as expressing his own relentless powers. All the opera's hectic energy comes from a single insight on his part into how he could crush together two great forces in contemporary music. Mannheim's musicians had pioneered ways of integrating virtuosic playing styles with emphatically tight and dynamic ensemble disciplines, anticipating the ways in which the symphony orchestra at its best in centuries to come would seek to operate as a sort of virtuoso instrument. At the same time the great German composer Christoph Willibald Gluck had been restlessly and strenuously spreading his vision for a holistically refined operatic aesthetic across some of Europe's most prestigious musical centres. Mozart's recent travels had drenched him first-hand in the Mannheim sound-world, and thrown him into circles that were loquaciously preoccupied with all avenues for reforming the art of opera. In *Idomeneo* he learns from both these tendencies with an electrical excitement, but there is also something violent in the vigour with which he makes them his own, as if a threat is being staved off. The Italian libretto can make the piece seem more committed to the *seria* tradition than it really is. Rather, it uses *opera seria* as a battered but robust framework within which to probe away at flashy and pugnacious new types of instrumentation, and new possibilities of more sharply contoured dramatic structure. The hungry orchestral amplitude and the narrative exuberance that result make *Idomeneo* no longer fully at home itself in the world of *opera seria*.

Mozart's opening scene for Ilia is full of grim splendour; we can hear both him and her embracing as well as wrestling with a deeply shaky world. He wanted the opera's beginning to have a sense of abundance and momentum capable of making this isolated woman into a spring from which three acts of high drama rush out. Opera audiences in the eighteenth century were full of chatter and general sociable noisiness, and the overture thus had the job of not just catching the attention, but funnelling all the restless energy surrounding a performance into the opera itself. Listeners in Munich especially knew and loved the lavish instrumental possibilities that Mozart's overture here invokes, and would have been especially sensitive to the ways in which he uses the explosive colourfulness that their orchestra was capable of, as a source of new sorts of dramatic tension and momentum. The overture's structure is if anything simplified, but this allows its agitated harmonic language and teeming instrumental colours to become so dense without losing shape. The same formula lies at the heart of the whole opera, and is what Mozart was getting at in trying to streamline the libretto. He did not want *Idomeneo* to be on anyone's idea of a small scale. Paring down the action was a way of heightening its dramatic movement, and of giving its almost painfully rampant musical inventiveness a drastic clarity. Streamlining the overture's formal structure likewise means that it can avoid resolving the intense load of musical tension that it generates without losing focus. In fact it gains focus and momentum as a result and can then pour them directly into Ilia's music, getting them to reach right through what would normally feel like more of a break between the sections.

The same combination of overall streamlining with a craggy proliferation of complex harmonies and expressive leaps is at work in Ilia's aria too. Her quicksilver shifts between despair at what she has lost and the stirrings of erotic hope come across with such crackling sharpness partly because the aria's basic shape is actually relatively simple. Likewise, the swirl of instrumental mass that binds the overture, her heavily orchestrated recitative and then the aria all together has the effect of making Ilia's condition a sort of dramatic incarnation of the fluid and polystylistic musical world that the overture sets up. Passions of love and hate and of jealousy and revenge and of bewilderment and pride course from her throat in ways that would have been more than familiar from sprawling quantities of eighteenth-century music. But Mozart's music does not just want to depict these states with renewed opulence and fervour. The princess's farewell to homeland and family has been forced on her by history, but the aria shows the character seizing hold of the meaning of her experience on her own rushingly distinctive terms, and its music maps this process intricately onto its own quest for a new sort of dramatic wholeness that will emerge precisely by way of turbulence. She grasps the contradictions of her situation on an island that is for her both a prison and an erotic paradise, and Mozart's music likewise reveals its own doubleness, the ways in which its turbulence opens onto possibilities of change.

Mozart's feeling for structural unity is often what allows him to investigate diversity and change with such depth. If this opening scene carries crackles of energy forwards from the overture's unresolved orchestral fervour, the recitative is correspondingly rich in the sheer amplitude of its instrumental writing, and in the motivic freedom that this allows. The point of the recitative as a convention was to give an opera's characters a more sketchy musical forum in which to tell its story before launching into the brilliant, shapely arias themselves. Composers were tempted to make these passages as short as possible, and as distinct from the arias as possible; the more straightforward musical pleasures would then never be far away and would stay relatively unimpeded by their surroundings. The rewards in a culture that craved vocal feats were obvious, but dramatic coherence was constantly endangered. Mozart here rethinks both these tendencies, at once expanding the recitative and blurring the edges between it and the aria that follows. In his hands recitative allows the more open instrumental textures and the jerky rhythm whereby Ilia's ravaged, probing psyche attains a stenographic vividness. But since moving into the aria still involves increasing the expressive intensity and formal power, the drama there becomes invested with how it feels for someone like the exiled Ilia to find her voice at all.

Yoking together recitatives and arias was often a fairly threadbare process, but Mozart here turns the movement from one to the other into a revelation of psychic self-discovery and freedom. The consequences for the rest of his operas and for opera more widely were incalculable. He could not have done this if he had not been able to rely on these particular orchestral musicians to release into their playing all but recklessly unsettling forces of freedom and instability in ways that were also deeply and finely controlled. The intricate phrases of the recitative are crammed with sonorities that seem to be straining with expressive energy without leading anywhere definite. But this is a version of homelessness that the musicians must be capable of grasping and redirecting and recoding, and the aria must gain momentum from the more formally shapely terrain that it finally sets out, without ceasing to extrapolate from the recitative's wiry tensions. As Ilia pauses after calling for her own unhappy heart to be torn asunder before launching into her song of farewell, one dazzlingly brief transitional passage has to work as a fractious source of unity, at once summarizing the recitative's sense of errant tension and introducing the more resolute dynamism of the aria itself. Richly chromatic sonorities and compressed harmonic leaps and segues can then proliferate in the aria in ways that do not just assert Ilia's complex, flighty emotions. Rather, she navigates and exploits them in ways that bring her complexity and intelligence alive. The aria is drastically hybrid, and still positively drips with the styles of liquid vocalizing that *opera seria* had thrived on for decades. By its end, no one can think that this is just one more flimsy and desperate heroine. If Ilia opens up the opera's vision of a world racked by loss and displacement but also thronging with promise and creativity, Mozart's music doubles down on both convulsion and potential. Maybe writing an opera of such structural heft could feel like a blazing homecoming for someone whose whole life was pervaded by music. But in the end it does become possible to feel a little disengaged from the fervent and rather relentless splendour of the thing.

It is still a fairly early moment for the composer, though. The opera's first audiences were both struck by its immense qualities and unsure of just what it amounted to; *Idomeneo* uses up quantities of tempestuous artistry to reanimate forms that it also suspects are nearing exhaustion. Its premiere was postponed because of its complexity and scale. Six performances had been intended but only three were carried out, and it became a sort of homeless opera over the decade of life remaining to the composer. His attempts to revive it did not succeed beyond a single outing in March 1786 at the private Palais Auersperg in Vienna, although on at least one occasion he put an aria from it into one of his concerts.

Mozart's greatest achievements in opera would come in styles closer to the comedic *buffa* tradition. Of course these works do also further his investigation of musical homelessness, and their comic exuberance asks serious questions of seriousness itself. Dramas of homelessness and its assuagement also migrated into Mozart's purely instrumental music. His basic tactic as an instrumental composer in fact involves again and again setting up sound-worlds and phrasal patterns that a given movement moves away from and develops and then finally, in ways that can be tortuously complex or richly so or sometimes both simultaneously, returns to. 'Sonata form' is the name that musicologists use to refer to these copious, flexible processes, and especially to their interaction with some developing harmonic argument across a movement. Mozart's finest concertos and symphonies can reveal themselves as brilliantly flexible narratives of errancy and homecoming, can amount indeed to existential allegories of the fates of psyches and societies pitched into change. Across the following century or so, musical homelessness would emerge in the broken psychic narratives wandering through Schubert's songs and in the ambivalent dramas of unhousedness and the destruction of worlds that storm through Wagner's operas. We can imagine some possible narrative of musical modernity with homelessness at its heart, but this homelessness itself veers around.

Seria style reappears in bursts and waves over the following years in Mozart's great comic operas, so that Donna Anna's high anger in *Don Giovanni* and Fiordiligi's labile sensuousness in *Così fan tutte* and the raging agility of the Queen of the Night in *Die Zauberflöte* generate shattering energy by slanting across its norms. Displacing and recontextualising the style are the composer's ways of keeping its full fervour alive.

Someone was absent from Munich as Mozart unfurled his vast opera that winter. It had been in Munich that Aloysia Weber had rejected him in the last gasps of 1778 after his months in Paris. But her talent too was restless, and by the winter of *Idomeneo* she and what the composer called her 'beautifully clear voice' had moved to Vienna along with her family. His months of work on the opera surrounded Mozart with many of the same people among whom he had found and known her; the surging acclaim that these cognoscenti now gave him must have been inflected by the absence of the person whom he had most wanted to impress and the voice that he had most wanted to fill with music. She had sung arias in *seria* style by him during his time in Mannheim, and he continued to associate that side of his musical personality with her. On at least one occasion during the 1780s in Vienna she would even sing music from *Idomeneo* as part of a concert in which they both participated. While the opera was coming into being, her voice must have been lacking and yet palpable, a memory and a lure that the work's raging expressive colour at once draws on and dispels. Mozart would marry her sister Constanze soon enough. By then the flaring energy produced by *Idomeneo* had helped him in breaking away to Vienna himself.

7

Being Praised

Piano Sonatas in C, A and F

Someone who is often praised is often someone who is deeply alone. Living up to praise can be one sort of shiny burden, and praise can be charged with premonitions of a time when it might vanish. It can sound insincere or focus on the wrong things or invoke hated rivals as reference points; it can finish too soon or extend to embarrassing lengths. Someone who is praised is normally being told what to be, or at least what to continue being, and also how important the person doing the praising is. Performing artists set up their lives as laboratory experiments in which the questions that teem around praise and recognition play out in expansive, brightly lit versions. Being praised had been a way of life for Mozart for a long time before the move to Vienna, and his work often sounds pleased by the praise that it is about to receive. So too this must have brought him sooner rather than later to some unusually high realism in assessing the meaning of praise.

How did Mozart strike people in the early 1780s as he made his way in Vienna? The composer was small and rather nondescript in appearance. But his demeanour was eager and quick, and often fidgety. It was as if his flesh were engaged in a constant, hustling protest against how unimposing he was. Swift pivots between masterfulness and obsequiousness would often have been required; sometimes he needed to be a salesman or even a huckster. Mozart liked dressing to impress, but his idea of urbaneness probably struck a few as gauche. It can be hard to make buttons or buckles shiny enough without rendering them too eager to dazzle. The composer came from Salzburg and from the whole of Europe; he could seem to be a bumpkin, but was more cosmopolitan than the slickest grandee. Music had been his passport to seeing about as many high and low sides of the social barnyard as his world contained, whisking him into exalted enclaves while also plugging him into the broadest movements and changes. On entering a room he probably often looked around for a keyboard; without one he may have felt like a sailor whose sea legs let him down on solid ground. The quantities of impact and panache held within the intensity of his talent probably suggested themselves to some before he even started playing, but maybe for the most part only through the hints of hauteur within his restlessness, and the ease of his chatter. In plenty he inspired simple and lasting affection; his swivels between boisterous bonhomie and flows of concentration must have been impressive and endearing. A knight who really knows his quest can find it easy to be generous and fun. Solitude may still haunt him like a dragon. Mozart's speaking voice was normally gentle, but could become insistent when directing some musical occasion; he occasionally stamped his feet then too.

We can imagine Mozart rising from his instrument on occasions when he knows that he has not been at his most sparkling, and finding himself garlanded regardless. But so too raptures of response to some especially successful display may have seemed specious or septic when they did not translate into practical results. Needing to figure out which torrents of praise implied real prospects of help must have been good exercise for his psychological powers. Singers typically got the most rapture in the spheres of opera and vocal music that Mozart often cared most about. Composers may find themselves at the edge of the limelight, wondering whose music the audience takes itself to be acclaiming. Hearing others being praised can be annoying to the point of horror for someone whose life has been based on being praised himself. Mozart must often have seen how misleading, unsettling or aggressive praise and its gyrations could be in the lives around him too. Weighing when and how much to praise others must have been a constant job.

A freelance of the sort that Mozart became in the 1780s may often feel only as good as his last round of applause. But then his decision at last to pitch himself fully into such a life was powered by praise in the first place, in particular by the storms of admiration raised by *Idomeneo* among Munich's meticulous musical circles. The city's singers and musicians were at once hard-bitten and renowned, but their responses were unstinting. No doubt the virtuosic players of Karl Theodor's orchestra were keen to show how richly their powers could unfurl in the operatic arena with all its glamour and prestige. Rehearsals for such a keynote commission were open to interested parties, and the atmosphere seems to have been euphorically excited. One of the star sopranos was so pleased with one of the scenes for her that she wanted to hear it three times in a row; a clever young count told Mozart how high his expectations had been and how entirely they had been surpassed. The oboist Friedrich Ramm claimed that no music had ever made such an impression on him. Finally the elector himself outdid the heights of praise by wondering how such great things could come out of such a small head as Mozart's. A daft remark can count for much if it comes from the right person.

The effects of this effusive atmosphere can be felt everywhere in the work's expansiveness and opulence. It may be that the actual performances when they arrived early in 1781 after many weeks of work were something of a comedown; maybe only those most immersed in the musical scene of a great and progressive centre like Munich could grasp how lavishly the work stretched and rewired opera's possibilities. Mozart had two versions of himself jostling within him in Munich; in one he was Salzburg's court organist on a tenuous furlough, and in the other a master redefining the possibilities of music. While the process of creation had been in train and with excitement building, it must have been easy to fold the facts of the first of these versions into the lustres of the latter. His work on the final act became hesitant. Maybe he was lurchingly reluctant to cease being the man who was working on *Idomeneo*. Writing the opera finally emboldened him to cut loose by moving to Vienna, but the boldness of the decision was undergirded by a horror of having to shrink back into Salzburg.

The little city's ruler had only unenthusiastically granted his court organist leave to pursue the opera, and this must have redoubled

Mozart's keenness to find a way of life in which no one could bar him from chasing more such triumphs. If *Idomeneo* seemed a triumph in a vacuum, a marvel that few could fully marvel at and which left his life in danger of staying right where it was, the same keenness must have been further whetted. His big move was expedited when Colloredo had to spend time in Vienna in early 1781 and called for his employee to join his entourage, so as to provide high-calibre entertainment and hospitality in the imperial capital. Mozart ended up travelling there not from Salzburg but from Munich, and was a semi-detached member of the archbishop's crew from the outset. The promising season of spring was just about to start when he arrived.

Right from Mozart's arrival in Vienna, the haughty archbishop and his brilliant employee ratcheted up their mutual distrust and resentment, and their grinding interactions were weighed down further by the quantities of court etiquette involved. Layered agendas were common to the two men, and Colloredo's attentions were split between tending to his severely ill father and testing how far Joseph's sway as sole ruler was changing the city's political weather. In some ways being summoned even peremptorily suited the composer, particularly as it became clearer that no grand job offer was imminent in Munich. Carrying on serving the Salzburg court in the imperial capital meant that he could weigh his chances without committing himself straightaway. Likewise the archbishop got a lot out of showing his young star off, while treating him as a bizarre underling who needed to do his bidding. Mozart's prowess at the keyboard was doubtless the pride of Salzburg, but it also pulled him into the circles of posh salons and grand admirers that promised a different future. He started issuing petitions stating his wish to resign, but could not even ensure that they pierced the zone of officialdom surrounding the archbishop. He never exactly got Colloredo to give him the boot in official terms. Instead the boot of a certain Count Arco gave him a famous kick in the backside, as this official sent the young musician packing from the ante-chamber where he patrolled their boss's interests. Mozart had already been called a scoundrel, a rogue and a cretin by Colloredo himself.

But he tells his father that it is being kicked in the behind by this lordly obstacle 'that means in straightforward German that Salzburg no longer exists' for him.

The anecdote has been a biographical favourite ever since. Mozart quickly gave it a cunning interpretative arc, since he needed a way of justifying himself to his father. Leopold seldom passed up chances to be didactic, whether at the music stand or while lecturing his way around the continent's architectural highlights, and one of the nostrums that he drummed into his son's head was the importance of honour. Yet honour came back to haunt him when that kick helped make it the outraged watchword of Mozart's final disaffection with Salzburg, and of his final refusal of his father's anxious and sometimes angry attempts to get him to rethink. Leopold worried about where the move would leave his son, alone in the big city with no set future or regular income. It would leave him isolated too, in the distant placidity of Salzburg. Count Arco would eventually have been back to regale the little city with his own version of the debacle.

The first of two substantial letters that the composer wrote to Leopold on 12 May has a vignette that is heady with these ruptures and their impact. In the evening after one talk with the sneering archbishop he went to the opera, but the strain of their interview left him trembling so feverishly that he had to leave halfway through the first act; the composer 'staggered about in the street like a drunkard'. He evidently knew in his bones how much change he was embarking on, and how much of his world he was challenging. Maybe he was drunk partly on the exhilaration of what he was becoming, as the heart of Vienna wheeled fervently around him, and summer began to emerge from within spring. Sometimes Mozart's mood over these months can seem bombastically serene and sometimes brightly warlike.

Praise meant everything and nothing to Mozart in the Vienna into which he was pitching himself. It was both his daily need and a mercurial currency that was often hard to weigh, let alone to cash out. Of course, empty promises and stingy patrons and the plethora of competitors could all make it hard to monetize acclaim. But the problem was also structural, something internal to the drives of Mozart's artistry. The ways in which he wanted to keep pushing music further meant that he stayed relentlessly dazzling, but the heights of praise from connoisseurs do not often provide the steadiest terrain on which to build a career full of income. A certain will to insecurity is audible in the very panache with which his works both sharpen and dispute their own capacities to delight. An odd doubleness ends up pervading Mozart's life in Vienna, as unprecedented acclaim and noisy applause are continually shadowed by shortfalls of income or feelings of neglect.

His friendship with the prominent diplomat and administrator Gottfried van Swieten shows that Mozart did not solve these questions but kept them cascading productively through his life after his move to Vienna. Swieten's father had been the Habsburg court physician, and the son had used his connections to get a prestigious appointment in Berlin representing Vienna to the insurgent Prussian powers. A diligent musician and full of fierce intellectual conviction, he was there able to join circles devoted to preserving baroque style at its most demanding. He tasked himself with spreading this almost musicological project after returning to Austria. In Vienna he organized gatherings of musical enthusiasts drawn from the creamiest of the capital's elites regularly at noon on Sundays, and soon after his move there Mozart began religiously attending. Swieten's stiff character was hardly suited to the sometimes downright bubbly composer, so their shared musical passions must have done much to make the strong accord between them possible. At the same time they both needed allies among the city's slippery factions; Swieten may have seemed to swim among the elites as a native, but he and his father were both really technocrats who were on the heights by dint of such dubious means as hard work and merit. During the 1780s he was in effect a minister for education and culture under Joseph, a role that would have attracted flack and bile at least as much as it brought any prominence worth having. The rigour and the volatility alike that Mozart found in music could be made sense of in Swieten's circles, partly because his own music was not the centre of attention. Rather, in this world he was one admiring and curious explorer of the baroque past among others. His main role seems to have been to hack his way at the keyboard through whatever sense he could make of Swieten's antique scores.

Vienna became the place where new visions of music could unroll partly because of Swieten and others like him whose experiments in culture and identity paralleled Mozart's creativity. Swieten was a brilliantly thorough avatar of new ways of life that the century was opening up, an entrepreneur of his own personality and expertise like innumerable others who crisscrossed Europe's cities and courts seeking advancement or new trends. His influence especially must have lodged itself in Mozart's psyche in part because of how neatly he seems to have replicated aspects of Leopold's character and roles. The composer seems to have known that he needed, as he took on Vienna, something like a conscience for his musical mind to work with and against. Swieten was as full of himself and as grandly pedantic as Leopold, and doubtless the pleasure to be had in pleasing him could be large. No doubt too it was important for Mozart to be able to see round and beyond these figures of conscience easily enough; he seems to have liked having someone around whose belief in him was stimulating partly because its officiousness gave him much to react against.

One early trophy of those Viennese years came when the composer was asked by the emperor Joseph, around Christmas in 1781 and hence not long after he had finally settled in the capital, to come to the palace to participate in a sort of keyboard duel with Muzio Clementi. Clementi long outlived Mozart and himself composed important music for the early piano; his work continues to find dedicated players. But at the end of his twenties as he was when this championship play-off occurred, he was best known as a virtuoso performer travelling around Europe to show off his technique. Mozart and he had done the rounds of many of the same inevitable grand places like Paris and Munich, and the keyboard contest must have felt for them both like an encounter with some flickering double. The glamorous rigmarole of concert life in London had shaped the course taken by Clementi, after the glaringly fashionable

Beckford family brought him to England as a teenager to be a sort of prize continental specimen for them to show off. A suave presence and a shrewd thinker as well as a commanding player, he combined an acute understanding of what musical culture wanted with the dexterity and feel for hoopla to provide it. Clementi was one of the first to grasp how fully keyboard technique could be remade for the age of the fortepiano, the versions of flamboyance and address that the instrument opened up.

Joseph needed to impress a titanic pair of Russian visitors whom it had fallen to him to entertain that winter, Grand Duke Paul and his consort Maria Feodorovna, who was in fact of German origin. Something of the twitchy rivalry between the two empires in question must have been in the air, as the two masters of the keyboard were pushed into a rivalry with each other of which both may have had reasons to be wary at least. Joseph chose to exploit the fact that Maria Feodorovna was herself a noted keyboard enthusiast by making a bet with her as to who would most impress. He would back Mozart as his Viennese champion in the joust. In his correspondence back to Salzburg, Mozart's account of the event glows with an excited ambivalence in which annoyance at the presumptuous demands of this definitively ruling-class audience mixes with disdain of his rival's claims, and some mischievous glee at the pumped-up occasion. Clementi said later that the elegance of Mozart's appearance made him assume that he was one of the emperor's chamberlains.

Mozart seems to have been happy enough with the first part of the encounter, in which the two men in turn played solos, not least because for now he was playing an instrument that he had brought to the occasion himself. Outrage takes over when they then have to improvise duets with each other, now both on instruments belonging to the emperor. Joseph insisted on this point; his idea must have been that duetting instruments should be fairly matched. But Mozart was sure that a faulty mechanism was making his keyboard sticky, and stopping him from responding as he wanted to the exuberant right hand runs for which Clementi was renowned. Further, he seems to have thought that the emperor was either testing or teasing him by giving him this instrument; a cryptic pleasure in such travails would not have been incompatible with Joseph's tricky character. Mozart must have felt like some medieval champion whose lady makes him switch his fine steed for a nag. His protests were waved away and he was required to keep wowing the audience. He seems to have been unsure whether the whole event was a slightly funny pinnacle or a vexatious farce. Being praised can mean being demeaned.

All art does implicitly want praise, though it may interpret this fate scornfully. Reading the dissection of Clementi's technical flamboyance and what Mozart thought were its failures of taste and expressiveness that follows in his correspondence with his family, we may forget how often and richly he bestows praise elsewhere. He explains why he dislikes Clementi's playing in a letter intended to dissuade his sister from learning to play the other man's sonatas. Clementi's showiness is stultifying and ingratiating, and is built into his compositions in ways that will erode the playing of who- ever takes them on. The dangers of an artistry that solicits praise meretriciously are contagious; the tips of Mozart's fingers would have known how much emptiness easy reactions can exude. Being a performer as well as a composer exposed him to these dangers, and let them energize his constant drive towards structure. Mozart in effect argues that falseness and deterioration lie in wait precisely for those who can claim mastery. Excellence is not enough any more than being praised is enough.

During his first few years in Vienna in the 1780s teaching the keyboard was vital to Mozart. It is not surprising that the questions facing him as a composer and his strong ideas about the right ways to play the instrument flowed in and out of one another. Right around the time of the duel with Clementi, one of his most important pupils was a young woman called Josepha Auernhammer whose family had helped him out during his move to Vienna. He is in his letters at least as caustic about her personal qualities, and about what may or may not have been her romantic designs on him, as he ever was about the claims of any musical rival. But the music for two keyboards that he wrote for them to play together conjures a bracing and affectionate partnership. The equality of demand that it extends to the two players constitutes an implicit act of praise and recognition towards a woman who would have a significant musical career of her own. In Mozart's writing for two keyboard instrumentalists, whether for two keyboards or for four hands at one, the relationship between the two players is often the deep concern. Rather than layering sonorities or textures in quest of a completely different sound-world from that of solo piano music, he is interested in how two different voices relate to each other, and especially in the sorts of symmetry and reciprocity that can come when they make space for each other. It is not that his music ever wants to escape entirely the factors of rivalry and praise that were spurred on by the keyboard match with Clementi. Rather, he wants them to feed into collaboration and connection. The pulse of symmetrical phrasing that sustains so much of Mozart's music opens in such pieces onto highly various visions of what symmetry can amount to, and of the ways in which players can be equal. Symmetry becomes a way of praising other people's possibilities.

At the heart of Mozart's composing over these years was a set of three solo keyboard sonatas that he eventually published with the high-end firm of Artaria in 1784 as a single oeuvre. No doubt Artaria's preference for publishing substantial oeuvres had something to do with this arrangement, and the three sonatas may well have originated in distinct contexts and even at rather different moments during these first years in Vienna. So too they are widely known now in their separate manifestations of the K330 sonata in C, the K331 sonata in A with the famous rondo in so-called Turkish style as its finale, and the K332 sonata in F. But they were sent out into the world together first, and together they constitute a composite, playful and cogent picture of the state of Mozart's art at this crucial juncture. Throughout eighteenth-century music there was a widespread tendency to think in terms of larger units made up of sequences or conglomerations of individual works, and Mozart consistently did so at vital turns in his artistic progress. Units like these could crystallize artistic drives all the more richly because their unities were so loosely defined. Creating unity and diversity out of each other was one of the endless tasks and joys of Mozart's art.

But then during these years he was also preoccupied with how all the diverse currents of his creative and professional life could flow together, and solo keyboard music had a paradoxical social versatility that made such questions both apt and urgent. Mozart would have wanted to be able to play the sonatas at small-scale performances himself. He would also have wanted to use them for teaching purposes which would probably have included composition lessons. Likewise he would have wanted to be sure that they were right for publication and so for the use of others, not just in music-making in domestic or salon settings, but also for their own pedagogical purposes. Publishing meant sending them off as ambassadors for Mozart's art in unpredictably expanding circles, not least when done under Artaria's prestigious auspices. It is no wonder that they sound now at once like subtly various anthologies of the ramifying musical possibilities of that moment, and also like analyses of what fundamentals of style and attitude would help anyone to negotiate such a plural world. In them we find someone who wants his work to be resolutely splendid but also elegantly available to different sorts of audiences and players. All the reams of brilliant talk and social display that filled the eighteenth-century salon relied on the willingness of its denizens to listen to one another too, to make room for other views and further perspectives, to value balance. It is this that made the salon the incubator of classical sensibility with its desire for balance and flexibility and a light touch. In these sonatas, Mozart balances the strenuousness of his ambition for his art against the needs of other people's ears and hands, and against his own willingness to please too.

Successions of simple but brilliantly assertive motivic ideas are thus processed in the first of the three with an oddly curt bounciness. It works as a sort of switching point whereby Mozart's own character as a keyboard musician intersects with the capabilities of lesser technicians. Heights of style and range overlap and interact with the mundane necessities of learning skills and understanding structures. Flickering changes of rhythm and tart dynamic contrasts give players chances to test their techniques and to make expressive choices, while held within structures whose sense of sharp containment is itself a form of wit. The whole sonata in C especially works as a distillation of all the playing and collaborating and discussing, all the learning and listening and appraising, in the gatherings in packed salons and so on that Mozart frequented in search of both fun and renown. It is a summary of all these switching identities and tasks that idealizes them too. But this swingingly sociable world was full of tensions, and in especially the outer movements of the following sonata in A Mozart tugs harder at the vision of unity that he has set up. It starts with a 'theme and variations' movement rather than the more or less expected sonata allegro; the movement is sent wheeling through a variety of styles and approaches that also probes the theme and variations genre itself for how it can connect to a more rigorous compositional approach. The three sonatas used to be wrongly dated back to the period of Mozart's stay in Paris a few years earlier, and critics accordingly explained away this sonata's surprises as aspects of some sequential looseness that it was thought to borrow from the French keyboard suite. Rather, the theme and variations genre helps Mozart here in making a belated assessment of his earlier exposure to French styles, as well as in assessing his years spent dazzling audiences more widely as a keyboard pyrotechnician. The speed with which he kept travelling through its musical possibilities made him exemplify his age, and made him a permanent exception within it.

Several sections of this first movement take the form in effect of double variations, whereby the initial theme is given two somewhat separate treatments within a given style of reinterpretation, and this gives the sequence a sense of tender expository clarity that the genre can tend to rush away from in its search for thrills. It is as if the music wanted to explain at each turn what it is doing and how it is doing it. Mozart is here rethinking how desirable virtuosity is at the same time as providing the occasion for some new version of it, and this culminates in the fierily delicious strangeness of the notorious rondo finale for which the sonata in A is famous. No more uncanny passage of music can ever have been taken to define a composer's style. He is likely to have discovered this theme and how to treat it while improvising for friends and admirers, and it is easy to imagine what whirls of praise and applause were reaped. But the theme's power lies not just in the zany intensities of tonal colour and rhythmic bombast that it releases, but in the almost brusque structural efficiency with which it does so. Mozart has pared down to a sort of limpid essence nothing less than virtuosic exuberance itself. The movement amounts to an argument in miniature about wanting a version of structural clarity that will remain nourished by performative brio and riskiness, and a version of playfulness that structure will revel in and want to uphold. Structure is of course one of Mozart's favourite ways of eliciting praise, but this may be partly because it also guards against its more narcotic, exhilarating effects.

In the central adagio of the final sonata in F Mozart zooms in both severely and lushly on the beauty and pathos that his slow movements widely specialize in. Its austerity somehow only makes the movement more radiant; testing these qualities for what they will become under the laboratory conditions of these sonatas turns out also to extend their power, and the heuristic and the indulgent flow together. The almost fierce melodic starkness is driven by the same fusion of pedagogy with dazzlement that instils the Turkish rondo with its svelte gaudiness. Choices about ornamentation formed a massive part of how keyboard technique was conceived in the eighteenth century, and the bareness here throws them into luminous emphasis. A drastic intensity seizes every decision that the player takes, yet the movement could not make it clearer that technical facility and performative brio will be at best empty if they do not serve what is feelingful, purposeful and cogent. Virtuosity is heard in these sonatas in the course of being reinvented as a source of meaningful expression rather than mere flamboyance, and this means that expository clarity and dramatic impact can run together. The sense of harmonic bareness and exposure is actually frightening when treated on such an expansive scale. If what emerges in these sonatas is a picture of the whole musical world of amateurs, con-noisseurs and enthusiasts that Mozart encountered in early 1780s

Vienna, the music here shifts between categories of the simple and the complex with something like sumptuous volatility. Right at the end of 1782 and so about a year after the encounter with Clementi, Mozart told his father that he would 'be really interested in writing a book' about music himself, a sort of theoretical treatise expounding his ideals alongside examples. It is easy to wish that he had gone ahead. But maybe we should be glad that his urge to think systematically about what music is and can be carried on streaming straight into music itself.

Whole tides of eighteenth-century music were powered by the culture's love of virtuosic display; it was one of the vital ways in which that culture was discovering its own extending powers. Mozart's devotion to folding the most exuberant virtuosity into more generously based sets of pleasures and exchanges may have stayed unmatched until the 1920s gave the world Louis Armstrong. Echoes of Mozart's own playing resound in this set of sonatas, but they also reverberate with what it was like for him to listen to others or to hear a pupil slowly or suddenly improve, or indeed to hear a fellow virtuoso who is being praised for the wrong reasons. As talk about music jagged around him at this or that glamorous gathering, his pleasure at such occasions must have vied with the possibilities of mordancy and disenchantment that they brought. The eighteenth-century salon was a place for experimenting in taste and style, and above all for endless commentary on which experiments were working. Mozart's complex love of this world is part of how sociable these sonatas feel and how acute they are about their own sociability. Walking into a room where he might find some rich potential pupil or some pushy rival, or some grand aristocrat effortfully hunched over a keyboard, he was always having to be as smart and quick as possible in assessing the arrayed talents and sensibilities. The sonatas are about asserting himself in that world stringently but with a cordial openness to the capacities and wishes of others.

Around the time of his duel with Clementi, Mozart describes his days as so exhaustively packed with composing and teaching and domestic life and the social rigmarole that music involved him in that he routinely had to stay up writing until one in the morning.

The whole thing would then start again early the next day; his hair was done at six, since any day of being visible as a man about town in the eighteenth century could otherwise not begin. A schedule as draining as this must have contributed to the illnesses and physical complaints that multiplied during the 1780s for the composer; in 1791 they would culminate in his untimely death. Episodes of headaches or stomach cramps or fever or toothache or fatigue or a bout with a cold or a chill clasp him in plenty of recorded instances, and it seems reasonable to assume that there were plenty that we do not know about. A lot suggests that he was also often even exuberantly healthy, but some trend of frailty and suffering was an undertow throughout these years, pulling away at Mozart and his music. Illness was a flickering underside of the world of creativity and praise, one that may have been exacerbated by his devotion to that world, and may in turn have deepened his take on his life's brighter factors. Maybe it also brought relief from them sometimes. In the eighteenth century bright dreams of technocratic progress abounded alongside the daily, tangible and corrosive facts of frailty and disease on which they had still made little impression. Mozart was an often suffering embodiment of this paradox. His music's realism about people or bodies or social life does much to make it so praiseworthy, but its realism draws on a shattering openness to desuetude and loss and roughness. The adagio in the third of these sonatas shows how determined his music was, amid its own radiant power, to stand up for fragility and delicacy and sadness.

Clementi would have had little to gain in his prosperous middle age from disparaging this sometime rival who had died so early but become so widely exalted. His praise sounds sincere though when he is reported as recalling decades later the 'grace and elegance of Mozart's playing'. England turned out to be a handy place to have links to during the Napoleonic upheavals, and he was well suited to its commercial zippiness; during the early years of the new century he turned himself into probably Europe's foremost entrepreneur and arbiter of the keyboard repertoire. He became an elder states-man of the classical style, and played an important part in establishing the canonical status of Mozart's keyboard works. He got involved in piano-making, characteristically becoming engrossed in the ongoing enlargement of the instrument's scope. Beethoven's works too benefited from his curatorial zeal and his mogul acumen as a publisher. Mozart might not have been shocked to find that works by Clementi himself found themselves in Clementi's exalted editions.

II

8

A Time When Europe Was a Beautiful Question

Die Entführung aus dem Serail

In the eighteenth century Europe thronged with singing voices and with the raptures that they provoke. Day after day and night after night across the culture, not just theatres and concert halls but palaces, churches and salons filled with the sounds of human flesh endlessly testing and extending its relationships with cultural meaning and musical form in that most direct of forums known as the throat. Italy remained the heartland of these lavish outpourings, and it was from Naples that they were kicked into being with the most momentum. But the sheer communicative zest with which vocal styles moved across borders and into centres, cities and ears across the continent was not just an incidental product of their pleasures and versions of panache. Rather, the century's vocal music shows how powerfully this culture was imagining newly liquid, connected and metamorphic versions of itself. In the great musical form of the aria Europe could amaze itself with the sometimes hectic quantities of power and change that it harboured, and at the same time try to figure out how to contain them within shapes and descriptions.

But was there such a place as Europe in the eighteenth century? Versions of unity had come and gone since the Roman empire had shattered. The upheavals brought by the Reformation had turned into fixtures of a jumpy, chequered landscape by this point. France under the Sun King had fancied itself as some sort of hegemonic heavyweight swaying the political map, but any serious prospect of this fizzled out early in the century, and the cheaper sphere of culture took up the remaining hopes. A splintered, diffuse equilibrium prevailed across much of Mozart's Europe. Vienna under the Habsburgs was the addled but still unbowed vehicle of what remained of the Holy Roman Empire and its klutzy loyalty to some idea of Christendom. The impressive flexibility of the forms of rule tessellated across the Habsburg domains made the empire at least as prophetic of some coming world of fractious pluralism as it was a throwback to motifs of imperious wholeness.

Naples itself kept slipping in and out of the grasp of the Habsburgs. The multiplications of Italian vocal music echoed the multifariousness and slipperiness of politics all over the peninsula as the Napoleonic explosion approached, and in Naples the great powers of Austria, France and Spain played some of their most complex and ominous games. Vienna became the place at the heart of the classical style because the Habsburg capital linked resonances of so much of the continent's past with premonitions of change and historical shipwreck. But this music came out of the electric intricacy of Neapolitan vocal styles, whose inventiveness responded to the complex life of that teeming, often sweltering centre. In Naples the closeness of much of civilized life in the eighteenth century to violence and debacle pushed to the surface. Music there was thrown in tight alongside singular levels of squalor and penury, so it had to be both balm and rapture. Naples was full of aesthetes and diplomats and musical stars and teachers; but travel was dangerous and the political life unpredictable even by the standards of the day. Outside Vesuvius smouldered, to the freighted delight of visitors; the ancient remains of the places that it had buried began to be properly examined during Mozart's lifetime. Opera's dominion in great cities like Naples and Vienna came partly from how skittishly it drew on the ancient world for precedents and narratives. Eighteenth-century Europe never knew whether it wanted to be dazzlingly new or imperiously old.

The aria itself was really the great art form of Mozart's century; it was the swerving vehicle by which again and again this culture most amply expressed itself, across operas and concerts and recitals and oratorios and mass settings and cantatas both sacred and secular. It was a form that kept on coming because of how charged and plastic the eighteenth century kept finding singing to be. A virtuosic voice of the sort that this culture adored was an endless opportunity for versions of expression and storytelling and meaning. Within its arias the period combined ebullience with a seething appetite for loss and catastrophe in ways that may capture its character better than yet another recitation of the facts of its small wars and political intrigues and class discontents. Flights of vocal brilliance from Neapolitan singers like Farinelli or Anna de Amicis made them renowned in a culture that wanted to hear power melded with beauty at the limits of what the body could do. The aria had to push the voice into innumerable feats of acrobatics or embellishment or refinement, and it also had to hold it steady. The century's arias pour out images and moods of loss and confusion and shattering; storms and tears and threats and so on run through them as if the culture's desire for beauty brought a violently obsessive sensitivity to transience. It can be hard to know whether language is being exalted or torn apart by the ways in which its sounds open out. At the same time the aria was a sort of wobbly bridge between the secular and the sacred, during a period when the church's roles were in constant, charged dispute in places like Vienna and Naples. A spinning cultural hedonism started to infiltrate the music of faith, but no more surely than reckless vistas of spiritual and moral expansion emerged out of the feats of singing in opera. Maybe the single finest work to come from a Neapolitan composer was Giovanni Battista Pergolesi's *Stabat Mater,* and it is full of a bold expressive sensuousness that keeps seeming on the verge of completely overrunning its ecclesiastical framework, but then keeps heightening the Lenten solemnity after all.

But Pergolesi was only twenty-six when he died in 1736 near Naples; he never heard the work performed. Mozart emerged into a musical world dominated less by any one major composer than by a renowned librettist. At the heart of the century sat the icy and inscrutable figure of Metastasio, the great Italian poet whose coolly refined words contagiously defined what arias could be. Pietro Metastasio had had the beginnings of a poetic career in Rome early in the century, quickly becoming celebrated amid the papal city's high-toned and finagling cultural elite, around the time when the ban there on the controversial art of opera was lifted. The brilliant aptness of this tyro's style for musical setting was vital to bringing him soon right to the heart of all things Habsburg in Vienna. Metastasio would live there for half a century more before finally dying not long after Mozart's move to the imperial capital. Vastly remunerated, and celebrated across the continent, he called the great castrato singer Farinelli his twin as if he wanted to clasp their versions of garlanded solitude together. The friends both died in 1782 as if contriving to close an era. Towards the very end of his life Metastasio could reportedly still strike a visitor as the most handsome man in Europe.

Bringing Metastasio to Vienna meant investing the place with a living summary of the cultural heights. His position as court poet was a version of the ancient institution of laureateship as re-invented a few centuries earlier for Petrarch. If he was a sort of cultural sovereign of the era, his art was also alive to much of its secret doubleness. Musical settings of the poet thrilled the deepest redoubts of the old European regimes, but his lyrics were also read in revolutionary Virginia by Thomas Jefferson. Mozart's own library featured Metastasio too. If enlightened despotism was the political form that pulled the period's ambiguities together, the Metastasian aria was the nearest cultural equivalent as it both charmed and overwhelmed listeners. Metastasio suggests a splendid last-ditch attempt at a sort of equilibrium that Europe has often dreamt of, one in which delight and meaning could feed and guarantee each other. Perhaps his was the last moment when such an image could be projected. Metastasian arias flared with possibilities of liberty, pleasure and progress, while also being highly congenial to the period's great blocks of wealth and might. His stanzas streamline the age's often frantic repertoire of images and affects with a sumptuous pithiness that can feel both like an effort to control them and like the zenith of their power. The eighteenth-century aria sang out of an ongoing and oscillating argument about whether aesthetic charm is on the side of equilibrium or delirium in the end.

The story of modernity is one in which communication accelerates and extrapolates from itself and doubles down on itself. Naples was renowned for freedom of thought during the period, as well as for being a centrifuge for vocal styles. The eighteenth-century aria was an addictive carrier of some frenzy for communication, a peak of stylistic infectiousness in which repetition and novelty could somehow keep singing in unison. So too this Europe was trying everything to make its roads and coach services slicker, and it sped letters and books and pamphlets and indeed musical scores around in a perpetual rapture of chatter and exchange. An improvisatory inventiveness worthy of Sebastian Bach was remaking the machinery of wealth, as paper money and new types of bills of exchange began to outmanoeuvre the older compromises between gold and promissory notes and barter. Cosmopolitanism required constant, jiggling feats of switching among currencies and versions of credit. On going to conduct his pursuits of happiness in England Casanova found that there it was the hard cash of gold that was looked down on, not the fluidity of paper currency; clinging to metal seemed somehow impolite. His desirous and eloquent wanderings made Casanova a secret sovereign of the era worthy to be matched with Metastasio. He counted the famous poet among his friends, as at one point he probably did Mozart.

Wherever someone like Mozart went in this Europe, colleagues and acquaintances and sisters of wives of close friends showed up, because music was the thread of the culture's most ramifying networks. Vocal music of the Metastasian sort met with raptures, because this society hungered for vistas onto its own giddiness that could also still seem stately, refined and precise. Singers were pressed into encores deep into the nights of this Europe; across the continent riches dangled before the most popular. Large meanings and consequences were attached to fugitive qualities of beauty and pleasure, turning on the acrobatic capacities of things as frail as throats and breaths. Stories tellingly used to describe how Farinelli had to sing the same few arias night after night to assuage the Spanish king's mental torments. But in fact these stories are doubtful, and the raptures that music kept sparking suggest that it was at least as liable to energize whatever unrest was striking the European mind as to placate it. Mozart himself indulged, in a letter during his Paris summer in 1778 to a Salzburg friend, in some sarcasm about the overegged operatic culture that the great librettist defined. He proposes improving the operatic scene back in his home town by commissioning Metastasio 'to write several dozen operas in which the male lead and the female lead never encounter each other on stage'; one castrato singer could take both roles, and a commendably unphysical idea of love would result.

After he settled in Metastasio's Vienna, the composer seems to have kept his distance from the great man. The ageing poet was so celebrated that even the sober routine of his day to day existence accrued glamour. Mozart had been setting his stanzas and composing within a broadly Metastasian ambit on and off for so long by this point that the sense of musical routine attached to him may have outweighed the sheen of his words. The piecemeal essays in *seria* style that the composer occasionally produced through the 1780s never exactly repudiate the old repertoire of scenarios and images. But they use them so precisely as springboards for new types of acuity and freedom that repetition becomes the very sponsor of change. In late November 1780 the death of the sedulous empress Maria Theresa had finally left her son Joseph to rule alone in Vienna. Metastasio had saturated the culture of the period that she had staunchly helmed, and then in the spring of 1782 he followed her into death. The empress had been fussy and cautious, but a fine manipulator of Europe's dynastic intricacies and an incessant, tinkering lawmaker. She did not exactly unleash change, but her rule created the momentum for reform that cut loose in rather unfocused bursts once Joseph was in sole charge.

Mozart arrived in Vienna in the year between these two deaths, at the start of a brief period of expansiveness and civic gusto during which music appears to have flowed more and more freely around the city's spaces. During the previous decade Joseph had opened the Augarten imperial park to the public, and in the summer of 1782 an impresario called Philipp Jakob Martin started to organize concerts in a refreshment pavilion in league with the composer, who performed at the inaugural one. Mozart was in demand in rooms and halls and public spaces across the city's expanding bustle, and the biggest dilemma was knowing how to turn popularity and esteem into solid prospects or regular income; it was a knack that he never fully got. The sheer proliferation of chances to make music across private gatherings and public occasions was part of the problem. Haphazard little bands or orchestras came and went night after night. It must have been hard to know when to play up his flamboyant uniqueness and when to smooth out his relationships with listeners or other players. Was he meant to make the classy amateurs who admired him feel lifted up to professional levels, or grateful to be hearing him at all? Mozart relied on the hype and goodwill brought by his constant availability to fuel demand for ambitious concert series that could yield a real income. Of course this meant placing exuberantly intense demands on himself within these concerts. Vienna during the 1780s was an ear trying to pull music more and more deeply into itself. Mozart had to prove that he belonged there to himself, his father, and the memory of everyone in places like Salzburg and Paris who had not listened to him hard or joyfully enough. But this meant not just belonging to the city but overwhelming it, playing more continually and dashingly and penetratingly than all comers.

As the decade developed the beating heart of his answer to all this was in how fiercely ambitious his vision of stage comedy became; at the heart of this in turn was his skill at rigging up arias that move fluidly within a nimble narrative while keeping on imparting massive dramatic or expressive energy. Mozart's arias play this double game over and over again during this period, and his characters get much of their multidimensional vividness from how simultaneously funny and serious their fates seem as a result. But it was a circuitous route over often murky institutional terrain that took Mozart during his first few years of living in Vienna towards his great collaboration with the librettist Lorenzo Da Ponte on their three comic operas. His last opera before relocating there had been *Idomeneo*, his grandest exercise in and assault on *opera seria*, but its wheeling verve may have been helped by the fact that its librettist Giambattista Varesco was a Salzburg acquaintance and not much of a writer. Working with a more prestigious collaborator might not have let Mozart attack the genre with such sovereign, colourful freedom. *Idomeneo* can feel exhaustive in ways that may have left Mozart unsure where to turn next in the operatic field. Often towards the middle of the decade especially his ambition for opera was inseparable from a simmering uncertainty as to how to deploy his powers. The seething orchestral ebullience of *Idomeneo* must have helped to convince the composer that the art was his to redefine. At the same time the piece's white-hot opulence evinces his passionate commitment to the largest values of some earlier operatic world, at least as much as it shows him straining against limits. *Idomeneo* is an exuberant recapitulation, and unrepeatable. His great comic operas plumb and revise the world of the eighteenth-century aria and its ideals of efflorescence and impact from more angles than staying within *seria* style could have allowed. Sometimes they engage playfully and sometimes they are agonized. We know too from Lorenzo Da Ponte's memoirs how drawn Mozart's vital comic librettist was to the Metastasian allure.

The crucial work that took Mozart towards the Da Ponte comedies was *Die Entführung aus dem Serail*, the one opera that he did complete during the first of these Viennese years, and a flamboyant and unsettling comic masterpiece in its own way. German rather than Italian was the language of the text that he took on, and this may have helped the opera to leap away from the Metastasian universe and into his own denser and more animated vision. It came together as a project fairly quickly after he moved to the big city partly because of the emperor's desire to encourage operas in German, and partly because a chance arose to write something for his prestigious Russian visitors. Mozart set about it at an exuberant pace that must have been fired by his sense of personal release in Vienna, inseparable as such freedom was from his eagerness to please. But there are other sides to the opera's hectic energies just as there were to the circumstances of its emergence. Vienna's opera establishment does not seem to have been unambiguously delighted by Mozart's arrival, and resentments and manoeuvres contributed to delaying the piece's staging for almost a year from the original timing. It was not until the summer of 1782 that it emerged to score perhaps Mozart's single most unambiguous success as a composer for the stage in the imperial capital. Meanwhile the Russian guests found themselves treated to a sample of Gluck's more tightly high-minded revision of operatic style. Their return journey late in 1782 happens to have let them catch up with Mozart's more loose-limbed riff on the future of opera too.

It is hard to be exact about the motives and intrigues that delayed the opera; the stakes were high for operas in Vienna, and the factors involved in organizing them various and arcane. Mozart's own complex, swelling ambitions did not help the process. A letter back to his father has a nice tone of slightly bashful boastfulness, as he reports of one performance after it has at last opened that 'in spite of the terrible summer heat the theatre was packed'; his sincerity is palpable when he says how good it feels to be acclaimed. A persuasive impresario and inventive all-round man of the theatre called Johann Gottlieb Stephanie wrote Mozart's libretto, and the composer was helped by collaborating this time with someone who must have been drenched in the liveliest traditions of the Viennese popular stage. The Habsburg capital was at the time amusing itself with a craze for anything linked with the Ottoman empire, the dynasty's neighbour in south-eastern Europe and its big rival especially in and around the Balkans. Mozart gaudily summarizes the Habsburg obsession with Turkish fashions and motifs in the opera, but tests it too for the resonances of admiration or even affiliation that it turns out to harbour. The exotic trappings of this music are nearly crassly florid, but the levels of raucous inventiveness that they give the opera also shake it loose from the norms that it relies on. The piece has an exuberant dramatic levity that oddly matches and counters the equally exuberant density of its musical means, until it no longer matters whether the world of the eighteenth-century aria is being travestied or refreshed. Mozart may often not have known whether he wanted to destroy or to regenerate the surrounding musical world. Moving to Vienna was bringing freedom and release, and he pours them into the opera. But a pulverizing recklessness lurks within it too.

We can zoom in on one particular aria's fusions of force with restlessness. The title tells us that someone is going to get out from a seraglio during the opera, and it turns out that the heroine Constanza is being held by Selim, an Ottoman potentate whose power turns out to be enlightened and merciful after the hero Belmonte's rescue attempt is botched. The aria 'Martern aller Arten' is a vast set-piece whirl of variously pleading, protesting and vitriolic vocal effects that Constanza delivers to Selim about halfway through the action, after he threatens her with dire consequences if she will not yield to his advances. He does not seem to know himself how wisely he will eventually respond to her defiance. The stormy power of character that her aria reveals jolts him into questioning the meaning of his own power; the opera's whole ethical world comes to revolve around the spinning intensity of Constanza's voice.

Constanza was first sung by a coloratura soprano called Caterina Cavalieri, whose talents and fame no doubt prompted the aria's fluorescent decorative swagger. Mozart himself remarked on what he called her flexible throat. She was in fact a grand instance of the sorts of hybrid, flexible cultural identities that eighteenth-century Europe proliferated, being for one thing decidedly less Italian than her name suggests. In a later letter about the shifting opera scene in Vienna, Mozart includes her in a little roll call of singers in the city who are 'Germans of whom Germany can be proud'. But it was Antonio Salieri himself, a pushy doyen of the Italian faction among the Habsburgs, who had done most to pull her surging talent towards the virtuosic styles of Italian vocal music. In October 1791 the two of them will make an important guest appearance together as Mozart's story nears its end. Surely her whole identity and all her talents alike can never have felt more fully drawn on than when delivering this aria's somehow both relentless and delicious torrents. At the pivot of this ardently German opera, the aria both exploits and measures the nearly crazy intensities that Italian vocal styles had nourished. Its zeal and its sensitivity must come in some ways straight from Cavalieri's throat.

The aria in question is Mozart's most fulsome attempt in the opera to give her voice the expansive, glittering things to do that people wanted to hear from her. But decoration becomes more than just a feature of the aria's swirling workings. The aria can also seem to have a merely or excessively decorative role within the structure of the opera, to the extent that commentators have sometimes wanted it cut in the interests of narrative clarity or stylistic homogeneity. It has continued to attract such responses, and we might end up wondering whether they reflect just how strange and unsettling it is. But the larger point is that they miss how drastically Mozart reinterprets the decorative impulse. Often for him decoration is precisely something to be reinterpreted, to be investigated for its real meaning. The Metastasian aria had become beset with extravaganzas of vocal technique; the structural vigour that it supplied meant that composers and singers could pile on the expressive embellishments that its underlying emotional power also encouraged. It is as if such arias worked from the outside in, their inner rationales propelled by their dazzling surfaces. Constanza's aria pushes this lovely but peculiar logic to unsurpassed extremes; rather than trying to correct it as some more reformist agenda might have wanted, she and Mozart together plumb what psychic turbulence and ethical ambiguity it may involve. Selim and any other listeners who find it disquieting have a point.

In fact the singer gets two opportunities to wheel through her powers, as the aria moves through successive versions of the two moods with which Constanza bombards Selim, one of indignant defiance and one nobly determined to appeal to his higher leanings. The sharply contoured phrases and brisk symmetries of Italian vocal style had ended up encouraging a certain quicksilver alternation between moods that makes emotional states seem both intense and transient. Constanza's aria takes this quality of emotional acceleration and turns it into an almost crazily sincere vision of a soul in turmoil. She rapturously shrugs off all fear of torture, and then glides into appeals to Selim's mercy and flights of emphasis on her constancy. Stephanie's phrasing in the lyric is more fitful, clunky and woozily rhymed than Metastasio would have allowed his robustly delicious stanzas to be, though the theme of protesting virtue was a big one in his world. But in a way this messier and more stolid verbal material may have freed up Mozart's attitude towards the underlying musical style. Constanza's moral and expressive zeniths grind against the casually comic storytelling and the lyrical lumpiness, in ways that tally with his mixed attitude of tribute and irreverence towards the musical world surrounding him. In a letter written to his father during his work on the opera, Mozart acknowledges with a certain rueful defiance that Stephanie's versifying is not exactly state of the art. He relates this to the wretched texts that according to him prevail in the rising genre of Italian comic opera, and which certainly do not damage its popularity, and may indeed abet it by ensuring that music 'reigns supreme'. It is almost a little improvised manifesto against Metastasio's eminence.

One interpretative trend has found signs in the aria that Constanza is really deeply attracted to Selim, or at least traces of sensuous manipulation on her part along with ethical appeal and rebuke. We do not need to decide how true any of this is; the point is the complex expressive vividness capable of prompting such notions. So the decorative expansiveness with which she dwells on and extrapolates from her words becomes, no mere set of flourishes, but a map of what it might be like for a clever and spirited woman to meet her own most extreme possibilities. We witness someone trying to figure out just how manipulative her sense of high moral probity can allow her to be, and just how overtly she can explore the larger sensuous and sympathetic life that her situation is opening up in her. We are also hearing a composer figuring out how manipulative he wants his music to be, and how overt or expansive or ambiguous his experiments with stock situations can become. Mozart tips the orchestra into these questions even before the voice enters, in an introduction that is as heftily layered as a concerto, and that sets up the aria's technicolour use of solo instruments like the flute to play off the singer's swooping flights. The opera nearly comes to an opulent standstill; it is a hard passage to stage, as the music builds towards Constanza's outpouring with an almost frantic proliferation of preparatory levels and frills. A hole opens up in the opera's dramatic fabric, and sheer musical abundance shows through.

Selim is in motion at this point, caught between responses of awe, bafflement and indignation at this increasingly amazing woman's defiance. In one way he typifies a larger trend in the period, as conventions of oriental villainy fitfully gave way to a new set of enlightenment stereotypes predicated on the wisdom to be found beyond Europe. But his complex and even dazed response makes him also an open-ended stand-in for anyone encountering this opera's seething mixtures. The turbulent pizazz of Mozart's music confronts opera itself with the drastic moral and experiential terrains that its pursuits of pleasure have always kept revealing. Constanza's sheer musical will to power and the swivelling variety of devices by which she incarnates it allow her to face down a version of the doubleness that powers the opera itself. Is the whole thing just a dazzlingly colourful entertainment in the end, or is it a deeply turbulent investigation of the topic of emotional freedom which its narrative of literal release from captivity merely suggests? Likewise, is Constanza merely the spirited but passive plaything of her situation's clichés, or can she grasp its opportunities and rewrite its meaning? In 1779 Gluck had moved back to Vienna, and Mozart was very aware of his example, despite the life of fairly entire retirement that he had taken up there after his years of austere triumph in Paris. The Gluckian answer to opera's teeming questions was to keep on paring down in pursuit of truth and impetus, but for Mozart this comprised only part of opera's quest for itself. In this opera Mozart chisels away at some of the excesses of the art, but also often embraces impurity and hybridity and paradox. Constanza's aria combines technical bravura with lyrical lushness, and mingles both with exotic frills and lush hints of titillating levity. Sensuous exhilaration and steely moral intensity can be heard here vying for the soul of operatic Europe, unless their aim is to end up allied.

Constanza affirms her constancy with an expansiveness that matches Mozart's own complex desire to keep faith with as much as possible of opera's potential as both art and pleasure. Exaggeration, gusto and a kaleidoscopic inventiveness would from this point guide him at least as vitally into dramatic truth as narrative rigour or musical purity did. But these forces also make the opera a portrait in motion of his first couple of years after moving to Vienna, as he sought to braid together his need to please and desire to impress with the complex, ardent strenuousness of his sense of artistic vocation. Mozart composed the work over months of comings and goings in and out of salons, musical gatherings and meetings with interested parties offering opportunities and advice and mixed messages. Sincere fun and the stern and needy pursuit of business mixed in ways whose confusions could only be processed by someone filled with both slyly enormous self-belief and much raw nervous energy. In no other opera does Mozart come so close to revealing a repulsion from the styles and pleasures that his music is of course mainly and deeply attracted to; the twisted moral situation of Constanza's aria and its musical extravagance make it the point where this ambivalence most richly scalds the proceedings. Is beauty under such grotesque duress a satire on beauty, or a protest against the need to supply it, or the final triumph of the capacity to do so? The composer spent those months discovering that he had more to say in the opera than he had known and that others wanted to hear it less than they let on; maybe they wanted to keep it from succeeding because they feared being all too impressed. Leopold did not pretend to want to hear it, however, and his stalwart indifference to Mozart's reports of its success greatly hurt his son. A few years later Leopold admitted to his daughter how good the opera was.

The elements of ebullience in Joseph's first few years as sole ruler find in *Die Entführung aus dem Serail* their giddiest product. The opera is as merry and resourceful an adventurer as its protagonists are. Within it Vienna claims to be capable of pulling in the whole of European culture and outdoing it, but elements of the claim are as gaudy and bombastic as others are fizzily thrilling. Mozart would have to wait a few more years to be capable of the comic operas that chew more fully into their culture's possibilities, but their relationship to Vienna is far more complex, and this opera is their precursor but not their model. Dozens of stagings across Europe from Ljubljana to Amsterdam would nevertheless assay it during Mozart's lifetime, and it was busily pirated; it may have been the single most contagious vector for his spreading reputation over these years. Writing a German comedy may at first have seemed a way of postponing a large reckoning with the possibilities of serious opera, but its levity became a route to acuity and power as well as acclaim. A drama set just beyond Europe's shores yielded an all but lurid freedom of attitude on Mozart's part which let him compose his way beyond the edges of what he or his culture knew his culture to be capable of containing. *Idomeneo* has something brimmingly transcontinental about it, as the dramatic panache and the orchestral abundance of Mannheim and Paris pour all over *seria* style. But there is a dead end deep within its splendour. Mozart was here showing Europe a different cultural direction, one that switches an aggressive potency for an uncanny, cartoonish nimbleness. He had probably already found that Vienna could not be bludgeoned with his greatness; it needed to be nudged and cajoled, and maybe he also needed to feel that he was teasing it.

While the character of Constanza blossomed in his mind and on the page into the exhilarating figure in the opera, in Constanze Weber Mozart was setting himself to marry her namesake. He had resumed contact with the musical Weber family not long after moving to Vienna, and his original icon of Aloysia was now immitigably wed to an artist and all-round bohemian called Joseph Lange who had already been through one marriage to a starry singer. Her younger sister Constanze seems to have been neither as beautiful nor as talented, but during their decade or so of marriage she would show herself to be resourceful and ebullient and splendidly solid. She could fold into backgrounds in ways that must have helped Mozart; she was herself a subtle and feelingful woman. Wooing Aloysia appealed to the parts of him that saw life through prisms of high-octane performance, grand achievement and ardent charisma. Living with her sister seems to have been a more subtly, soberly convivial business. Whatever symbioses these names involved, composing Constanza's opera and marrying Constanze were enterprises that fed each other with momentum and boldness. Getting married not long after arriving in Vienna was partly a way of assuring anyone doubtful that he had relocated irrevocably. The opera had its opulent first performance in the middle of July 1782 and their wedding was at the start of August. Although Aloysia was not part of the opera's cast at first, it was not long before she joined it in the inevitable role of Constanza. As reigning prima donnas on the imperial city's opera stage, she and Caterina Cavalieri were living lives so rivalrously entangled that they may have felt like sisters too.

Mozart's last direct, major engagement with Metastasio's legacy came a decade or so later when he was commissioned to set *La clemenza di Tito* as part of the accession celebrations for the new emperor Leopold II in Prague. Fugitives from the revolutionary violence in France no doubt numbered among the opera's first audience. Europe was changing ever more stormily, to the extent that history was tearing down its favoured ideas about how change should operate. Mozart worked with a new librettist called Caterino Mazzolà to give the drama clarity and pungency. Critical responses to the opera used to be largely dismissive, and it was seen as a skilful but stilted throwback to a generic world which the composer would not have returned to without such a prestigious prompt. The counterthrust probably remains a minority position, but there has been growing momentum behind viewing the work as a neglected masterpiece. Finally *La clemenza di Tito* is a hugely unsettled hybrid, at points in fact a fiercely unsettling one. His bold choral writing and the exuberantly sinuous woodwind passages show Mozart wanting to rethink opera even after his last great comedies. The piece seems to know deep in its music that the Europe of the eighteenth-century aria is becoming irrecoverable, and that the aria itself was going to have to internalize a new historical world. Yet Mozart does not want to give up on earlier visions either, or on the fusions of orderliness and lightning flash that they had promised.

9

A Swinging Woman

Serenade in C minor

The Wallace Collection in London contains crowds of the sorts of artefacts that would have gleamed within the most high-end places that Mozart played in, but even there Jean-Honoré Fragonard's frantically dashing, exuberantly charged painting of a woman on a swing gives a singular hit of the rococo. Its full title of *Les hasards heureux de l'escarpolette* means something like 'the happy accidents of the swing', but the painting draws us right into the style's complex undertones, as well as its often deliriously straightforward charms. Let us note the expression on the face of the young man lying propped in this shadowy garden as he reaches towards and gazes up at the swinging legs of his lover. His face may be this dazzling picture's least interesting feature, but may also be its key. His expression has an ecstatic blandness; the face was one of Fragonard's great topics, and he must have wanted something to seem missing or awry at this crux of the picture's delicious liberties. The man's face is at once the centre of the image's exhilarations and a dead zone at its heart. The woman's form as it flashes and ripples above her lover is a vision of rococo style at its most scintillating made into painterly flesh. She traces the sinuous lines to which the style was addicted back to their origin in the female body so directly and intensely that all distinctions between substance and decoration short-circuit for a moment. But while the swinging intensity of her form bodies forth the rococo's premises of hedonism and glitz, its premonitions of greed and fecklessness are also projected in the almost silly delirium that she inflicts on the man looking up at her.

Fragonard was in his mid-thirties and at a pivotal point in his art's swivelling progress in 1767 when he painted the picture. It seems to have been commissioned, and prescribed to a fairly lurid degree in its narrative details, by the young aristocrat who had himself included in the form of the recumbent figure. The young man seems to have wanted to remain a spectator even as he was absorbed right into the spectacle. But the mismatch between the intensity of the work's overall vision of pleasure in motion and the insipidity of the man's face is Fragonard's way of rebuking the terms of the commission, without giving up on the mania for charm that must have driven it. At the time of its creation he had been wavering between artistic directions, or perhaps trying to shrug off simultaneously partisans of all the styles of painting that Paris offered. He had nearly but not quite become the noble painter of grand classical subjects that the cultural establishment wanted, and nearly but not quite become the high-minded painter of upstanding bourgeois pieties that the newer intellectual elite headed by Diderot desired. But neither would he exactly end up propagating the high rococo style of his teacher Boucher; his pictures swerve away from Boucher's grand decorative exuberance and his unfussy reductions of mythology to disporting flesh, towards something more quicksilver and pungent. Fragonard's paradox is that a haberdasher's son who was taken up by so many of the big men of cultural Paris, a wildly pleasant man about town whose pictures are likewise crammed with charm, should have produced art that is also so strange. Maybe some underlying restlessness or anxiety drove his dislike of the public commissions that someone like him should have thrived on. The ceaseless appeal of motion, of literal and psychic versions of restlessness, is the deep key to his oeuvre. Paintings are static objects but his are packed with fluctuation and fantasy; he seems never to have painted still lifes. He and Mozart were both latecomers to the rococo party, split between plunging into its pleasures and assessing them soberly or acutely.

In the rococo, pleasure must take over the meaning of the world. The style was more a climate than a strict movement, and the decorative and applied arts were its most encompassing hives. Probably the nearest thing that it had to a single origin was in the fallout early in the century from one of the world's first great efforts of forcible modernization, the grand project of centralized splendour that revolved around the architecture of Versailles. All that grindingly definitive majesty turned out to be something that French culture could not sustain, or could not persuade itself to keep wanting. So the rococo gathered up the parts of baroque style that were most mobile, limber and diffuse, and recycled them within a looser and less strident vision. It cut away from the striving in the baroque for moral stature and rhetorical might, and played up the elements of embellishment and theatrical élan that had been its sideshows. As it ferments materials like lace and porcelain or insists on the most colourfully dappled types of marble, or sprinkles lapis lazuli around to spice up what would otherwise be the merely shiny metal surfaces of clocks or other mantelpiece ornaments, we see a world of things commandeered by charm.

Rococo style suspended itself in a brilliant halfway state in between past values of courtly splendour or artisanal integrity and some coming regimen of mass-consumerist baubles, as it wound itself around the whole world of small courts and urbane salons into which Mozart emerged. It was the right style for a world unclear about whether wealth and power were dissolving or proliferating, and its flimsiness and adaptability made it lithe, fecund and multiple. A musician working at the social heights would keep having to be grateful for the trinkets that grandees exchanged for pleasures received. Watches and snuff boxes were doled out as if sheer shininess could perpetuate old aristocratic worlds of conviviality and largesse. Mozart joked about adapting his clothes so that he could keep more than one watch at a time visible, in order to stop being given them when what he really needed was money. But the rococo showed its more acute, sceptical side in the hands of someone like Fragonard. Culture in the eighteenth century kept throwing ever more charge into values of charm, politeness and licence, and then kept finding them just as fallible or as despotic as the grander and more hierarchical values that they were meant to displace. The liberal vision of modernity has always been slow to see that pleasure can be just another tyrant. Fragonard's picture is about a world in which everyone wants to be a new sort of absolute monarch, in settings that may have been scaled down but were pumped full with irresponsibility. It shows how hectic such a world's airiness will be, how fused its versions of darkness and brightness will be, and how fraught and inventive its ethics will have to become. The sheer brilliance of delineation that encases the leaves on the dark and grotesque trees comes to seem zanily drastic, and Fragonard's painterly flamboyance becomes no more and no less than the play of forms thrown off by a pervasive vertigo.

Fragonard's picture is like Mozart's music as it moves between at least two worlds. His swinging woman is seen in a moment of motion between two men, as she is pushed towards and over the fellow lying in the foreground by a darker figure lurking behind her. The picture wants the patron who commissioned it to feel that he has got what he wanted; he can see himself transfixed beneath her as she swings, engulfed by the flashing confidence in the availability of delight that is clearly one of the painting's registers. In the patron's fantasy version of the picture, the man in the background may be the woman's husband, unaware of the presence of his wife's lover hidden in the foreground. But he may be a servant under instructions for the sake of the scene's stagecraft, or he may be someone grander who is manipulating some more complex story of betrayal. Did Fragonard feel like a master or a servant as he painted? The work's pictorial surface has a clarity so drastic that it underscores doubt. All that we can be sure of is the magnificence of the woman's swinging presence, as if the rococo curve construed by her form in the air was the only grounding that Fragonard could commit to. In fact part of the picture's wit is the use to which it puts the most basic facts about how swinging works; right at the moment when the woman comes closest to her prostrate devotee, the arc begins to lift her up and away from him. The world turns into pure spectacle and pure unsustainability in the same breath.

Figures like Mozart and Fragonard can relay pleasure while analysing it and withstanding its blasts and torpors, and they both saw that sexual libertinism was a key capable of opening up the fluctuating historical world that they shared. It was itself a force swinging between two worlds, rooting itself in aristocratic licence and privilege as much as it reached forwards into coming hopes for pluralistic personal choice. Stolidly and inevitably, Leopold disapproved as Constanze Weber began to feature in his son's letters, and in the gossip about him that travelled back from Vienna. Maybe Mozart was insisting on his father's disapproval when he chose to fall for another Weber daughter; without it desire may not have felt like desire. Leopold had been aghast at his son's smitten plans for a life with Aloysia a couple of years earlier, and now here that ramshackle family was again with another daughter sowing unhelpful thoughts. Maybe Leopold had come across as feeling all too vindicated when those earlier plans collapsed; being right was something that he thought himself particularly good at. In taking up with Constanze, Mozart was rewriting that debacle as a more carefully considered story designed to end happily.

Mozart tried hard in his letters back to Salzburg in the months leading up to the wedding in the summer of 1782 to soften his father's mood and to explicate what he was up to. Confronting Leopold's stubborn consternation may also have given the composer a focus for overcoming anxieties of his own about making this change while his life in the big city was still so unsettled. The wedding took place in a cathedral whose Gothic vastness may have highlighted the patriarch's absence. Marrying was a way of trying to earth the energies that life in Vienna was releasing and requiring, but partly too a way of insisting that going there had been the right decision. Writing to Leopold to try to justify the decision, Mozart is almost awkwardly clear about the backdrop of sexual opportunity and general dissoluteness that the city offered and threatened, and against which the sway of wedlock had to be measured. The weird fusions of charm and urgency that power much of his music especially during his first couple of years in Vienna take their bearings from these fluttering and severe questions. A large part of what we hear is a brilliant and passionate young man meditating on his gains and losses as he moves into new phases of life and especially into marriage, and into the new relationship to his own desire that it brought. A marriage is a work of art, a way of turning desire into an enduring shape.

A year or so into Mozart's Viennese life and sometime around the time of his wedding, he composed the K388 serenade in C minor, a focal point for his transactions with the rococo. The serenade genre conjures the world of hedonism and social whirl to which the style belonged, because all that it takes for a piece to be a serenade is that it should be a fairly loose suite of movements suited to being played amid the general diversions of an evening. But here the genre's fluidity does not mean that the piece stays light and pleasant; instead Mozart exploits it to write something shadily suited to this period when his social life and its entailments were up in the air. Delight moves in streams through this music, but also reveals its headiness and its rigours. The pleasures of form and an almost turbulent sensuous intensity converge in the piece in ways that his music would never surpass but did keep drawing on. We can infer that some breathy, darkly toned and oddly solemn new understanding of pleasure emerged for the composer over the course of that summer's evenings and nights. Pleasure in the C minor serenade is something loaded and causative, something that can jackknife suddenly out of distraction or flirtation and assume grave entailments or suggest severe reflections.

Commissions and invitations and possibilities rushed at Mozart in Vienna, and it is not as clear as many commentators have wanted to suggest how exactly this serenade came to be written. Its power comes from the amplitude with which it listens in on and grasps the fraught hubbub of the city's social whirl. Mozart had thrown himself into a city filled with musicians scrabbling to seem indispensable to its greed for musical pleasures. On good days this made it an ideal place to be; on other days it may have felt like the opposite. Concerts and performances of all sorts were diffused into the city's social flow and commercial culture, and the grand domestic set-ups of aristocratic dynasties like the Thuns or the Liechtensteins or of the more aspirational bourgeois families like the Greiners or the Trattners or the Auernhammers vied for the exploits of figures like Mozart. The more expansive and clamorous these circuits became, the further musicians could drift from feeling that any place in them was settled. The general surmise is that the C minor serenade was written for one of the great connoisseur princes of the capital, Alois Joseph

Liechtenstein. He was setting up a wind band of the sort that the piece furnishes, and it seems plausible that Mozart may have meant it to catch the princely ear even if it was not directly commissioned by him. Towards the end of July 1782 he tells Leopold that he has found himself needing to come up with a piece of night music 'in a great hurry' amid some already rushed work on a commission for the Haffner family; probably this was our serenade. Elegance and extroversion are offset in the piece by a fierce urgency, a sense of having been not just composed but unleashed. Not content with belonging to a glitzy social world, it cuts through and unsettles it.

Within these circles such an unsettling serenade may have been all the more darkly delicious a novelty. Music gave the likes of Liechtenstein points of congress between sheer pleasure and heights of sophisticated, prestigious culture. The serenade is a map of Mozart's dual artistic identity at this point; staying popular as a purveyor of high-class fun was vital, but his more artistically ambitious or wilful side needed nourishing and could in any case bring no less profitable renown. Partly because it is scored for an octet made up entirely of wind instruments, the basic structures of its phrasing are mostly very conventional and hence fully compatible with the readily digestible pleasures that serenades suggest. But this swift, easily comprehensible phrasing assumes a double purpose, letting the music switch between expressive modes with the speed and stealth of a trapdoor. The rococo spirit in music had encouraged the catchy motifs and nifty phrasal hooks that became, paradoxically, the linchpins of the classical style at its most searching. Often they ended up forming the best ways by which the style's headiest pieces can build and signpost dauntingly complex arguments. The appeal to the ear of the serenade's phrases is lavishly direct; but this is also how the piece cajoles listeners into territories full of twists and shifts. A spirit of ceremonious poise at one moment can open with stunning rapidity onto blurting nervous energy.

Rococo style is filled with a desire for teeming and ingenious surfaces which endlessly provoke more desire. But this drive is also behind the spirit of agitation and doubt that moves across the serenade. Mozart composed it during a time of expansive popularity in Vienna of *Harmoniemusik*, social or occasional music for groups of wind instruments. Works of this sort were ever more in demand; a *Harmonie* of prestigious instrumentalists was founded at the imperial court around the time when the piece was composed. Mozart's serenade is finely geared to declare how up to date any gathering adorned by his music would be; Vienna seems to have started sucking in woodwind virtuosos around this time from across the empire's Bohemian lands and beyond. At the same time the serenade wants to show what subtleties lurk within such high technical possibilities. So the abrupt juxtapositions of smooth and staccato textures in the oboe writing in the first movement, or the monu-mentally extended rhythms extracted from the bassoons in the finale, do not just show Mozart squeezing all the juices of skill out of the available players. Writing like this wants to show the charges of sensuous unease that emerge as technical musicianship and the decorative impulse itself are extended. The serenade genre most easily lent itself to either chugging dance rhythms draped in unisonal textures and colours, or to soloistic and pleasing melodic simplicities laid out on a steady bed of harmonies. Mozart's piece instead shifts its developments and textures among the instruments; it wants to prove that this instrumental grouping is not preordained to be decorative or reductive, but can release flickeringly specific colours and a swivelling expressive density.

The fashion for wind bands was accelerated by Vienna's hunger for new operas. Bands like these would play catchy arrangements of the music from hit operas, turning their tunes into pervasive, contagious presences. A rich household could make itself fashion-able twice over by playing the latest numbers in this nifty guise. A week before the letter in which he seems to mention composing our serenade, Mozart tells Leopold that he is working helter-skelter to make such arrangements himself out of his 'seraglio' opera, now that it has opened and is already proving so popular. If he does not get them done quickly himself, someone else will get there first 'and collect the profits instead'. His father does not appreciate 'how difficult it is to arrange an opera for winds'. The serenade is crammed with ambition and drama and expressive swagger in ways that may well have drawn on Mozart's experience of trying to get a wind band to carry the force of operatic music. But its sense of dense largesse shows the relish with which Mozart could turn to exploring the wind band's copious resources on their own terms. Abbreviating his opera's riches until such an ensemble could manage them might not have been much fun even without the jostling commercial pressures involved, and the serenade's sense of bristling involution may have been a way of extracting himself from or correcting the previous project. The piece in any case mines the feelings of subjection to the wishes and pleasures of others that any artist of the social whirl may be prone to. But then this is one of the pieces that demonstrate most richly what a complex, paradoxical undertaking pleasing his audiences often became for Mozart. It turns out to mean writing such unexpected and assertive music that being serenaded can feel like being upended. The compression of phrase brought by writing for a wind band helps the serenade sustain an appealing, flashy directness, but also yields a texture that is hard-bitten and acerbic.

Rococo pictures or bibelots likewise pull hard at whoever encounters them with their all but crazy loveliness, but their extremes of refinement and artifice make them keep their distance too, and insist on their own unattainability. Mozart's own devoted, often reeling sense of fun fairly spills down the pages of his correspondence and in reminiscences about him. Names of socialites doubtless spangled his conversation as they do his letters, and we read of his love of punch and billiards and party games and dances and fashionable clothes. All of this was perfectly sincere while also being a mask by means of which he could penetrate further into his world than a more aloof or solemn artistic perspective might have allowed, and from behind which he could observe it, sharply and lovingly. We know how much he enjoyed a good masked ball and all senses of dressing up. But other people's fun was a serious business for him, something to be endlessly pondered, anticipated and redefined.

The wiry solemnity of the C minor serenade so wittily rewrites the genre's promise of smooth entertainment that it becomes a form of backhanded mischief. Maybe Mozart wanted to make sure that his most impressively advanced listeners could not miss how impressive he was, at this tender moment in his progress. We can also hear in this music dashes of brashness, anger and resentment on the part of this young man faced with needing to impress so endlessly. Rococo sensibility at its richest often tilted social celebration into satire or even moral mordancy; we can think of artists like Hogarth in London or Longhi in Venice as well as Fragonard, or of writers like Pope and Laclos. Mozart's serenade keeps blasting open the terms of its social world by its passages of passionate vehemence, before sashaying back into that world's good graces with phrases of dashing niceness. The third movement combines the charming rhythm of a minuet with a version of the strict imitative writing of a far older stylistic world. Hearing how the rhythmic lilt does and does not accommodate itself to the hard phrasal intersections of the canon style is like hearing easy sociability and severe artistry jostle and test each other. Likewise, the allegro finale swings with elegant briskness through a succession of variations on a theme that is itself austere to the point of bristling rigour. After the thrilling menace of much of the piece's music, the burbling levity within the last variation feels both highly conventional and slightly uncanny. Works of great artistic difficulty sometimes end on such notes because they want us to know that it is all right to return to the world.

Consciousness of ragged edges and dark trails animated the pleasure gardens of the rococo. Far from some anodyne or decadent accompaniment to any slide into lassitude on the part of the old Europe, or the symbol of some perfumed decline which the upheavals of modernity would eventually punish, the rococo thought on its quick feet as the world changed or buckled beneath it. On its way was a period of revolutionary and Napoleonic upheaval, but the best accounts suggest that it was less a comeuppance visited on an emptily hedonistic culture than the culmination of the restlessness and recklessness opened up by the eighteenth century at its freshest. Fragonard's swinging woman envisages the rococo as itself a form of ambiguous motion. Within the darting cosmopolitan audacity of figures like Casanova or Frederick the Great of Prussia or indeed Thomas Jefferson, the rococo reveals its historical density. Its fashions drenched all these sensibilities, in which anomie, irresponsibility and exploitation merged with wit and cultivation and the capacity to build worlds.

Frederick the Great was the period's most effective statesman and also a vital commissar of rococo trends. Prussia was in a strong position in 1740 as he came to the throne, but his steely outmanoeuvring of the Habsburgs among others set new terms over the middle decades of the century for what German political unity could yet become. His military acumen was matched by his devotion to the most delicately advanced musical fashions; his trenchant character made him an explorer in both pursuits. A dedicated flautist, Frederick grabbed the great guru of the instrument Johann Joachim Quantz from Dresden no less insistently than he used his remorseless statecraft to drain power from Saxony or Vienna. Quantz was a whirlingly productive composer for the flute, and in 1752 published the treatise on playing the instrument that became a landmark in the century's musical thinking; he also had the daunting privilege of indicating to the king how well or otherwise he had played. The burstingly decorative arias of Johann Adolph Hasse likewise reigned in Berlin, as Frederick's opera house became a centre for performing that most fulsome German exponent of Italian vocal styles. Frederick was charming and chatty and justly proud of his collection of pictures by Fragonard's great, delicious precursor, Antoine Watteau. He gave a masked ball on the night before he invaded Silesia during the first winter of his reign, and in 1744 the resulting war was at its height when he decided to build the palace of Sanssouci which summarized his fusions of majesty with wit and wiriness. If Versailles was once the acme of baroque will to power, the new palace was charged with rococo doubleness. Its name could be translated now by something like 'no worries', but there was a seething meticulousness to its construction of a new model for royal pleasure. The place was dauntingly splendid but also full of inviting intimacy and meandering sorts of decorative fizz and twitchiness.

Rococo style was an education in the forces of versatility and nimbleness that the Prussian king's statecraft thrived on. Frederick

was the era's most thoroughly disillusioned ruler, and he outma-
noeuvred the grander French and Habsburg monarchies in ways that
parallel how the rococo thrived as the tides of baroque grandeur
foundered. By the time of Mozart's move to Vienna, the city had
an emperor in Joseph who took Frederick as his model. Across the
century's middle decades, networks of affinity that were spun from
the delicate stuff of charm and taste revolutionized sensibility.
Frederick's great confidante, the Prince de Ligne, was another adept
of rococo style, and his career savours of its uncanny mobility and
nimbleness. Belgian if he was anything, the prince became a key
military leader for the Habsburgs, but was also a brilliant conversational
skirmisher in Paris and Saint Petersburg and a thinker admired by
Voltaire just as he would be by his eventual editor Madame de
Staël. During his twenties he made a reputation as the most dashing
soldier in the Seven Years' War while in fact fighting against
Frederick. But he spent the rest of a very long life skipping among
courts, circles and versions of political and literary life with a voracity
as flexible as a rococo floral motif. At one point late in the century
he declined to head a revolutionary riposte in Belgium to the
French upheavals on the grounds that he never revolted in winter.
He was a friend of Casanova's and a vital early audience for his
writing, and it was under his aegis that Casanova's painter brother
Francesco became a court favourite in Vienna, after moving there
from Paris where he had been a close associate of none other than
Fragonard's. He specialized in battle scenes and his Viennese circles
overlapped with Mozart's.

Who would really gain from the world of the rococo in the end?
We are getting close here to Mozart's great Italian comic operas, as
they swing between revelling in the era's pleasures and revealing
their destinies of loss and emptiness. The composer was steeped in
the style's love of delicacy and proliferation, in its restlessness that
can leave no stone ungilded. But he was also capable of paring down
its largesse, of concentrating its possibilities almost ascetically into a
few essential strokes, in ways that suggest a grasp of the discontent
spiralling through the rococo's swirls. A mirror is not just a mirror
in the rococo but a giddy fantasia on themes of visibility, and a

portrait is not just a likeness but a desperate argument about what constitutes personal charm and how to heighten it. Its stylistic extremes lead the rococo into deep questions and sharp powers of focus. The rococo and the enlightenment are often construed as opposing strains within Mozart's century, but the former became so quick and light partly in order to cope with the burdens of knowledge spreading across its culture. The two movements were really interfused; sometimes they were frenzied friends and sometimes intimate enemies. Mozart's feel for symmetry and stabilization was endlessly strong enough to let him both indulge and counter his own rococo sympathies, and his music thus turns the style's curiosity about giddiness or change into broad, grave investigations. *Don Giovanni* is the vanishing point of the rococo which also reveals the hard truths held in the extremes of its shallowness. The libertines that crowd the century's literature think that they pursue individualistic tastes and agendas, but they are threatened with turning into mere machines of desire, and Mozart's opera plumbs the emptying out of inwardness that results. The gleaming blankness of Giovanni's psyche is close to the bland face at the heart of Fragonard's picture. Likewise, in the serenade Mozart's writing for winds attains a freedom that is implacable to the point of fierceness. He treats their sound-worlds with a caustic amplitude that then resonates through much of the rest of his music.

The serenade itself represents a sort of endgame for its genre though. Mozart seems to have had little success when he tried rebooting it a few years later as a string quintet. Perhaps it had been a hit with connoisseurs which he felt should get a new hearing, after the fashion for wind ensembles had passed its zenith. Perhaps no one had ever liked it, and he was vexed or perplexed or intrigued by its unpopularity. His life in Vienna relied on finding the pleasures of others stimulating and fruitful, a hard task for anyone to maintain. The serenade's elements of shadow and asperity may comprise a clever sort of reverse magic; maybe Mozart could carry on wanting to give pleasure only so long as he could entangle it with gnarly, complex ingredients or with arguments about or against itself. Sometimes in the early 1780s he must have felt in danger of turning into something like a rococo machine; his days were devoted to squeezing out delight and inventiveness moment by moment as copiously as the style covered its world with gleaming surfaces. His letters to his father from the summer of 1782 regale Leopold with his engagements and the names of the grandees that he is visiting. Constanze finishes one of them in his place when he has to be snatched off to see a countess. Vienna's wandering wind bands went around pulling music into all the city's social events and niches; the same group could play the same fashionable music at a few different places during the same night. Mozart's music often came out of ongoing and casually laborious negotiations with haphazard entities like these groups, and out of endless processes of moment-by-moment music-making that scattered into the city's air. In the C minor serenade the complex, fluctile pleasures of Viennese nights in the early 1780s live on, but it also yearns for a more fully alert, comprehensive and dramatic vision of musical argument. Is this a new version of rococo hedonism or an exit from it?

In the end the style's adventurousness always pointed beyond itself, whether the rococo knew it or not. His highest contemporaries like Blake or Goya often learnt to turn its athletic piquancy and oblique zest to darker purposes as history heaved onwards. Likewise, the composer sought to carry on learning from it and perpetuating its pleasures, however expanded and scarred his horizons became. During the summer of 1787 Mozart would have heard of the musician Carl Friedrich Abel's death, around the time when he was rebooting the serenade. The deceased had been a close contemporary of Leopold's, and had exemplified some vision of the musician as a svelte, successful man of the world. As well as probably the last great virtuoso on the viola da gamba and a supple composer, he had been an entrepreneurial and bibulous ringmaster of London's highest and most commercially sleek musical circles, running an epochal concert series alongside one of the great Johann Sebastian Bach's sons in the city's burgeoning west end. Mozart responded to his death by incorporating into his great, expansive K526 violin sonata in A a riff on some music from a trio by the older man. But the passage from Abel is a piece of such merely dashing elegance that a sort of double stratagem emerges from Mozart's sampling of it within the whirling amplitude of this sonata's presto finale. In effect Mozart is saying that the rococo world can bear such pressure and yield such charge, but only if treated with all the intense structural imaginativeness that he could rouse. The rococo world can provide its own elegy here so long as it does so in Mozart's way.

The recycling of Abel's original allegro revolves on its sense of rhythmic attack and its all-over decorative vibrancy; if anything Mozart makes its merriment even more skittish. In this presto the rococo sheds even its elegance, revealing itself as an art of something like pure transience or pure transition, or pure headiness. At the same time a ricocheting exquisiteness emerges from Mozart's use of his paired instruments, and his feel for deep-lying patterns allows a subtle shapeliness to maintain itself across the movement. As a result Abel's theme can yield so much giddiness of surface without losing equilibrium; classical balance and euphony turn out to be the paradoxical inheritors of the rococo's febrile panache. It so happens that Abel's own father had worked under Bach back in Leipzig, and was probably the soloist for whom much of the latter's music for the viola da gamba was written. His son's grippingly fluent solo writing for the gamba may thus be one of the best guides that his culture produced to living amid the remnants of baroque grandeur. Charm can be a last-ditch ruse for coping with loss or metabolizing it. Can this turn loss into something that it thrives on, or even invites?

10

The Enlightened Labyrinth

The 'Haydn' Quartets

Within Vienna in the 1780s the convolutions of the enlightenment could be seen at the heart of the cityscape. It was not always an edifying spectacle. The emperor Joseph was captivated by ideals of reform that aimed to make his rule more rational and streamlined. One result was that large portions of his palaces were shut down and boarded up, in efforts to economize that reflected his discomfort with the empire's grand old images of majesty. Joseph's reign can read like a tangled parable of the threats and temptations that the enlightenment movement dispensed to the period's rulers. He churned out new policies as if the spirit of reform could replace awe as the centre of power. Certain reforms did fare well enough; in 1785 Vienna's excellent military hospital was built, during one of Mozart's most productive years in the capital. But the reforms tended to spiral away from his intentions, partly because neither his deeper loyalty to the Habsburg past nor the intricacy of the imperial bureaucracy could often support any wholesale commitment to liberalization. One widely disseminated propaganda image was an engraving showing him working a plough, watched by various gaudy courtiers and an impressive yeoman farmer. Joseph is meant to look like a man of the people and a man of action; the plough is a technologically advanced one. The image is as absurd as its effortfulness is noble, and this combination has its own pathos. Goethe claims somewhere that Joseph eschewed state beds when on royal trips, sleeping on the floor beside them instead.

The revolution in France that closed the 1780s throws an intense glare of meaning back onto the churn of ideas and networks that had made up the enlightenment over the preceding several decades.

But as the century's second half wandered on, Europe could not decide how enlightened it was or wanted to be. The guillotine that eventually struck the Bourbon king's neck may suggest a society's flashing determination to remake itself, or a blind resurgence of violence. Often the continent's great monarchies seemed determined to claim that they could be enlightenment's ultimate carriers. But all this largely showed either how ready the movement was to be waylaid or how densely certain versions of will to power had suffused it from the outset. 'Enlightened despotism' is the tag that has kept being ascribed to Joseph or Catherine in Russia or Frederick the Great in Prussia, and the despotism could normally be counted on more than their enlightened aspects. So when Joseph began to dethrone the values of magnificence and display that the continent had dazzled itself with for centuries, his reasons for reform were as opaque as the mystique in which the old ways had been shrouded. If he probably was sincerely convinced that some new rules were needed for new times, power plays and shifting momentums among cliques and factions and indeed larger groups in the city and the empire were involved too, as was his own watchful and laborious personality. Joseph liked people to have to second-guess him. He worked with the sober zeal of a natural bureaucrat during the day, and spent his evenings straining to redefine kingship by jerkily impersonating a private citizen. As his blandly haughty looks were spotted amid the Viennese clubs and salons that were busily imitating Paris, it is hard to imagine that conversation flowed easily.

But the enlightenment itself was a labyrinth by now. Up in Königsberg, towards the very north-eastern tip of Prussia, the philosopher Immanuel Kant appended the date of 30 September 1784 to a short essay which would appear later that year in the *Berlinische Monatsschrift*. A recent essay from a different pen in the same periodical had mentioned in passing that the author had never found the question of what is enlightenment answered anywhere. The title that Kant gives his essay both poses the question and rather pedantically tells us that he will answer it, but then his outlandish meticulousness notoriously extended beyond his brilliant philosophical rigour as far as the timing of his daily walks. His neighbours knew that it was half past three when the professor in his grey frock-coat strode by. He was in his sixties by this point, and we can assume that versions of the question had been nudging away at him for years, as the enlightenment movement poured its waves of discussion and controversy and chatter across Europe. He had spent the previous couple of decades working away with ecstatic relentlessness at a vision of critical thought capable of both summarizing the largest reaches of the enlightenment and turning them inside out, one designed to push away so hard at the spirit of remorseless inquiry that it ends up proving constructive rather than dissolvent. Rousseau's moral idealism had deeply impressed Kant as it made its turns towards inwardness and sensibility, and his obsession became with showing how free-thinking and a heightened individualism can turn out to draw people all the more fully and richly into habits of reasonableness and universal forms of thought, as well as almost exuberantly stringent moral principles. No one saw further into either the powers or the dangers of modern thought. He knew how diffuse and corrosive its expansiveness could be, how the pursuit of knowledge could either dissipate into mere accumulation or shatter into dispute and doubt, if thinking was not called back to its most basic powers of construction.

Part of what is so powerful about his essay on enlightenment is all that it leaves out. The famous encyclopaedia that Diderot presided over and the likes of Rousseau and Jean le Rond d'Alembert worked on may have been the signature project of the heights of enlightenment ambition in mid-century Paris. But Kant's essay is the opposite of encyclopaedic, eschewing any hint of a catalogue of the gains of modern knowledge or any attempt to sort through the kaleidoscopic strands and schools of enlightenment thought. Instead he concentrates with fastidious glee on the most basic terms on which the question of enlightenment can be addressed. He starts by defining enlightenment as man's emergence from what he calls self-incurred immaturity, and explains that this immaturity is 'the inability to use one's own understanding without the guidance of another'. The key for Kant is that this makes enlightenment less a state to be attained than a process to be endlessly renewed, an injunction to think both freely and responsibly whose findings cannot be predicted or fixed. One result is that neither his own nor any other could be what the essay carefully uses italics to call 'an *enlightened* age', because that would suggest that some promised land had been reached. Living in an age whose ongoing aim is enlightenment is Kant's ideal, and he uses the little Latin tag '*sapere aude*' as his motto for enlightenment values. So the idea is that we must be daring to gain knowledge; the enemy is less ignorance than the lack of the courage needed to break away from it. Daring to know is all the more vital because no final, utterly solid knowledge can be reached. Ignorance and irrationality must be combated, but simply knowing is not an option; knowledge is something that we have to keep embarking on and attempting endlessly. The enlightenment movement can be as turbulent, cryptic and fallible as it likes, because being enlightened comes down for Kant to something both grindingly simple and rapturously cogent. It involves a bedrock faith in the mind's constructive powers which is also an almost manically energetic goad to using them as relentlessly as possible.

His student and eventual antagonist Johann Gottfried Herder relates how urbane and charming Immanuel Kant really was, how he could be much more sociable than his reputation for dowdiness and a life based on clockwork routine suggests. In fact the great philosopher was a sort of pivot within the enlightenment movement, someone who wanted to swivel it away from a period of hectic expansion, and into a more fraught but also more subtle and durable version of itself. Interpretations of his historical role accordingly veer around, sometimes seeing his work as an exacerbated last stand for eighteenth-century norms, sometimes as a heady conduit into romantic subjectivism and rampancy. Reason could renew itself for Kant only by seeing how close it always comes to upending itself or tying itself up in knots, and so by rededicating itself to the forms of thought that drive its claims in the first place. Someone like Herder could set himself up in opposition to the enlightenment as a defined school of thought. But even his intricate pluralism extends aspects of the movement precisely by disputing others; his is a cosmopolitanism that questions itself by finding patterns of thought other than its own so compelling.

After his months in 1778 within the tricky heartlands of enlightened Paris, no one will have had much to teach Mozart about the forces of sprawl, dispute and disillusion that had spread through the enlightenment movement. Voltaire's death that year darkly crystallized the sense of disappointment and fracture colouring the period. But what Kant's essay marks is the point at which the idea of enlightenment no longer belonged to any given movement or proponents or any set of works or ideas; instead it had become at once an atmosphere, a horizon and an ethos. Ambition and controversy had driven the likes of Grimm on in Paris, but also dragged their version of the enlightenment into innumerable rancid displays of crossed purposes and sheer crossness, and into accommodations that were themselves highly creative with the surrounding zeniths of power and wealth. The elements of the movement that featured in Vienna in the early 1780s would not have seemed as overripe, but they were no less diffuse, jagged and hybrid. The emperor Joseph wanted his capital to be a progressive cultural centre; inevitably music would be vital. Gluck and Salieri were more stable quantities to enlist than Mozart, however, and the emperor's qualities of intelligence and ranging sympathy had downsides of fickleness and prevarication. He does seem to have greatly liked and genuinely appreciated Mozart; the composer might have preferred a princely backer who was less sincere but cannier and more determined. Anecdotes about their relationship abound, but they seldom make it sound simple. In the most famous one Joseph tells Mozart that *Die Entführung aus dem Serail* has too many notes, to which he is meant to have replied that it had exactly the right number. Da Ponte claims that the emperor thought that *Don Giovanni* was divine but unsuited to the Viennese; in the best-attested vignette he calls it too difficult for singers.

Mozart's music was a carrier of the vertigo of the enlightenment as well as of its core values. While this gives it all the more to say now about the raging complexity of being enlightened, it meant that it was not the most useful counter in any game for someone like Joseph whose plans wavered between technocracy and idealism and downright megalomania. He wanted to be a dynamic, lucid, modern ruler on the model of Frederick the Great; in Kant's essay the Prussian king gets a very honourable mention. But Joseph was stuck with the Habsburg empire and all its lumbering frailty, and he was stuck with himself too. During the 1780s the grand families of the empire's aristocracy spent less and less time in Vienna, unable to imagine a social world not based on festive showing off, but unsure about outdoing an emperor who seemed bent on crossing out such splendours. Vienna was becoming dominated by a motley alliance between new social cadres from the spheres of business, finance and imperial technocracy and the more progressive, cosmopolitan elements of the lower aristocracy. The flux was exacerbated by Joseph's trick of selling off aristocratic titles and privileges to the most successful, and pushy, representatives of these new cadres. Maybe the emperor could not help wanting to lay bare the vacuousness of the old systems of power, but he relied on their allure to fill his coffers and to win supporters. He wanted to streamline his systems of revenue, but the logic of rationalization is voracious, and can eat up both what it means to use and what it aims to protect. The new classes whose support he needed could not yet supply a cultural scene capable of supplanting the old courtly splendour. Mozart got caught up in some of these contradictions as the second half of the decade imperilled his own finances; not enough money was flooding or even trickling from imperial sources, but neither could Vienna yet reliably nourish a free-standing civic culture. The city was conjuring with energies that it could not fully commit to.

By the early 1780s the bright colours of the early enlightenment movement had been mixed in with so many other cultural and political realities that Vienna's confusions make it into a sort of showcase, typical precisely because enlightenment drives there took on such mixed-up and unpredictable versions. Did all this mean that the enlightenment was prevailing across Europe or failing? Its ideas were pervasive but in forms that were everywhere diluted and compromised; the sunny geometry of Canaletto had morphed as a guide to the continent's mind into Piranesi's style of fractious, occlusive fantasy. Enlightened types always eventually encounter either their inability to change the world or the world's unwillingness to be changed, and so tend to end up moving from overexcitement to secret depression. A movement that feeds on being adversarial may end up being manically embattled, or terminally embittered, or its proponents may become mere gadflies flickering around in salons and periodicals. The constant desire for new ideas made the intellectual landscape unstable; the validation of specialized knowledge broke it up. The enlightenment was a centrifuge, as fellow travellers and minor adepts multiplied argumentatively in all directions, often inventing new variants on its themes as they wandered amid the culture's small courts and pushy little cities and rooms full of chatter. Minor grandees like the removed Polish king Stanislaus I at his ersatz court in Lorraine or Goethe's duke Karl August in Weimar wanted to be surrounded by the finest and most current intellectual raiments. Across the various German lands, versions of enlightenment reason intersected with those that looked to pietism for a streamlined theology or with the craze for Spinoza's philosophical pantheism that had swept the more precocious literary circles. The life of Casanova as he moved towards finally settling during the 1780s as the librarian to a Bohemian count had become an incarnate experiment in splicing together enlightenment lucidity with grasping fantasy, a commitment to culture with a sprawling cult of ego. Scholars veer between punctiliously spotlighting this or that local branch of the movement and loftily insisting that only Paris ever had the real thing. In Kant the European mind was making its great effort to hold itself together, but the strain of the attempt is part of the texture of his thought.

The enlightenment was a flexible way of life and it was a network of complex networks; it was not a set of doctrines. Mozart's father was typical of many in his generation who were imbued with bits and pieces of the enlightenment spirit, without feeling any need for a full subscription. It was partly Leopold's relentless didacticism that gave Mozart such a deft feel for the enlightenment in all its pedagogical frenzy. Loyalty to the desire to understand the world could jostle in him with a tough filial scepticism towards such drives. His central circles of support during his Viennese years included the Countess von Thun und Hohenstein whose drawing room came close to its Parisian models of refinement and wit, and whose Stein fortepiano Mozart particularly liked, and the ruminating array of writers and cosmopolitans and students of the era who met within the Masonic movement. The composer began spending evenings around the middle of the 1780s with the city's remarkable Jacquin family, and in their circle serious and uproarious music-making abutted teeming discussions of the Linnaean system of classification, in which field the father of the house was an international expert. His friendship with the great clarinettist Anton Stadler seems to have thickened within the ambiance of these evenings, and their pursuit together of new technological options for the clarinet probably owed much to the fusions under that roof of musical and more broadly experimental passions. So too his letters to the young Gottfried von Jacquin, and the sometimes luridly merry songs that came from those evenings, remind us how fully such circles could mix the enlightenment spirit with goofiness and flirtation and mischief. In one letter from Prague back to Gottfried, Mozart addresses him as his 'dear Hinkiti Honky' before running through gaudy nicknames for other figures in their world. The composer's Viennese circles also overlapped with those of the famous doctor Mesmer from whom our ideas of being mesmerized derive, and whose theories combined medical intricacy with exuberant sorts of cosmic caprice.

Mozart was nothing if not plural, and in his correspondence enlightened thinking is not exempt from his drives of ambiguity and mischief. But mixed feelings typified the movement's later phases, and the composer stayed filled with enlightenment traits of thought that put talent above social status and upheld the universality of taste and reason. He craved a milieu filled with debates and inquiries, but also with fun and hints of mayhem. His own growing commitment to Freemasonry around the middle of the decade particularly shows both the intensity of his craving and the absence of any more perspicuous vehicle. Nowhere did the ambiguities of the enlightenment in 1780s Vienna show themselves more richly than in the rise and fall across the decade of the Masonic brotherhood. Its esoteric origins in the world of medieval guilds and its hodgepodge of oaths and rituals made Freemasonry an ungainly vehicle for enlightenment hopes. But probity and truth and fraternity were meant to be central to it too, and indeed this unlikeliness may itself have helped the Masonic movement become the nearest thing that this Vienna offered to an institutionalized version of enlightenment values. It played roles that were similarly both vital and rather chimerical elsewhere. The great, starry playwright and essayist Lessing had made himself from the 1750s on the nearest thing that the German language had to an official representative of the enlightenment movement, and he had also joined the Freemasons. Lessing typified enlightenment tendencies towards polemic and intellectual battle too, however, and he soon became a critic of the brotherhood.

Ignaz von Born was the mighty doyen at the complex heart of Freemasonry in 1780s Vienna. His enigmatic presence within Mozart's life is sometimes reduced to the question of whether he was the model for Sarastro, the philosophical ruler at the centre of *Die Zauberflöte* and its mazy parables of illumination. In *Die Zauberflöte* the composer would indeed bring the enlightenment to an exuberant reckoning with its own most cryptic or topsy-turvy elements, right at the end of his life and while news of the revolution in France flooded Europe. Charm and authority seem to have radiated from Born towards all who met him, though the whirling range of his learned pursuits can make him seem to have been daily engaged in blurring distinctions between enlightenment and sheer crankiness. He was a brilliant talker renowned for his outpourings of both good cheer and coruscating invective, and he was ethereally handsome too. He was also an expert mineralogist whose special interests in coinage and metallurgy were neatly geared to connect recent scientific trends to past ages of alchemy and magic. Under his auspices Freemasonry sounds as if it operated more like a learned society with the odd oath or ceremony added on than anything too elaborately ritualistic. But the resulting alloy of cosmopolitan intellectual ambition with abstruse make-believe did not make the brotherhood's prominence less controversial in Mozart's Vienna, and by the end of the 1780s its links with political freethinking had helped pitch Freemasonry there into decline.

Vienna was both porous to the enlightenment and resistant to it; it hungrily drew on enlightenment trends and tendencies while blocking them or sending them into circuitous routes or odd compounds. All this helped make it the ideal, fertile and complex setting for the classical style in music to emerge in. The complex power of this music became the great expression of this pivotal historical moment because intricate, tender and ambivalent ways of wrangling with the meaning of enlightenment are in effect built in. Music and the enlightenment had been febrile dance partners throughout the century, in great cities and little centres across the culture. Paris must loom large in all accounts of their tangles. But Naples had its own rich version of an enlightenment movement, as well as being a hothouse for the most up-to-date musical styles. The centrepiece of that version of the enlightenment was Giambattista Vico's mighty attempt at a 'new science' capable of unifying ancient myth with modern historical research, though his teeming city only slowly grasped what it had had in him; heady parallels suggest themselves now between his project and aspects of *opera seria*. Music stands as an open but elusive invitation to rational description, and enlightenment Europe had piled up manuals, theories and treatises. A certain sleek resistance to analytical schemas inhabits it that tends to pull them on towards it too, while at the same time it was a source of such intense and general versions of pleasure and prestige that it bound the enlightenment to all that it ostensibly opposed. In the odd musical biographies that he wrote as mixtures of labours of love and hackwork, Stendhal eventually provided a sweeping dis-tillation of this world of fandom and promotion in which opinionated brilliance and raptures of pleasure kept mingling. Mozart was one of his subjects, and his admiration of him was both vast and insightful; he found his music full of violence.

If the triumph of the classical style was powered by ambivalence towards enlightenment ideals, so was much of what was best in the enlightenment itself. Sometimes Mozart's music seems so rational as to be all but abstruse, but it thus also suggests how weird rationality is in the first place. Within the layers of sonic thought that make up Mozart's so-called 'Haydn' string quartets, we hear something like a change in the demands made on hearing itself. Mozart worked hard over much of the first part of the decade on these six pieces, and then published them at the end of the summer in 1785 as a set, not long after Kant's essay had reached its public. A famous dedication to the older composer in which Mozart describes them as the results 'of long and laborious endeavour' accompanied them in the sumptuous edition. The complexity of composing them was a marker of how volatile the quartet form then was; it was still emerging under Haydn's tutelage from the breezy, courtly ambience of the divertimento and the serenade into the place pulsing at the heart of chamber music seriousness that it has largely kept since. Combining two violins with one viola and one cello had until recently still been just one of many ways of organizing music-making on a small and manoeuvrable scale; it was largely Haydn who made the string quartet an archetype. He coaxed its four voices closer to equality in ways that made it ideal for combining dense textures with lucid surfaces. In turn this opened the form up for the stylistic pluralism that he wanted to showcase; a brusque rigour can abut or interlace with the galant appeal of delicacy and wit. In the hands of Haydn and Mozart, classical music proposes a version of equality where its value is inseparable from its tensions and hazards. By wrestling with these gnarly factors, Mozart got his versions of the form to equal his friend's. A string quartet has to be engagingly persuasive in ways that pieces written for large ensembles or solo instruments do not, because it cannot just immerse listeners in drama or volume, or dazzle them with technical feats.

Haydn's early quartets had evidently thrilled the younger composer. No other works in the Europe of his youth suggested with anything like the same zesty lucidity how the culture's variously lovely and extravagant musical styles could galvanize formal rigour. Haydn turns freedom of phrasing into the driver of new types of expansive structure. He and Mozart had been aware of each other for years, but until the 1780s they seem not to have actually met.

Pieces by both men were included in two grand concerts put on in December 1783 by a newly formed society for Vienna's musicians, and these would have been snazzy circumstances for them to come together in. Haydn was spending some time each year in the imperial capital, and the affinity between the two men easily flowered into an intimacy sharpened by intense mutual respect. Around two and a half decades separated them in age, and much distinguished their characters; Mozart was fulsome, profuse, and extravagantly chatty and suggestible and waggish, while Haydn was gnomically canny and tenacious, if also witty and full of a more choppy, rugged bonhomie. Becoming close friends with someone who for once was in so many ways a genuine match for him might have been too much for Mozart if plenty of asymmetries had not been in play too. Haydn's origins were in a wheelwright's cottage in fairly lowly rural Austria, and when Vienna had latched on to his outrageous talents, his endlessly tough and bouncy personality kept its forces from drowning him. As a young man clinging on among the lower rungs of the Habsburg empire's musical ladders, he learnt to compose in a spirit of oddly robust openness to risk and change. All this meant burning through social worlds, stylistic habits and not a few forms of patronage or employment.

Latterly, though, the older composer had largely been immersed in twenty years or so of seclusion at the far-flung Hungarian court of the very grand Esterházy princes. His career there gave him a singular, patient angle from which to listen in to the rhythms and possibilities of Europe's music, and he became a composer of what can feel like casually abundant originality. During the early 1780s Vienna was starting to find the power and appeal of his works undeniable, but he was distrusted and resented within the high musical echelons surrounding Joseph. Maybe this doubleness was part of his charm for his young friend. Haydn's work combines a sort of swinging ease with terseness and acerbity in ways that make it seem imperiously aloof as well as deeply fun. So too he was a privileged courtly employee engrossed in rather backwards versions of hierarchy and splendour, but he was also becoming a celebrity freelance in demand in the zippiest metropolises, and this layering of roles helped feed his work's great investigations of what it is like to live in a plural world. His music is full of hiatuses and tripwires, but its thrills are all the more hefty because they are juxtaposed with doubts. He was now around fifty and new levels of success and renown were claiming him, but his quartets had remained imperturbable in the ruggedness of their charm, and the playfulness of their rigour. It was impressive that Mozart had stayed capable of apprenticing himself to anyone; Haydn's quartet writing was the only contemporary body of work that could make sense of that boldly humble endeavour.

Pulsing through Haydn's music there is a yearning for artistic liberty that keeps wanting to realize itself in harmoniousness and sociability. Around the middle of the decade Haydn in fact joined the Freemasons, though his lodge was not the same as Mozart's. Writing string quartets was a good way of bringing such desires together, because the ensemble raises questions about the relations between togetherness and freedom. Mozart's 'Haydn' quartets themselves amount to a fulsome act of reception of the older composer. He renewed his interest in the genre soon after moving to Vienna, during a period when the two men were so aware of each other's work as to be almost collaborating. Plenty besides music gelled their friendship, but its essence lay in how deeply they both saw new ways of combining structural stability with twisting dramatic freedom that the most up-to-date musical styles could bring. The pair do seem to have tried to see a lot of each other whenever their schedules brought them close, but this was not often. The two of them regularly played in quartets alongside each other when they could get together. But the music that they composed comprised their finest dialogue. As Mozart's ideas slide in and out of what he took from the older man, the quartets are both touching and shocking as they show how intimate with another mind's workings someone can be. Directing the sequence to Haydn was Mozart's way of saying that the enlightenment will go nowhere without friendship. Musicians seek further versions of affinity and mutual reception as they play these pieces.

The classical style was negotiated point by point between the two men rather in the way that Braque and Picasso would together press and nuance cubism into existence in painting not that much more than a century later. While the 'Haydn' quartets are never less than accomplished, tension and even choppiness keep turning their suave surfaces complex or fraught. Mozart made abortive sketches for several movements, and found himself working simultaneously on different movements from across the sequence. Their tight turns and bracing edges can feel painfully close to declaring how knotty writing music could be even for him sometimes. The quartet group was large enough to throw up complex possibilities of argument or register, and small enough for the resulting choices to be starkly palpable. In these pieces every quality of sound is tinkered with or taken apart or anatomized or combined with some other element. A rapt intellectual tortuousness keeps threatening, as if these instruments belonged to a laboratory rather than a musical group.

Critics have used the metaphor of conversation to describe classical quartets and to link them to enlightenment trends. But this does not really capture the plunging density with which the instruments investigate their relationships in Mozart's set. Few conversations push so hard at each word's depths. The quartets cannot pretend that a cello is as suited to melodic leading as a violin; the equality sought is meant to throw throbbingly intense light on each instrument's actual aptitudes. So too the popular dance rhythms of the minuet will keep a movement in touch with social pleasantness, but the music will also visit such processes of probing and involution on those rhythms that they too start to brim with intellectual impatience. Who, in a world trying and failing to be enlightened, can fail to want to be both involuted and elegant? In some moods the enlightenment believed its own beaming hype about progress and lucidity and tolerance; in others it chased after reason's more delirious flights, or prophesied the violent debacles to which modern rationality has indeed proved prone. Within these quartets many such moods become strenuously and movingly audible.

Of course a conversation can resemble a laboratory or a labyrinth; the analogy may originate with Goethe, so we should hesitate to discard it. The quartets move with a newly charged combination of density and flexibility, since the relationships between the different instrumental lines are made so complex and mobile. The same artistic decisions that carry all this investigative energy are the sources of structure too, in a hydraulic version of enlightenment thought. So the divisions between melodic themes or stylistic ideas tend to be more starkly contoured than in the piano concertos, say. No soloistic instrument is there to give dramatic clarity, so the thematic units cannot take the form of long cantabile melodies, but are pressed out as more tightly focused shapes. One result is the often almost choppy fluidity of the dynamics with which the instruments set out their progress, as if some new sort of musical grammar or punctuation was needed to make this elaborate terrain legible. It is like being in a labyrinth crammed with elaborate signposts.

Mozart often ends up conceiving of works in distinct groups like this set when he has some large-scale shift in compositional practice to explore. So it is generally a marker both of depth of artistic need and of expanded artistic capacity when he does so, and it often comes when he is unsure of exactly who he is writing for and on what terms. It may have been only gradually that the first two or three in this sequence suggested a joint project, but the looseness of its unity helps make the sequence so gripping and suggestive. Mozart's mind is full of both exhilarating expansiveness and a tense awareness of problems and knots. The string quartet had been closely linked with the sphere of courtly, aristocratic entertainment that Joseph was busily degrading, but no alternative culture of widespread and lucrative bourgeois connoisseurs had taken hold either. It was as if these quartets were being composed in the face or the ears of a vacuum. The prominence given in their published edition to the dedication to Haydn carried real artistic piety. But Mozart and his publisher were being strategic too, wanting to slide them towards the fans of the form's great pioneer, and towards whatever versions of connoisseurship Haydn's works had tentatively nourished. In some ways the sheer seriousness of the set communicates the hopes for a sophisticated public sphere that we associate with the enlightenment's best energies. But their elements of convolution and density convey how fraught such hopes had tended to become.

Enormous weight is placed on the last in the sequence, the K465 quartet in C that is generally known as the 'Dissonance' quartet. We can try to imagine Mozart as he sat down to write it, trying to think of some way of setting it going that would both give it a powerful agenda of its own and set it up as a partial, raking summary of the whole compositional effort of the quartets as an oeuvre. The bright allegro movement that opens the piece is itself prefaced by an adagio passage that in some ways is no introduction at all to what immediately follows, but a broodingly distinctive puzzle in which the instruments search with a certain halting relentlessness for a place to begin. The search itself becomes the place; but Mozart's feel for phrasal clarity is so powerful that it is vividly agonizing when it is withheld. Notes and phrases nudge one another hesitantly around without settling into any one shape. But placing this glistering music at the start of the last in this sequence of quartets also lays bare the deep rules that have really been guiding them all along. The restless probing of notes and harmonic relations takes on such stark, dramatic emphasis that we suddenly realize what we have been hearing all along across the sequence. At the same time an uncanny double effect takes hold of the music, because the lack of the normal sources of momentum and melodic flow turns out to allow the emergence of a different sense of quivering equilibrium and balance. It is like watching the glistening tension of a meniscus. The notes do not arrange themselves into the sorts of patterns that say where they are likely to be heading; a sense of churning potential instead obtains. Writing music must time and again have meant bringing together two different drives for Mozart, as the notes coming out of his pen pushed into the free creation of their own sequences at the same time as they pulled towards orderliness and shape.

Across the quartets a yearning for structure in fact keeps investing the melodic lines of individual voices; the finale of the K387 quartet in G that was the first of the set is a lyrical case in point. Listening to the start of the quartet in C can feel like being soaked even more deeply in some basic, inchoate desire for structure that is not normally fully audible itself. The passage has the downward pull that we have associated with the viola and its appeal within the act of composing, as the lower instruments prevent the first violin in particular from breaking off into melodic clarity. The music keeps wanting to stay in a state of sheer compositional potential just for a few stretched moments longer. Mozart's music here is both pared down and infinitely expansive; it is as if it were listening in with amazement to the compositional freedom that underlies it. It is both exhilarated and slightly aghast to discover that the world will not tell it what to do.

So this sense of teetering freedom is doubly heightened by its position at the start of the sequence's last quartet. The passage's flickering shadowiness works as a culmination of all the investigations and remouldings that crowd through the earlier pieces. On the other hand this is also the beginning of a new piece and has the sense of dramatic suspense which Haydn himself often used slow introductions to build. The passage pulls in two directions, backwards into the five quartets that have preceded it, and forwards into the final one. So when a crisply singing theme breaks free in the voice of the first violin and sets the allegro in motion, the sense of transition and suddenness is stark, and the melody's freshness feels uncannily freighted. Mozart's entire art is alive in the little swivel of movement between the adagio and the allegro; the whole spirit of the enlightenment may pivot here on the tiny shimmer of transition whereby these two sections play against and interpret each other. In fact the violin's little sequence of rising notes links back very loosely to thematic hints in some of the introduction's very earliest phrases. An almost stubbornly bright clarity lights up the rest of the allegro, and the piece turns into one of Mozart's most vivid and gracious quartets; but none of this erases the revelations with which it began. Rather, we learn to hear them brooding within the shifts of harmony, recalibrations of melody and experiments in instrumental colour that proceed.

Perhaps it is the audacity of the enlightenment that Mozart's quartets make audible, the daring to know that Kant exhorts us to and which cannot be reduced to any fixed set of ideas. Accounts of the enlightenment in our culture now veer intemperately between idealization and dismissal, but Kant wants to rid us of our preoccupation with whatever the enlightenment might have been or failed to be, and to set us instead to trying to illuminate our own lives. In the strains of this set of quartets we can hear something like artistic courage itself, as we can too in the volatile monumentality of Beethoven's quartets over the following half century or so, and in the abrupt recklessness of Leoš Janáček's too another century or so later. Mozart's work is full of such constructive audacity and also of a Kantian understanding that drives of development thrive on being probed and rethought and all but dismantled. The textures of Mozart's six quartets are often finely woven, of course, but they are also sometimes jumpy and sometimes cramped. A labyrinth can be an exciting place to think in. Early in 1804 Immanuel Kant died shortly before he would have turned eighty, in a Prussia that would soon be humbled by the version of France that Napoleon was dragging out of the revolutionary period. A couple of years before his own death, Haydn is reported to have said in 1807 that he could not help crying when he heard the name of Mozart.

11

Eternal Questions

Great Mass in C minor

In Salzburg Leopold followed his son's progress with sharp devotion, but only received one visit from him after he had moved to the imperial capital and then married. It was late in the summer of 1783 that Mozart embarked on this one return. Salzburg was full of unfinished business that he had closed doors on. He was working around this time on his great K427 setting of the mass in C minor, a piece that he never completed. Its fragmentariness has ended up seeming to contribute to its unsteady, colourful pathos, but of course Mozart cannot exactly have intended such effects. The mass is also imbued with such a powerful will to formal finish and stylistic substance that its incompleteness feels all the more charged and revealing. Mozart's duties as a court composer during his later years based in his home town had meant writing large quantities of church music, so a work of this sort would have brought a reckoning with large aspects of his past in the context of this return. The mass combines surging monumentality with a giddy athletic zip in ways that exist nowhere else in the period's church music, as if it wanted to outdo and to speed away from a whole world of other mass settings, including his own. It has the feel of a church whose features lift the eye so high that architecture merges with vertigo.

No one has established a commission or any other external prod behind this music. Mozart had turned twenty-seven in the year when his return to Salzburg appears to have occasioned its first performance. He was sure that throwing his lot in with Vienna had been right, but so far the results there had not answered all the questions of anyone determined to be hard to convince. Somebody turning up as a married man and a householder and a breadwinner may in fact strike some as having made failure a more likely and fraught prospect. His family saw Constanze as a frisky soul who had inveigled herself into her husband's life by way of his own airier attributes. The grand names and hectic engagements that crowd his letters from Vienna probably seemed to Leopold to evince giddiness at least as much as solid progress. The journey back to his home town had been long planned since the gradual process in the previous year by which he had got his father to see that he was getting married, sometimes cajoling him into accepting it and sometimes confronting him with the sheer necessity of doing so. A certain stony recognition that the thing was being done did eventually issue from Leopold, but no one from the family attended the wedding. 'My wife weeps tears of joy whenever she thinks of our trip to Salzburg'; so Mozart writes to his father only three weeks or so into their marriage. It is conceivable that other emotions were involved in any such tears, as the thought of her adamantine father-in-law loomed before the young spouse.

Mozart's letters to Leopold over the following months froth with effort as they try to make it seem obvious that he really does want to visit him; the composer may have needed convincing himself. But they also abound with reasons why he cannot set out. So, in the same letter from just after the wedding, the grand Russian visitors for whom Mozart had performed in his keyboard duel with Clementi are returning, and need to be entertained this time too, and Mozart may in any case be just about to become music master to the Princess of Württemberg, and for slightly inscrutable reasons this would make the trip much easier later on. Later in the year he badly wants to make it to Salzburg for his father's name day in the middle of November, but he cannot miss the lucrative season when the upper classes return from the countryside to pile back into music lessons and concerts. He claims that he and his wife would in any case have had to go back by the start of the following month. Effusions and regrets continue in these veins. At one point Mozart says that legal fears are keeping him from the journey, because of the irregular processes by which he had extracted himself from the archbishop's service.

The misgivings that he must have had about the trip proved to be largely right, after the couple eventually tore themselves away late in the following July from a dead season in the capital. The nostalgia of return can become uncanny when it applies to somewhere that was largely disliked all along. Mozart was back in a place that he knew to its bones but he was a new person in it, a married man in his father's house, and surrounded by old friends and acquaintances whose opinions and news had lost resonance. Leopold's patriarchal reception of the no longer newlywed pair was at best grudging, and Constanze failed to hit it off with her sister-in-law too. Mozart's sister Maria Anna must have struck the new woman in the family as an odd, unyielding compound of provincialism and haughtiness, and she never accepted her brother's choice of wife as a suitable one. A hugely talented keyboard player herself who had of course been zoomed past by her slightly younger brother, she was at this point in danger of stiffening into a dowdy spinster priding herself on the technical rectitude with which she taught the instrument; doubtless part of her resented her brother's cutting and running to Vienna. Mozart's father had filled his house with a handful of young live-in pupils who may have struck the composer as rather shrill ways of filling in the hole left by his departure. Stretches of high artistic achievement often come when large accesses of experience combine with an odd sense of distance and coolness, and going back to Salzburg meant just such a fusion. The effect did not kick in straightaway. In 1784 he would have a year of rampant overachievement even by his standards, but the couple's three months in Salzburg were mainly spent in an odd spasm of unproductivity.

The mass was the major work that Mozart worked on during the arc running from his marriage through the following year's winter and to the couple's return to Vienna. Whatever stages of this period it may have variously emerged at, the mass demands to be heard in the context of a vastly shifting emotional world. All inner lives teem with fragments and abandoned bits of selfhood and trajectories that have never been finalized; we should not be surprised when a really comprehensive artist creates something that tells us so, and any inadvertence in doing so may only double the point. The C minor mass combines exuberant stylistic discovery and giddy reaches of expressive power with a certain lurching uncertainty in ways that amount to a portrait in motion of the composer's mind early in his marriage. Experts have drawn conclusions from a letter to Leopold from the very start of 1783 which mentions his marriage, an important vow, the purportedly imminent trip to Salzburg and an unfinished mass setting. One interpretation is that Mozart has made a vow to compose a mass in thanksgiving for his marriage; it could indeed then be the C minor mass that he means, and perhaps he really had already written much of it. But the letter really only shows that these matters were all mingling in the mind of the composer, and we can only be confident that the torso of the mass as we have it emerged sometime in the period from the final months of the previous year through to the months in Salzburg, possibly fitfully. Constanze does seem to have sung at least some of the soprano solos in the one performance that the mass torso seems to have had in Salzburg, the sole outing that the piece appears to have had under Mozart's own auspices.

The timing and the venue of this performance are telling. The monastery church of Saint Peter's was the setting, one at least somewhat removed from the direct remit of the little city-state's controlling bodies. Maybe this was partly a way for its renegade ex-employee to keep a tactful distance from the court; but then the archbishop could presumably have stopped a performance anywhere within his precincts if so minded. But to be mounting a mass setting of all things, and one on such an exorbitant scale and with such an expressively revolutionary agenda, was a way for Mozart to fuse powerful drives of rebellion or disdain towards his home town with some ongoing desire to impress and indeed to engage. Having it performed somewhere removed from the heart of the city would have tallied with the split feelings that the mass conveys, towards Salzburg and plenty of other things. Its soaring technical grandeur suggests deep bonds to authoritative values and commitments; its fragmentariness and revolving styles state a surging openness to the new.

The couple's stay in Salzburg became surprisingly prolonged, and it was not until the very end of October that they finally departed, not many days after the performance. It seems probable that these two events were connected, and that hearing at least some version of the mass performed had become for Mozart an important yet fraught element of being back in Salzburg, something that he wanted to get done but found tricky and time-consuming to achieve. He may have tried to write more movements and failed; he may have patched together a complete setting for the occasion by recycling movements from his earlier church music. The Austrian winter was louring by the time of the performance. Maybe it had become clear that the mass had no straightforward future in Vienna. He may have wanted to make at least some version of a major musical statement before leaving. But maybe again something in the complex attitudes held in the mass towards authority and the past and the church made him keen to regale Salzburg even with a shaky version of the thing, and keen especially to hear it resound there himself. Mozart was stunningly sure of himself but as yet stubbornly uncertain what it meant to be him. The mass combines towering, sometimes even garish splendour with a hectic, patchwork jumpiness in ways that make it the epitome of its composer at this twisting point in his progress. Of course, its veering omnivorousness unites these elements.

The uncertainty about the meaning of religious music that powers the mass must also have helped stop it in its incomplete tracks. The impact of the enlightenment on religious practice was proving stark in Joseph's Vienna. His main idea was to undermine the wealth of the monastic orders and their continued grip on educational matters. The controversies were such that in the spring of 1782 the pope himself descended; the city's powers were tasked with smothering the Holy Father's consternation in pageantry. Joseph's reforms were having consequences on ritual and liturgy which meant that far less church music was required, particularly of the elaborate sort that Mozart valued. His failure to finish the C minor mass may well have been directly linked to these changes; maybe specific plans or possibilities for performing it no longer seemed plausible. Since he broadly sympathized with Joseph's reforming spirit, Mozart may have been especially sensitive to its ramifications for a piece like this one. While enlightenment trends kept butting up against the impressive remains of the Counter-Reformation's cultural offensive, the urge to monumentality in church music may have seemed to many retrograde. But Mozart's desire to do two things at once often only increased if they seemed contradictory. In the C minor mass he writes church music that is both burstingly grand and niftily modern.

If we move back again to the late 1730s and Pergolesi's great, gymnastic and brightly Neapolitan *Stabat Mater*, it is easy to imagine that the century should have been flooded in its wake with church music achieving some such equation. But Pergolesi's piece has become so famous because there is something almost freakish about how successfully it crushes together ecclesiastical rigour with dramatic agility and gleaming melodic pleasantness. During the decades that followed, ecclesiastical music tended to get ever more vaporous, either because it grabbed at melodic levity too keenly, or because refusing it left it unmoored from the period's furthest advances in style. A composer like Florian Gassmann is not bad; he wrote important and skilful church music around the 1760s from his grand position in Vienna and Mozart admired him. Mozart stayed in the imperial capital in 1773 around the time of his death, and many thought that he must be on manoeuvres. In Gassmann, music donned the bright elegance of the middle of the century, without gaining enough agility or melodic verve to compensate for the loss of texture and structure. A few composers resisted bringing progressive, lightening strains into church music, but at the price of giving up expressive vividness. One figure in the Roman Catholic world whose eclectic forcefulness might have recharged the field was the great Bohemian composer Jan Dismas Zelenka, but his startling achievements in the couple of decades up to his death in 1745 were intensely idiosyncratic, and scholarship has shown how jealously his employers in Dresden guarded against circulation of his works.

The vast achievements of Sebastian Bach's cantatas and passions in Leipzig during the first half of the century or of Handel's oratorios in London around its middle decades were far removed from the mainstream of these developments in ways that their renown since blurs. But Mozart's desire for scale and reach in the C minor mass logically raised the question of the larger, rockier styles that had preceded the recent climate of sweetness and suaveness. In fact the mass came as he was looking into the world of high baroque styles with some devotion, encouraged by his older friend Swieten. Its music is filled with the crisply severe impact of the same vistas on the Neapolitan or galant vocal styles that his earlier church music had specialized in. Works by the likes of Bach and Handel came to him more as things to be pored over and studied, rather than through any sort of idiomatic immersion, so his mass has to engage in its own bendy ways with their immense suggestions. Swieten did own a copy of one of the monuments of baroque church music, the Sebastian Bach setting of the mass in B minor, allotted to him by Emanuel Bach in his role as pious curator of his father's legacy. But that work's nearly celestial levels of anomalousness and reach could hardly have given much overall guidance, and Mozart's mass instead rummages around in the baroque at the levels of stylistic variety and local technique. It teems with fragmentary borrowings and glancing allusions; the recapitulatory zest of a fugue or the careful tread of a chorale can be heard merging or jostling with propulsively operatic types of singing melody. Its fervent, jumbled sense of stylistic largesse may be itself the new form of musical drama that the piece proposes. The mass does not launch itself towards the eternal by trying to transcend time and history so much as by throwing versions of them together. It believes in the musical past and so resurrects it, albeit piecemeal.

The proposition behind all church music is that time and eternity are made for each other, can slot together and reveal each other's richest meanings. In writing the mass Mozart listened back to his own personal and musical past with new and acute ardency, as if being back in Salzburg brought a reckoning with time's very passing. The danger that he runs is of composing something whose swooping stylistic variousness will abrade or subvert the definitive meanings and devotion to authority that church music is pledged to. Instead the latter are energized and renewed at every turn by the music's dynamism and unpredictability; we can think of the richly expansive but also technically intricate use of fugue right at the end of the 'Gloria', as vocal and orchestral levels densely and gloriously interact. Art joins itself to the eternal, not by ascending to some sphere of crystalline immobility, but by pressing on ever more eagerly into its own possibilities and its own germination in the continuous present tense of creativity. Mozart's music here can sound as though it is made half of supernal fervour and half of laboratory tinkering, two spheres that end up sounding uncannily matched. He is trying to be both deeply modern in his thinking and a committed man of faith, and all the forceful freshness of eighteenth-century music ends up suggesting that each of these things may require and propel the other. Music makes itself the perfect medium by which the most peppy and updated aspects of late eighteenth-century sensibility can turn back towards and test themselves against the past and traditional faith. It propels, cajoles and pores over the church's formulations without having to turn out distinct verbal statements of its own. Mozart outmanoeuvres anyone in Salzburg who doubted him or his decisions by moving off in two directions simultaneously, throwing the mass open to progress and the future while grasping the church's traditions with more force than their most backward defenders could have mustered. It is hardly surprising that the piece has elements of bravado and brusqueness as well as refinement and structural grandeur.

The aria 'Et incarnatus est' is the endpoint of the work as a continuous setting of the Roman Catholic mass liturgy. Further movements do exist at various levels of completion, but it is here that the pluralism within the music ceases to push it forwards and the mass becomes the fragmentary work that it is. The aria in question breaks away with an almost bewildering swerve of formal freedom from the density and monumentality given to the first sections of his mass by Mozart, and music of such beauty can seldom have proved so controversial and critically divisive. The words describe the doctrine of incarnation in which Christianity tries to bring time and the eternal together. The composer gives them music whose tuneful, pastoral earthliness and tenderness come directly from Neapolitan and even operatic styles of vocal writing, and this has gone down badly over the years with partisans of the German baroque. Their preference would seemingly have been for a version of the mass in which Mozart would have more unequivocally declared his most austere affiliations. But the point of the aria is surely also to be found in the sheer commitment with which Mozart expands the possibilities of this simpler, updated vocal style, without relinquishing its plangent directness. Baroque monumentality still impinges on the aria and feeds it, precisely by inspiring it to give substance and structure to its more tenuous and sparkly melodic freedom. The aria makes of its sweetness something gripping in a way that reverses the silvery levity with which the mass elsewhere recycles its gleanings from the sturdy templates of the baroque.

Mozart makes wildly elaborate use of obbligato wind accompaniments to turn the aria's lyricism into cogency and power. A small but densely scored array of wind instruments sings and echoes and burbles alongside the soprano. Elsewhere the mass paints itself with layers of counterpoint, but here density of texture comes by way of a more mobile and darting interplay of almost soloistic elements, all of them held together by their common element of human breath. At one point the soprano and the winds enter together into a high-wire reverie on a single syllable of the word 'incarnatus' where decoration itself, extended far enough, becomes the food of the largest musical substance. The voice gives expressive resonance to the instruments, and in turn they give it winding structural heft and a kaleidoscopic sonic backdrop. Constanze was very probably the soprano in the monastery in Salzburg that autumn. Mozart is in effect supporting and giving substance to his own young wife's voice, turning it into a new revelation of musical bodiliness itself. His home-town listeners were probably at least dimly aware of what a charge of new identity and of complex reconciliation with the past her singing would have conveyed for the composer. We can imagine her singing before whatever audience of old acquaintances and poker-faced relations and watchful townsmen the occasion had mustered, weaving his life's strands together in her voice.

Returning to Vienna from this return to Salzburg would have brought further layers of reckoning. During their journey, Mozart and his wife made a stopover lasting a month or so in Linz as the autumn of 1783 turned into winter. It became an oddly and tellingly expansive interlude. He was welcomed there by the mighty Thun family whose patronage had already been important to him in Vienna, and the contrast must have been endearing after he and his home town had shown how alienated they had become. Straight-away he took up an offer to present a new symphony at a concert a few days into November at the city's Ballhaus. The piece now known accordingly as his K425 'Linz' symphony shot from him with extreme haste, at least according to what he tells Leopold. Maybe he needed to prove to himself that his mind had moved on from Salzburg. But otherwise it is hard to avoid concluding that a certain spirit of prevarication was taking hold of him. No doubt the prospect of winter roads and darkening days prolonged the sojourn, but throwing his energies back into Viennese life was not something that he seemed eager to begin. Nothing much seems to have detained them in Linz after the initial hyperactivity. Years later Constanze claimed that Mozart one day drew an Ecce Homo for her, and the subject of Jesus facing the populace of Jerusalem during his trial would have fitted any mood of maybe even anguished uncertainty that was descending. Coming back to Vienna just as winter hit may have seemed a more extreme hiatus than moving there had been in the first place, because Mozart now knew that he had nowhere else to go back to. Early 1784 was when time's arrow hit the composer. He was not who he had been any longer, but was suspended like an empty bridge between the now utterly lost past and an as yet insolid future.

During the rest of the 1780s Mozart made no more sustained efforts at church music, and he only really seems to have taken it up again a little way into the following decade when its possible roles within both his own life and the culture shifted. The C minor mass stayed as unrepeated as the trip back to Salzburg. The feelings clustered around its performance there cannot have been easy to consider reviving, whether or not its conception had been closely linked to Salzburg in the first place. Often enough the little city-state will have seemed lifetimes away once Vienna again surrounded the composer. In other moods his links there must still have felt crushingly intimate. He avoided returning again even in the wake of Leopold's death a few years later, leaving his sister to deal with the estate unhindered and unhelped.

If he had gone on with the mass setting, Mozart's next task after this aria of incarnation should have been the account of Jesus's crucifixion that follows in the creed's sequence of avowals. Maybe this image of the eternal as it falls even more deeply into the clutches of time would have pushed the questions raised by the piece too far. The composer did grab and then reupholster much of the music from the C minor mass for a Vienna charity concert in 1785 in aid of impoverished musical families, making a cantata called *Davide penitente* (K469) that applies many of the same settings to passages from the psalms. The job is neatly done and we get a couple of new arias that are pleasant enough, but the thing as a whole is strikingly unnecessary. Its main value may have been to revive in Mozart the questions that the C minor mass had raised, since they are then reanimated so fully in the one great and anomalous piece of religious music that the middle of the decade drew from him, the K477 funeral music performed later in the same year at the ritual for two of his fellow Viennese Freemasons. The deceased do not seem to have been at all important to him, and this music is outlandishly general in the fervency of its reach.

Since Freemasonry was highly controversial then as well as pledged to secrecy, the details of Mozart's involvement are elusive. He signed up sometime in 1784 and never ceased to be committed to the movement, as he remained to the Catholic creed too. He would have regularly gone to meetings, and Viennese Freemasonry at the time was suited to being used as a hub for intellectual and progressive fraternization; rituals and esoteric doctrines may not have got much emphasis. But the middle of the 1780s was probably the high point of any optimism within his circles that fusing the two forms of thought and ritual might drive some sweeping cultural renewal. Masonic culture can seem in retrospect to have been a sort of gaudy displacement of the spiritual projects that institutions like the monasteries could no longer sustain, but it had a deep and ingenious appeal for a tentative Viennese intelligentsia in need of new spiritual and institutional bearings. Being a Freemason could never have exactly solved the problem of the eternal for Mozart; it may have helped to keep it stirringly alive as a problem. The flow of inspiration from the mass to the funeral music shows how the composer's mercurial side could feed his unfussy sense of generality.

The two works share the key of C minor, and the raspingly sumptuous plangency with which the later work gets going migrates directly from the start of the mass too. The funeral music is another piece whose concern with the mysteries of life and meaning finds a corollary in the mystery of its own origin. Nothing that has been established in Mozart's relationship to these two departed colleagues can be driving its grand surges of pathos; the reckoning with crucifixion absent from the C minor mass seems to surface here instead. If it was not in fact originally meant for their November funeral, its qualities of dirge and lament and its processional rhythms cry out for some such occasion. But what is crucial is the sheer grinding impetus of its techniques, kneading together the stately tread of an underlying chorale form with the more animated feel of the measures of a funeral march. In one way the striding expansiveness that results carries some of the ardour of enlightenment optimism in its Masonic guise. But the piece also pushes so hard into its confrontation with final questions that it ends up seeming to leave Freemasonry behind; maybe Mozart knew that the movement would end up having been more of a spur to him than a total answer. In this sense the funeral music clears the ground for the delicately exuberant riffing on Masonic doctrines and images in *Die Zauberflöte* half a decade or so later. Mozart's last great comic opera treats matters of belief and ritual with a freedom that is exquisite, nearly cruel, utterly bizarre. Its whirling chiaroscuro of homage and pastiche is unlike anything in the mass or the funeral music, but could not have been reached if they had not come first. The 1785 funeral piece drives itself vehemently on as a protest against oblivion that somehow ends up going nowhere. Within the heady antiphonal writing that moves between string and wind groupings there is a yearning for ritual that is unsure whether it can claim ritual meaning itself.

An unfinished mass setting was in effect the gesture with which Mozart finally left Salzburg behind. The C minor mass was among the most ambitious works that he ever attempted, a sort of total statement on everything that music could be, at this point in the 1780s at least. It was a total statement that he could not complete, any more than he ever found completely satisfactory ways of being both Leopold's son and Constanze's husband, or a church-going believer and an enlightenment freethinker. The mass is by turns poignant and stern, twinkly and sweeping, serenely sensuous and tightly argued. Not long afterwards, the Masonic music shows him still yearning for some solidly ritualistic vision of sacred music that he can also be moved by, but the restlessness has become hard-boiled and gnomic. Maybe he failed to pursue the mass once its momentum had lapsed because he found that its energies could pour into secular music. The lengthening melodies and the cascades of harmonic argument throughout his later works can seem to carry a dispossessed feeling for the eternal.

12

Blowing and Scraping and Hitting Are Fairly Simple Actions

Quintet in E flat

Minneapolis in the early 1980s may not seem a place for parallels to classical music. Brash highways, frantic bars and the coming of cable television and of Reaganite economics do not fit with some ideas of eighteenth-century Vienna. But then the point is how flimsy such ideas can be; Mozart's city was raucously full of controversy and mutation. So too the songs of the pop star Prince can turn out to be both wildly and finely open to the variousness of their historical world in ways that teemingly parallel Mozart's achievement. The breakthrough hit that signalled Prince's ascent was the song 'Little Red Corvette'; it was here that he finally left behind his origin as a controversial cult performer on the black music circuit and moved on to a vaster version of stardom. He also showed with this song how sweepingly he would remain open to the tightly packed musical worlds that he had come out of. The song faces in two directions across history in some of the ways that we have seen in Mozart, and gives its own account of how music can announce and cope with and play with motion and change. In 'Little Red Corvette' Prince wants both to inherit all the fierce energies of the funk and soul and blues traditions and to twist them into new shapes of his own; he ends up giving us an almost garishly intense meditation on cultural freedom.

The song does this by way of a smart, stark inversion of the normal stories of seduction or conquest that flood pop music. It tells the story of a standard nightlife pickup that does not so much go wrong as go so wildly right that it ends up derailing the basic drives behind such tales. A man who sounds used to playing fast and loose finds a woman who plays faster and looser than he knows how, and he is duly sent spinning. The male seducer is seduced and outdone and upended, and this turns the song into a contradiction in motion, an epitome of cool and prowess whose cool has been scorched and whose prowess is turned inside out. Prince's own dazzlingly ambiguous artistic identity is in play throughout; his music endlessly probed the ores of fluidity and reversal and pastiche that he could find within the forms of which he was such a forceful master. As a performer he switched between the most extreme absorption in his art and a lovely pleasure in pleasing others with a livewire suddenness that both disarmed and daunted. He could move between the slightest charm and the densest rapture, or between the most vulgar goofiness or obscenity and the sheerest technical prowess, in just a breath or two. Watching footage of him on stage may be a good starting point for trying to guess what Mozart was like as a performer. In this song the forces of music and eroticism that make up the mythology of the modern urban night are no longer mere playthings at the disposal of male pleasure, but energies that might sweep it aside or denude it. Of course this also makes them opportunities for psychic growth and artistic renewal.

The singer starts by saying that he should have known even from the way that she parked her car that she was trouble; he describes the room that she takes him to as full of trophies from previous conquests. He starts to wonder if he has enough class for her, a troubling notion within the lines of identity that such a song draws on, as much of a reversal as any of Prince's sliding games with gender and passivity and vocal identity elsewhere. All the great values of sensuousness and potency that flow through pop music are present, but the song strikes into their reservoirs of vulnerability and transience. Excitement fuses with mourning in the singer's voice as he remembers this night. He keeps on rhyming the words 'fast' and 'last' all but obsessively from the song's opening lines, endlessly trying to get a handle on the speed of this woman's lifestyle and to warn her of the need to find a love or a life capable of enduring; he sounds desperate to prove that at least this rhyme is capable of lasting. He sings that she will have to slow down but the warning carries a raw envy shaded with awe.

The richly original wash of sonorities with which the song colours the sound-world of early 1980s dance music imbues that world's pulsations with a melancholy that somehow also holds it steady. We know now that black American music was in the throes of a metamorphosis as Prince emerged, the process that would feed rap and hip hop, and all their clamorous reinventions of voice and its rhythms. Any number of new directions are already held in something like gleaming suspension by the large, echoey sound design, and the blurry expansions of syncopation in the relationship between the synthesizer and the drums. Prince's voice is overdubbed with versions of itself in ways that produce a sort of polyphonic layering of different attitudes towards the song's story. A glitchy, fraught expansiveness results that is the track's way of mirroring a state of obsessed rumination in sound. It is also one way in which all the song's energies turn into a meditation on musical art itself, on music's power and sensuousness and transience, its dense speed and heady regrets. In the expansive live version that he performed in his later years, Prince intoned the words 'slow down' more to himself than to anyone listening. He sang them over and over again as layers of music replicated themselves.

A lot of complex engineering went into the sweeping sonic textures in Prince songs of this period. Central to this was the sheer variety of instruments that he played on them himself, but this is also one reason why the resulting extravaganzas of sound kept a vital unity of feel and purpose. The sense of openness and high-stakes volatility that runs through Mozart has parallels in the fusions and transpositions by which Prince braided together often violently opposed forces like rock and disco. In this song only a solo guitar and some very restricted backing vocals are credited to two other performers. But this also makes 'Little Red Corvette' something like a disquisition on Prince's own bodily and cognitive multiplicity, and so on the sorts of magical surplus that some versions of artistic identity can set out. The song's big hope is that play and steadiness can turn into the same thing; it wants to be capable of both going fast and lasting. It is neither fast nor slow itself, not really a soul ballad but not a funky dance number either. It hovers and grows in between.

Musical instruments are ways of giving bodies new versions of themselves, and each one opens the people who play or listen to it to the physical and historical worlds that the instrument comes out of. Blowing into a wind instrument and scraping the strings of a violin with a bow and hitting the skin of a drum are fairly simple actions. But the wild complexity that music is capable of comes from the fact that these actions are the joining points between bodies and worlds, between all the psychic lives that bodies and worlds are filled by. A musical instrument waits patiently to be picked up or struck, but then brings new accesses of freedom and self-knowledge to the flesh that touches it. The revelry and the sadness in 'Little Red Corvette' show us Prince both coping with and exulting in the dazzling extensions of selfhood that music brings. The historically informed performance movement has added much to our under-standing of Mozart since it started redefining how to play music like his in the later decades of the twentieth century, and one of the biggest gains has been how keenly the sheer pleasures and the sometimes frenzied complexities of sound production have come into focus. Mozart loved the sensuous intensity that instruments contain and release, the types of wit that they enable or sometimes require, the ways in which playing one can variously feel like an obstacle course and a labyrinth and flight. His writing for solo horn is driven by his fascinated love of the fact that an instrument whose function within an ensemble is to smooth and to fill out the overall sonority suddenly becomes full of blurts, twitches and curdling when used on its own. Likewise, his clarinet writing can never get over how rapidly the little wooden tube can shift between the most svelte cantabile sound and the most blippy wit. Numbers of outlets for talent and insight and charm kept being all but zanily opened up for both Mozart and Prince by music; in both the imperi-ousness was accompanied by stunning levels of need and a vital strand of clowning.

Early in 1784 in Vienna Mozart started keeping an agglomerative catalogue of his own, around three years before he composed Leporello's aria about the frantic list of Giovanni's conquests. Mozart's list documents his own music as he composes new pieces, and he began it just a couple of months after getting back from his final visit to Salzburg. He chose a fairly small notebook of fairly high quality; it is partly bound in leather and its covers are decorated with some pleasantly modest floral motifs. Pasted on to its front is a sliver of paper stating its purpose, in the same grandly scatty handwriting that Mozart used within. He lists each composition along with the date of its completion, and the odd detail of the piece's scoring or occasion. The right side of each spread of pages is ruled with staves, so that he could write out the opening bars of each piece opposite its entry. Silent flashes of music thus cascade through the notebook. Excellent electronic reproductions are provided by the notebook's current holder, the British Library, and of course there are facsimile editions. The thing itself lives behind the carefully lit glass with which such institutions encase certain treasures, a fate that has its own pathos. The thoughtful decision to keep this little catalogue of himself must have been linked to the distance from the past that was made palpable by the visit to Salzburg. No doubt he wanted to rely less on his father's help in keeping track of his works.

Mozart was gathering intensities of purpose and self-fashioning as the early months of the year brought flurrying engagements to perform at the houses of people called things like the Prince of Kaunitz-Rietberg and Count Pálffy-Daun von Erdöd. Towards the end of March he sent another list off to his father, one naming the many dozens of subscribers who had signed up for a series of concerts organized by him in a private hall over three of that month's Wednesdays. A keyboard concerto furnishes the first entry in what became the packed little catalogue of his works, and this beginning could not have been more apt, because it was the vital form in which his most expansive sense of personal artistic identity could come together and declare itself. The keyboard was his chief instrument, but the concerto meant joining it up with larger and sometimes very large ensembles, and projecting its possibilities into large performance spaces. In fact he may have begun the K449 concerto in E flat more than a year before finishing it and making it this first entry, and it seems to have been inspired as much by the playing of a highly talented pupil called Babette Ployer as by his own. Mozart needed a form that could ever more richly tell the Viennese who he musically was, and endlessly extending his artistry meant keeping it endlessly open to others too as fellow musicians and as listeners. He needed to wow audiences, and the concerto was a form calling out to map how large he had become.

Since the keyboard was soaked in his personal past and professional history, the concerto form brought songs of himself directly together with the drive to expand his work and reach, and with the desire for new and complex contexts. Motifs and rhythms and harmonic ideas move backwards and forwards in a concerto like this between the soloist and the orchestra, and likewise among the orchestral parts, until every sound is testing and enjoying every other sound. The electrically fresh interactions that result cut across oppositions of self and other. Mozart's great discovery is that a musical idea becomes what it is by being moved around and changed; it finds its meaning and its real unity by means of reinterpretation and renewal. By such commerce chaos is undone, or rather transmuted. Vital to the feel of his music in the middle of the 1780s is his incalculable knack for phrases that create a sense of balance out of the ways in which they keep pointing forwards and moving on. One result is that his rapid productiveness becomes no mere incidental feature, but part of the inner momentum of his music. Further change can always be on its way, and then it always needs stabilizing again too. The three keyboard concertos that he wrote in quick succession after finishing the E-flat concerto call for larger orchestras than their precursor envisaged. Mozart's version of classical style is one in which order protects no one from metamorphosis and transience, but creates itself out of their insatiability.

As the Viennese winter turned to that year's spring, Mozart wrote a piece that must have struck him as not just one more example of his music, but as something like music itself. The K452 quintet in E flat for piano and winds gains much of its vitality from the ways in which it learns from and then plays with the styles that his keyboard concertos had developed. It is soaked in their discoveries and possibilities, while also seeking its own oblique, gyrating version of their visions of dialogue and dramatic drive. Mozart himself was at the keyboard on the extravagant occasion of the piece's first performance right at the start of April. The small ensemble called for by the quintet gets it categorized among his chamber music, but the circumstances of its debut could hardly have been more public and imposing. The concert took place towards the end of a run of weeks that had made up a more glittering and congested period of popularity than Vienna ever again brought him. He would play at the salon of the Russian ambassador Prince Gallitzin on Thursday evenings, in his palace covered with works of art, to which he seems to have been ceremoniously fetched in one of the prince's many carriages. By the start of April he must have been packed tight as a bullet with confidence, and sharp with nervous energy. But this was an especially charged evening, because its setting of the Burgtheater was the glitzy heart of Vienna's most exalted versions of culture, a space tricked out with the trappings of court life and gilt decorations and aristocratic boxes. Its capacity may have been well above a thousand, so the audience could have been far larger than in the more informal surroundings of the Trattnerhof where Mozart held his subscription concerts.

He designed the occasion as a lavish anthology of his talents; he was not inclined to withhold things from his public. It featured show-off arias for celebrated singers and keyboard improvisation by Mozart alone, as well as the first Viennese airing of his most recent symphony, a piece crowded with crowd-pleasing effects. The glamorous and much-desired singers who spent their lives benefiting from Mozart's gifts could throw the spotlight back onto him, in the shiniest context possible. Nothing was too much on this occasion, and the first performance of the quintet accompanied the premiere of a new keyboard concerto, in a juxtaposition that would have clarified what the stakes were in the quintet's highly distinctive rethinking of the most basic machinery of a musical ensemble. Mozart was so convulsively productive around this time that we cannot be sure which concerto this new one was.

The quintet was a stunningly odd as well as dazzlingly impressive addition to the evening. It has a sort of inbuilt implausibility that is partly Mozart's way of further wowing his audience, and partly a way of holding it at a slightly waggish distance. The piece combines basic elements from the two forms that Mozart had just been concentrating on, the piano concerto and the string quartet. Aspects of the concerto's dramatic interplay between soloist and ensemble mix with the tight interweaving of equal voices that the quartet was bringing. But the quintet does this while lacking the one thing that the two forms share; it excises the basic musical element formed by a section or group of string instruments. The resulting ensemble seems to have been more or less unprecedented, mixing the oboe and the bassoon and the clarinet from the woodwind family with the horn and then the keyboard. The wind groups that had been booming in Vienna typically used two of each instrument, but here no such doubling fills out the sound, and the resulting sense of soloistic exposure in each part is then heightened by the even more innovative stroke of combining them with the keyboard. The piece is always sinuously charming, but it is pointed too as it turns to the Habsburg grandees who had suddenly taken a voguish interest in wind music, and tells them that any real reckoning with its possibilities must face this piece's hyperkinetic nimbleness. Mozart takes the knowledge that he had sucked from the world of the Viennese wind band during the early 1780s and richly repurposes it, as he had in the great soprano aria in the C minor mass in a richly different way.

Lacking the basic musical glue normally afforded by the strings, the quintet has an inbuilt sense of excitement and vulnerability. The fortepiano ends up with nowhere to hide within the jumpy but finely grained sound-world that results, and none of its normal roles define it, whether as an accompanimental instrument or in a continuo role or in the concerto role of the solitary soloist. Feats of virtuosic display cannot swoop down to rescue this music from its own need for originality, since anything that the keyboard does must in principle be capable of being matched on the mouthpieces of the horn and the bassoon. Because its combinations of sound are so unpredictable as it pieces itself together out of the isolated voices of these instruments, its sonorities have a sort of openness or rawness that is dazzlingly impressive, and inherently touching. A touch of the high-wire pervades the sound-world, as if some basic elements of gravity or traction had been removed or bracketed; its harmonic equilibrium is so full of disparate factors and pulls that moving forwards becomes the only way of staying steady. A weird combination of liberation and constraint prevails, as it does for a tightrope walker; basic facts are being exposed about how a world holds together or supports anything at all.

Maybe the quintet was a deliberate adjunct to what seems to have been Mozart's project of developing more elaborate wind writing in his later concertos. Another result of the piece's laboratory is a new starkness in the double aspect of the keyboard's sound. Its percussive side and its link with the strings family are both thrown into new emphasis by the fluctuations of these wind sounds around it. One of the vital topics of research during the composer's lifetime, in the versions of actual laboratories that the eighteenth century developed, was the composition of air. Early scientists were prodding and scanning and harrying air to find out how unitary it was or how combustion worked just as the sounds of the five instruments here prod and scan and harry one another. Joseph Priestley's isolation of oxygen became a keynote event of the second half of the century; the craze for hot air ballooning that did not spare Vienna is worth noting too. The wind instruments that dominate the quintet's ensemble only make it more apparent that all musical instruments are ways of doing complex things to air. The work's relative homogeneity of pacing across the three movements and its eschewal of elaborate melodies help it double down on sonority itself, on the sheer strangeness of its own existence in and as air.

Why would the composer choose an event like this Burgtheater concert, under the gleaming scrutiny of Viennese cultural life at its grandest, to unfurl such anomalous music? The expansive canvas of such an occasion becomes something like the quintet's premise, the raw material that it works with and toys with and recodes. Partly, his own anomalousness was precisely what Mozart had to sell and to use. A certain freakishness was vital to his artistic armoury just as it would be to Prince's, and in both cases it was part of what gave their levels of commitment to ordinary pleasures such piquancy too. But the qualities of risk and exposure in the quintet are too intense for this to be the whole story. Mozart wants to advertise and to analyse his own singularity with a starkness capable of revealing the underlying pulsations of his art, and of asking those listening how deeply their lives share in such processes. The sound-world brought by the wind instruments is one that listeners would have known from the groups that blew nicely on in the background of innumerable polished Viennese evenings. But here that world of suavely relaxed recreation is both pared down and opened up; it must have been for many in the audience like suddenly seeing aspects of their lives spotlit on stage with rich but unsettling precision. We can be reminded of the intricate expansiveness wrought by Prince on the musical world that thronged around his audiences in innumerable bars and clubs. His song is both a dazzlingly superficial entertainment and an all but appallingly intimate exploration of artistry and self-hood. As Mozart's quintet revealed itself in the Burgtheater that night, the audience came into contact with something uncannily both public and private. Maybe such a space is what all great music creates. Mozart's life was given over to display, but there was something manically clandestine about the intensity of the gifts that pulled people towards him.

The quintet becomes an anthology of types of echo and so of types of inwardness, as some little melodic sequence or other offered by the piano is broken up and rejigged according to the characters and moods of the wind instruments. The different ways in which say the bassoon and the horn echo the keyboard mean that they echo each other in ramifying ways too, and so on through the group, and the overall harmonic argument has to stay very light so as to keep this more cellular style of interaction from becoming clotted. It is among Mozart's most original works, but it is made from very conventional phrasal building blocks; the pieces that it most resembles in its basic thematic material are his divertimentos and serenades. But this is all part of the quintet's unique atmosphere, in which tenderness and vertigo join hands. The audience at this concert would have been expecting novelty. But how can novelty be something that people expect? Mozart faces them here with something more like novelty squared, a piece that changes even the ways in which pieces are meant to innovate. If there is something flashy and bravura about its very unclassifiability, the piece is also marked by an overall sense of structure and restraint. We can imagine him projecting himself forwards as he writes this music into the vast theatre where it would be performed, and knowing that what he wants is a music that would be both audacious and rigorous. The essence of his style in the middle of the decade was how intensely it fused a dense commitment to his culture's bricks and glue with the most hectic originality. The quintet gives this intensity the clarity of a diagram.

In a letter to Leopold from a month earlier, Mozart lists twenty-two engagements that he has agreed to for the stretch from the last days of February to early April. Along with exclamation marks and grand names, his letters to his father from the period teem with protestations of hurry as he keeps being kept from writing to him. The headiness of his life at this point can be all but directly heard in the keyboard concertos, say in the braiding of soloistic delight into structural heft in the finale of the E-flat concerto, and they are there in the quintet too. He wanted to dazzle and he loved dazzling, and he knew how to do it, endlessly. But here it is as if Mozart turns inside out the presuppositions of kinesis and dazzlement that normally bind together an audience and the most ambitious virtuosic talent. Instead of pushing further and further ahead, the quintet pulls the audience down into the commotion and pathos of the basic constructive urges within Mozart's music. Instead of cutting through an orchestra or blazing ahead of it, he can be heard here negotiating point by point the interactions and the textures that bind his instrument to these others. Of course, turning his own adventurousness inside out like this does not mean abandoning it; instead we hear an uncanny doubling of adventure and flair. But the piece is also a new vision of what they comprise. It is for no known musical group, after all, and its keyboard writing is at once too rigorous for most players and lacking in the sorts of technical elaborateness that would allow Mozart's fellow virtuosos to do their things. It could exist nowhere but in some experimental overlay of possibilities that Mozart dreamt up for the occasion. In a letter written several days later to his father, he reports that the quintet was beautifully played and extraordinarily well received, and calls it the best piece that he has yet composed.

The quintet is a sort of self-portrait that pulls in many directions, one that shows Mozart's version of artistry precisely as it weaves in and out of groups of others, in and out of the facts of his world. In no other piece does he so delicately sketch the indeterminacy that the keyboard had for him, its flexibility of colour and rhythm and touch, the ways in which it can hover between soloistic and ensemble roles. Sometimes the keyboard dictates terms to the surrounding instruments, and then it listens to and learns from them instead. Flexibility must have been something that the composer both aspired to and felt condemned to daily. He was at a moment in his artistic development and his public career alike when he was realizing that all his breakthroughs to new achievements or acclaim would at best open up further options, new vistas for further works and metamorphoses. In some ways this opening onto endless further tasks is the final glory at the heights of artistic achievement; in others it brings their deepest pathos. The stage on which Mozart gave this irrepressible concert was the one where he had scored such a glamorous success two years before with *Die Entführung aus dem Serail*. While the concert must have been awash with memories of that triumph, in the meantime the plans for German opera that had generated it had collapsed. His letters from the period are crammed with success but also with restlessness, and with the closeness of success to vulnerability and failure. The ebullience of the Viennese music scene made a concert like this possible, but also meant that his audiences and indeed collaborators were liable to be lured elsewhere. He tells his father that the quintet was extraordinarily well received, but he never tried to repeat his feat of composing it.

Mozart is singing to himself in this music, reminding himself not to go too fast even while he is cutting loose into ever headier artistic terrains, telling himself to create forms that will endure even while he unsettles rules of sonority and structure. The quintet's three movements keep to an even pace in a concession to the music's demands and originality; the piece hovers like Prince's song somewhere in between speed and slowness, and one reason why it tells itself to slow down must be that otherwise its audacity simply could not proceed. But without these qualities of evenness and deceleration, the piece's endless originality would not become as pushily, richly clear. Our ears are pulled in to focus on the minutiae of sonority that the keyboard elicits from its comrades, and the points of transition between phrases become stark enough for us to keep being relieved by the slickness with which they are then negotiated. If Prince pushes so far into the hedonism of pop that he ends up discovering a paradoxical pathos laced with cautionary regrets, Mozart turns his own capacity to please an audience inside out here too, and reveals its essence in acts of sheer compositional precision and indeed in the bare bones of pitch manipulation.

The quintet's fate over the following years was singular. Nobody seems to have known what to make of it, but numerous parties seem to have wanted to turn it into something, often something distinctly different from what Mozart had written. Pirate editions and unauthorized versions for other groups of instruments spread, and Mozart's widow seems to have cobbled together what was almost a pirated version of its ending when trying to publish an authoritative edition some years later, after the manuscript of the final bars went missing. Mozart's world at once wanted this work and did not know how to receive it, and this disparity can seem all too suggestive of his ambiguous position in Vienna. He was an undoubted star who was also an often starkly confusing anomaly within the structures available to him. We may think of the paradoxes built into the form of stardom pioneered by someone like Prince two hundred or so years later, whereby reaching some celestial apex of success always meant also meeting bewilderment and scorn. The quintet unmistakably states its offers of excellence and pleasure, but it also whips away around every corner to get to its own mercurial space, out of reach.

Towards the end of its finale, the piece breaks open into a deeply rethought, splendidly loose but also splendidly careful equivalent of the cadenzas that Mozart's concertos typically feature in their outer movements. A normal concerto cadenza sends the soloist alone back into aspects of the preceding music to reconfigure phrases and ideas, whereas here all five instruments partake. But this means that what is perhaps the quintet's freest section in stylistic terms also has to be in some ways all the more tightly organized, as the flashy or flighty phrasing typical of cadenzas has to be adapted for the combined idioms of this instrumental array. If the melodic flair of the clarinet must have its say, the horn's richly tense mellowness needs to have its moments too; all the instruments must keep in touch and interpret one another's possibilities. Likewise, the brilliant digital manoeuvrability of the keyboard has to feel floatingly present without overwhelming the less nimble technical options of the other voices. Sounds and textures fluctuate here if anything even more wildly than before, but they also interlock with an intense steadiness.

At the end of May, as the coming summer encouraged this stretch of hyperactivity to wind down at least somewhat, Mozart treated himself to the purchase of a pet starling. He was a true animal lover; during the 1770s his family in Salzburg had done what plenty of complex families do in using a beloved dog to help them love one another. But birds were especially important to him, and this one somehow seems very quickly to have learnt to whistle a tune from the finale of one of that year's array of keyboard concertos. Maybe the composer tried teaching it to do so as a test before he parted with any money. His delight in its copying or echoing his music may have been a sign of how overspilling with musical energy he was during these months. It may also have come from how desperately eager he could be to have his music met, taken up, answered. Hearing it come back to him from a starling may have made him feel that his music had a place in the world, but one with a twist of jokiness built in.

13

Using Jokes

Ein musikalischer Spaß

Mozart has pulled many bit-players from his life into the historical record, but the process has not always been smooth. Of the three things that people tend to repeat about Joseph Leutgeb, one seems to be largely untrue. As well as being the horn virtuoso for whom Mozart wrote his most famous music for the instrument, and the butt of endless jokes from the composer, he is routinely described as having been a cheesemonger. The horn player was an old friend of the Mozart family from his own days as a working musician in Salzburg, and Leopold lent him money when he left the city in the 1770s to pursue more ambitious horizons in Vienna. He came from a family with links in the grocery business, and when he wanted to reassure his steely colleague and creditor back in Salzburg that his financial prospects were sound, he referred a little blurrily and perhaps only once to a plan to set up in the cheesemonger trade himself. No evidence exists that he ever did, but the combination of horn virtuoso and cheesemonger has continued to prove irresistible to scholars and programme note scribes. But there is no need to add colour to the story of Leutgeb's friendship with the composer. Mozart admired him as a musician and adored him as a man, and the exuberant reach of the virtuoso music that he wrote for him corresponds to and links itself to the lovingly silly jokes that their friendship evidently thrived on.

Leutgeb was probably not a particularly educated or cultivated man, and this may have been part of Mozart's ongoing merriment at his friend's buffoonish traits. In any case he must have exaggerated or played on such absences himself. The variously hectic and sly cleverness of the music that Mozart wrote for him suggests that he was easily smart enough to be in on all sorts of jokes at his own expense. But the bigger point is that a virtuoso horn player, at this juncture in the history of music and that of the instrument, was an inherently funny thing to be. It meant being a contradiction in motion, someone pledged to mastering especially stubborn difficulties without ever reaching the sleek showmanship that is meant to be the virtuoso's payoff. The horn had not yet started to use valves to give more control to the flow of air through its tubes, so its range of notes was very limited, and even these were hard to play with any great expressiveness or technical panache. The instrument was largely limited to providing orchestral colour or to filling out the harmonies of wind groups with chugging or blaring or blurting accompanimental lines. Whenever it was deployed as a solo instrument, its technical restrictions generally hemmed it in, and its associations with areas of life like the army or hunting tended to dominate.

Leutgeb was a sufficiently brilliant talent to have wowed connoisseurs in Milan when he happened to be there at one point in the early 1770s at the same time as Mozart and his father. He seems to have been a pioneer in two ways of extending the horn's power. First, his lips were capable of extreme feats of agility and stamina. By itself this would only have meant that he could play with unusual gusto and beauty the few pitches that the horn naturally produces. Perhaps even more important were the ways in which a player's own hand could act as a stopper in the instrument's mouth, allowing a range of notes in between the basic pitches to come into play too. The shaping of sound waves by human flesh can be taken as the basis of all music. But a loopy literalness starts to emerge when the horn is played in this way, as the hand blocks or squeezes or moulds or suddenly releases the sounds. The more virtuosic a horn player became, the more he was a reminder of the sheer haphazard physicality within any musical act, at a time when music was trying to be ever more elaborately nimble and dazzling.

Mozart's joking with Leutgeb has survived in the scribbles of scurrilous insults and mock encouragements that he added to some of his scores for the player. Leutgeb is called an ass and an ox and a

buffoon, and is coaxed or cajoled with teasing little calls of bravo
and so on through the more difficult passages. It is seldom funny
to throw such insults at someone unless they are largely untrue.
Mozart must really have had strenuous faith in his friend, and the
horns available to Leutgeb really did make these passages excru-
ciatingly hard to play correctly, let alone beautifully and expressively
and so on. The jokes become funnier if we imagine the collaborative
relationship that all this banter was part of, the dialogue between
friends trying to work out what this instrument was now capable of
and what was still beyond it, in an atmosphere of mutual reliance as
well as merry creative excitement. Failure is a big part of creativity,
after all. The composer would have wanted the music to be capable
of certain sorts of effects, and Leutgeb would have tried to comply,
and then had to explain that only some of them were feasible.
Mozart called him an ass and an ox and so on, but Leutgeb's
resourcefulness and deep musical intelligence were inspiring some of
the composer's most deeply, robustly pleasant masterworks.

The horn concertos were written over much the same spread
of time over the middle of the 1780s as Mozart's major sequence of
piano concertos, and they amount to a structurally reductive but
burstingly colourful commentary on aspects of that larger achievement. Mozart's discoveries in the finely expansive keyboard genre
could be tested in the pieces for horn to see what would survive
in their pungently and poignantly contracted arena. One difference
is that they are far shorter. Not even Leutgeb's lips could mimic a
keyboard's versatility for long stretches. But the humour and
sympathy of the relationship between the two men can be vividly
heard, and this underlying emotional richness helps them to bring
together their disparate expressive drives of peppy wit and breathy
lyrical suaveness.

Joking is often a way of having two attitudes at once about
something. The funny thing about working with Leutgeb would
have been that he was a brilliantly serious musician who would
nevertheless get a lot of notes wrong and prove incapable of certain
sorts of passages. Mozart was writing music that relied on his friend's
talent for its qualities of exploration and invention to be realized,

and then he teased him for the strain, clumsiness and glitches that no performance of these pieces on the instruments of the day would be likely to avoid. His jokey graffiti was meant to spur Leutgeb on rather than to trip him up, and the orchestral writing has a succinctness calculated to let the horn navigate the music's contours after all. The pieces end up meditating with burly vibrancy on a long-standing friendship full of odd, glitchy bonds. The horn writing is designed to let an audience take pleasure in the successes of the soloist if he can get through it with flair and poise, or in his travails as he tries to do so, or even in whatever sonic perplexities his fallibility might bring. By drawing rather merrily on hunting music for much of the material for the finale movements of the concertos, Mozart gives Leutgeb a set of tuneful, snappy payoffs neatly suited to his instrument's limitations and strengths. Leutgeb evidently had a character that could pull all this off with charm and vim.

Bursting evidence shows that for Mozart joking was not just a pastime or a way of letting off steam, but the passport by which he moved through his world. Beyond the outright jokes with which they are studded, a general climate of humour sweeps through many of his letters, splashing passages of news or observation with its atmosphere of tomfoolery or teasing or wit. Mozart's sheer nervous and cognitive energy seems to have needed this flickering outlet. He was someone for whom making sense of the world involved making nonsense out of its parts. One letter may feature a torrent of goofy nicknames, another a parodically sententious little poem on the subject of marital mores, and another a sparklingly verbose apology for being verbose. Mainly tender but sometimes barbed bursts of observational satire take on some of the figures passing through his professional or social whirl, and there are screwball whimsies aimed at this or that big title or pretension of etiquette, as well as renowned fits of scatological farcing.

Surrounding Mozart was a world whose social terms were becoming unconvincing and insolid, and it can be hard for anyone faced with such processes to know whether to be excited or distraught. It is partly because the horn's sounds carry illustrational memories of military ritual or the expansively aristocratic world of hunting that changes and frayings in the civilizational surroundings can enter into the concertos for the instrument. Within them the horn cannot escape from its grand associations but it cannot take them all wholly seriously either, any more than Vienna could then have pinned down exactly how far it was still meant to be defined by allegiances to the army or to the aristocracy's galumphing pastimes. The horn also had a lowly and rustic side that Mozart's writing for it plugs into in ways that are waggishly cultivated but also vividly energized. So the jokiness of these pieces may have been partly a way of testing how seriously their listeners took the values that their society was meant to be based on, and partly a way of coping with the possibility that they did not do so very seriously at all. Joking in a changing world can become addictive and voracious; the comedic elements of Mozart's music may have sometimes helped it to function as a defence against humour, one that could only contain it because it cultivated it. Using jokes could let him work out what he felt or thought about something, or play for time if he was not sure or could not say. His joking may show how close he sometimes was to cruelty, but also how he then rescued himself from it. In his music bursts of formal wit likewise tame some of the extremes of elegance or structural tension.

Mozart's famed scatology seeps into all sorts of discussions of him, and this is fair enough. He really did find turds and farts and bums and all things lavatorial and defecatory to be sources of endless, amazed amusement, but this may not be as surprising as people have often seemed to think. He found plenty of other things fairly hilarious too, and the main difference with the toilet humour may have been that plenty of people around him joined him in it. The right response is to wonder how his relish for scatology was allied with his creative power. It suggests, after all, a willingness to let the mind roam and extrapolate freely. His passion for such things was shared with his family circle, and even his letters to the often fearsome and pompous Leopold can throng with obscenities and merry references to muck and shitting. The famous letters that he wrote late in the 1770s to his spirited cousin Maria Anna Thekla in Augsburg are where the subject runs away with him, by way of a drive of outrageous fantasy that may aim low, but that parallels his music's feel for exquisite proliferation. She was the daughter of Leopold's brother Franz Alois Mozart, who ran a printing press in Augsburg, and she was very close to the composer's age. The two cousins became close during Mozart's stay in what was his father's home town during the autumn of 1777 as he tested the place for professional openings. His letters to her from around this time surge with faecal reveries and images, so that arses are variously kicked and licked, and muck is both sucked and chucked. We hear about one place 'where the shit runs into the sea', and another 'where they make the crooked arseholes', and about Mozart's amazement that he has been shitting 'out of the same old hole' for his whole life without tearing it. The composer finds a way here of both exercising the muscles of his talent and seeking refuge from its grand demands.

A talent like Mozart's must for one thing generate stores of irreverence and mischief, perhaps even of potentially destructive contempt. In scatology he could be both outrageously free and vividly pleasing, a transgressor who stays loveable. The heights of artistic form never really escape the earth's embarrassments and fractures; the real passion of art is for experiential wholeness. A joke is a sign of spare psychic capacity or of attitudes and insights that have not yet fully emerged. It suggests someone wanting to reconcile contrary desires, or to keep doing two or more things simultaneously, or to keep multiple ideas and attitudes in the air. By turning up as he once did in 1777 unannounced at the workshop of a renowned keyboard manufacturer, and only gradually letting him be sure that it was the famous virtuoso who wanted to test his wares, Mozart doubles his own identity in a way that mirrors all the disguises and betrayals in his operas. He tried insisting that he was called 'Trazom'. By commandeering the glockenspiel backstage during a performance of *Die Zauberflöte* more than a decade later, and adding an unexpected arpeggio on it when the character on stage who is pretending to play one pauses, he plays on the multiplications of reality that make all drama both possible and potentially absurd.

During the same year of 1791 Constanze's wobbly health took her to Baden in what turned out to be her husband's final summer, and he reminds her in a rather lonely letter that he always needs someone around to make fun of. She conceivably did not need reminding, but the rueful tone acknowledges that his own absurdity shows through in this extreme need for humour. He adds that the mice in their apartment are keeping him company. It is banality rather than seriousness that is the deadly enemy of jokes, since it gives them so much less to go on. But in a shaggy-dog story the banality negates humour only to end up regenerating it; the more perfectly unfunny such a story becomes, the funnier it is too. We find the composer telling such a story years earlier in a letter from February 1778 to his Augsburg cousin, a tale of eleven thousand sheep that may or may not ever succeed in crossing a bridge. He is 'in a hurry' as he writes, because he has 'absolutely nothing to do right now', though at the same time 'no one knows how this thing will end'. In fact it turns out that 'they could all have stayed on this side' anyhow. The 'very beautiful' sheepdog that turns up may not be especially shaggy, but the story is as exuberantly tedious as could be hoped. Mozart here wants to turn the very fact that a joke is not funny into laughter. Within the constant joking in some letters we can feel how intensely he loved the basic fact of communicating with others, but also how close this intensity came to turning febrile or revealing a sudden emptiness.

Mozart's music has affinities with humour built into its textures, as these turn formal patterns or traits of harmony or rhythm into new versions of themselves, and reveal them to have more and often weirder sides than expected. The musical material stays the same and yet is vertiginously altered, its blocks are transposed and reconstrued and given new contexts, and the deepest trick lies in how its largest transformations feel at the same time like revelations of what its essence had been all along. A phrase will turn up in a different guise as a piece develops, and, as with the gags in a good stand-up routine, its second appearance will rearrange the suppositions that it had previously set up, revealing a wider, perhaps more surreptitious logic that has in fact been in place from the beginning. A piece shifts and contorts its own components and inventions, and each time it also claims that the latest contortion reveals some essential shape more clearly. The best jokes reveal deep and surprising facts, and likewise his music convinces us of its rightness even as it twists apart the foundations that we have been standing on. Mozart's music can have the humour of limericks, in which outrageously mismatched elements are held together by the dream logic of rhyme, or of farce, in which doors swing open and characters reappear at such perfectly inopportune moments that they end up being, instead, perfect. The plots in comedies at the theatre or the opera go by way of wit, surprise and reversal towards witty and surprising versions of stability or reconciliation, and it is from such patterns that even Mozart's most densely searching works often gain their basic ideas of structure. His skittish, foamy K191 bassoon concerto from way back in 1774 has the fun premise of giving the high spirits of the still teenaged composer to the most dowdy and least fluent of the woodwind family. The great K622 clarinet concerto from his final year has a spinning amplitude that is not exactly comical, but its sometimes hectic shift of mood and its glancing stylistic omnivorousness can feel directly plugged back in to the earlier work's vibrant example.

One of Mozart's less funny achievements is the actual joke piece from the late 1780s which he designed as a mocking assault on established musical styles. The K522 work in four movements called *Ein musikalischer Spaß* consists of a series of deliberate bloopers and surprisingly laboured and inconsequential parodies of the sorts of musical incompetence that abounded around him. Mozart's real humour knew the wellsprings of his own styles and energies, and it failed him here when he meant to unleash it on the ineptitude of others. His is the comedy of an extreme intelligence alive to its goofball aspects, and it has no real interest in merely savaging the failings of others. In Haydn's music sheer formal sleekness does not permeate the humour nearly as fully as in Mozart, but its extra ingredients include a greater grasp of the robustness and punchiness of folk styles, and a larger tolerance for nearly ragged shifts of texture. The jokes and parodies and skits and formal trapdoors and stylistic shell games that they both loved were at their best when they fed, rather than mocked or dismantled, their highest efforts of musical remaking. Logic might suggest that there should be one phase in which a style develops and perfects itself, followed by another in which it can be subverted, parodied and dismantled. Instead the restlessness that produced these new styles meant that they were riddled from the start with their own jokes on themselves, their own ways of teasing themselves open or mocking their own pretensions.

Mozart's music cannot really be mocked or parodied because it was already laughing so hard at itself. The history of the novel shows a similar pattern, powered as it was from the start by masterpieces of subversive wit and formal parody like Cervantes's *Don Quixote* or Sterne's *Tristram Shandy*. The novel got going as an enterprise because it wanted to have fun, and its seriousness followed later, and took its bearings from a primordial amusement. Satire was vital to the more subversive strands of enlightenment culture, and it no doubt provides the most obvious route for humour to succeed in whatever aims of seriousness it may harbour. In Mozart and Haydn the levity may play along with and gain from critique, satire or subversion, but it goes far beyond their limits. It learns to rescue itself from the aggressive, corrosive aspects of joking by means of a more ample set of connections between humour and desire; Haydn's late symphonies should convince anyone of how a ruggedly comic perspective can animate endless curiosity about the world's mutations. Mozart's final comic opera *Die Zauberflöte* reveals a logic that undergirded his whole enterprise when it increases the levels of silliness in the humour on stage while also making the moralizing more didactically intense. If all the jokes were taken out, the piece's moral earnestness would shrivel. But the jokes would lose their piquancy and audacity if extracted from the opera's depths of moral investigation.

Mozart seems to have maintained good ties to Leutgeb throughout his Viennese years. If the horn-player's links to Salzburg contributed to the pair's friendship, perhaps they also added to the charge of the jokes he inspired. The composer may have often feared feeling, or seeming, clumsy or provincial in the imperial capital. In the music that he wrote for Leutgeb such feelings are absorbed and reconstrued; joking lets him project them onto his friend at the same time as it lets him turn them into sources of callously casual musical power. A life devoted to change can make the past seem even more unsettled than the future, and having someone like Leutgeb around may have helped Mozart both to probe and to disguise some of its open questions. An ongoing question through those years was how to write utterly sophisticated music whose polish would not suppress or shrink its drives of intensity and inquiry. Joking was for him a way of living in a world that was bombarding him and itself with changes and options, and a way of staying genial without softening his perceptions.

We could say much the same of music. A certain double perspective on his own output was needed as Mozart moved through, burned through, styles and achievements. Pieces of music came at him stamped with feelings of validity and authenticity. Yet each piece was also only a stopping point on the way to its future iterations in different performances or different versions, and he knew that he would move on to further creations, further creativity. A lot is said about the fears that creative artists can have of drying up or being blocked, but a deeper vertigo for someone like Mozart can come from the perpetual imminence of the next thing to be conceived or glimpsed, or finished. Bringing levity and absurdity into the heart of his music would have allowed the composer to know that each piece was transient, without ceasing to strive to perfect whatever was emerging. Highly creative minds may need all sorts of tricks so that they can both know and not know how far their perceptions could throw their lives asunder. The endless joking may well have made it hard to live alongside him, but it would probably have been harder still without it.

14

The Wandering Piano

Fantasia in C minor

If Mozart ever felt at home anywhere, maybe it was at the piano. But this was a home that shifted and skipped beneath his fingers. The years of his career were marked by an experimental ferment in keyboard instruments, a process that led only uncertainly towards the emergence later of the modern grand piano, however imposing the latter has ended up seeming. The piano that was lurching and tweaking its way into existence in Mozart's time has become since then more than a musical instrument. It has become a loaded symbol of serious musical culture, at once a foundation for teaching and an apex whose solo repertoire is meant to occupy the rarefied heights of all music. It has been charged with dreams of pleasure in bars and nightclubs around the world, as well as with the doughty fantasies of cultural authority that civic institutions or bourgeois families have preferred. Whether modern societies have wanted private joy or public improvement, the piano has sounded out the possibilities. The sleek surfaces of this opaque beast have resonated within so many rooms and halls and arenas that it has been one of the great dream machines of modern culture.

A vision of Vienna as an Elysium for keyboard musicians was what Mozart sprinkled before his father in 1781 as he began trying to convince him that moving there for a new sort of career would work out. His then friend Count Arco had warned the composer, at the point where their arguments about Mozart's Viennese plans were still friendly, about the fickleness of the public in the Habsburg capital. He told him in effect how easy it was to be dazzled by how easily dazzled the Viennese could be; their accolades might last a matter of months, but then they would want something new. In the letter in which Mozart relates the count's warning, he reassures his father that none of this can affect his speciality of keyboard music; he concedes how unreliable the Viennese are at the theatre. The next ten years of Mozart's life can seem to us to throng with mighty achievements. But Vienna's musical life spun an atmosphere that was both hyperactive and fugitive, and these years were marked for Mozart by only fitful bursts of progress, and more often by a churn of diffuse possibilities.

He was all too good at believing that these openings and directions might just slot together perfectly around the next corner. Vienna could seem to stream with opportunities, but it also kept revealing that they had been doled out already; it was a scene that blew enough bubbles to ensure that there were plenty to puncture. Extremes of talent can make all this harder to bear and to navigate. Vaster promises may be made and giving up on them may be harder. Allies may overestimate the likelihood of triumph, and rivals may manoeuvre all the more cannily. Mozart's life towards the middle of the decade especially whirrs with quick-fire factors and helter-skelter decisions as he darts between composing and engagements; 'musical taste is changing all the time' in Vienna, according to one letter from 1783 to his father. He is pleased, of course, and he is also justifying not being in touch more often. An artist like Mozart is in any case one reason why tastes do change so fast in places like 1780s Vienna. Yet his days would surely not have had to be so fully headlong if things had been going even better for him; his life whirls because it is dangling between success and failure.

The piano was at the heart of the whirl, a constant companion which was also a continual vector for making new links or moving on to further prospects. It must have felt like an extra body branching out of his own. His confidence that he could make a go of a freelance life relied on the variety of roles that he could take up, performing and teaching and composing as occasions arose. The keyboard was the nearest thing to a golden knot tying them all together. Staying afloat meant keeping the keys moving beneath his fingers. Working with singers meant accompanying them on the keyboard as they practised or rehearsed or tweaked performance ideas, and Mozart often led performances of his operas by playing a keyboard continuo part that brought him close to what later periods would make the role of a conductor. His powers at the keyboard opened up social landscapes; his capacity to sight-read complex scores made him vital to the gatherings of highbrow amateurs trying to interest themselves in baroque music. In a letter from early May 1782 to Leopold, he records playing the entire second act from his 'seraglio' opera at the house of the sophisticated and clever Countess Thun, saying that he pranced through it. But a trap waited for Mozart within the kaleidoscopic absorbency of his keyboard music. The more richly his artistry registered his life's mutating factors, the more deeply he exposed himself to them too. Keyboard music was his skeleton key, opening up any number of his culture's tastes and possibilities, but this exhaustiveness must itself have been exhausting. The pull of creation can get an artist through the day, but the cost is perpetual gyration. During March 1784 he told his father that he was having to perform somewhere almost every evening, and was in such need of new music to play that he had 'no choice but to write' constantly. Music took him towards people and away from them too.

The keyboard's flexibility took it all around the musical world surrounding Mozart, and in turn this was partly why it was going through so much flux and redefinition. His world wanted ever more from culture; so it wanted the keyboard to be more and more things. 'It is impossible to describe the confusion and commotion', according to a letter from Leopold back to his daughter in the spring of 1785 when he has made it to Vienna. But the most vivid detail from the flood of concerts and lessons and general music-making that he records is of how often his son's keyboard has to be carried and carted in and out of the apartment and to and from wherever it is needed. A piano is a moody creature with which to share an existence. We can imagine how much nervous tension, technical fiddling and affectionate cajoling went into these episodes, as the instrument went up and down stairs and along Vienna's battered, dusty roads. The fortepiano at the time lacked the strong inner casing that let the grand pianoforte become so imperiously meaty over the following century. Its relative slenderness made the carting-around feasible, but made it more vulnerable to jolts and bashes.

The harpsichord remained the culture's dominant version of the keyboard well into Mozart's lifetime at least, but it is telling how fast its aura of pre-eminence faded once the piano began to spread; it reminds us how avid for technological novelty the late eighteenth century was. Bartolomeo Cristofori was the Florentine inventor who made the initial technical breakthrough just as the seventeenth century was ending, right on time to make so much of the eighteenth century possible. The impetus for Cristofori and his circle was not really a directly musical one, and it did not stem from dissatisfaction with the harpsichord; no one at the time would have easily imagined an end to the sway of that instrument. Rather, the first pianos emerged as flamboyant feats of engineering calculated to prick the interests of Florence's intellectual connoisseurs, devotees of any number of curious avenues of technical and artistic advance. Maybe the invention was one of the last exhalations of the spirit of Leonardo in that capital of the Italian renaissance, and of his fusions of technological experiment with artistic ardour. Piano keys present their notes with a clarity as sharp as a scalpel; a thorough, diagrammatic empiricism invests the instrument's alchemy of sound. Of course Leonardo was himself a fine musician.

Reams of the history of classical music can be told as the gradual, splendid German takeover of Italian styles. Cristofori's invention did not really take off as a musical or commercial proposition until the basic idea was copied and altered decades later in Prussia by makers under the aegis of Frederick the Great and then even more fatefully in Vienna. Mozart's letters show how keenly he engaged with the granular changes that pushed all this along, immersing himself in the fine detail as well as the high volatility of technological progress. It was one way of opening himself and his music to the big technological rhythms coursing more generally across the culture. His keyboard music offers itself as among other things a sort of seismographic account of what it is like to live in a world seething with technological shifts. The workshops in which the fortepiano was scrutinized, prodded at and rejigged were allied to innumerable other workshops and laboratories and studies across the culture, in which everyday items like pins or advanced commodities like watches were being manufactured with new levels of inventive intricacy and industrial zeal as the century strode on. Henry Ford was already on the historical horizon.

Harpsichords and pianos alike produce music by getting strings to resound within their bodies, but the big innovation of the fortepiano is how this happens. Pressing a key on a harpsichord releases a plucking mechanism onto the desired string, whereas a fortepiano works by a percussive action that is in some ways cruder. The impact of the finger on a fortepiano key travels directly onto the corresponding string, rather than releasing a mechanism that then works on the string with inflexible regularity. So the player could now alter and vary the volume and hence the dynamic range of the sound in ways that were impossible on the harpsichord. The name 'fortepiano' refers to the different qualities of loudness and quietness that could now be summoned as a result, as of course does the arbitrarily reversed word 'pianoforte' pinned to the larger version later on. The difference may not sound big, but worlds of new power, freedom and feelingfulness were released by it. Further types of keyboard instrument contributed to the mix, not least the church organ, complete with its historical authority and its quirky variations from place to place. In homes, the harpsichord was often supplanted by the clavichord, a rival with its own distinctive features. At the forefront of change, the fortepiano itself was constantly being tinkered with or enlarged. Leather was replaced by felt as the cushion for its hammers, and expansive types of levers or pedals for sustaining notes were tried out. The story of music is partly about building ever more supple interfaces between solid objects and the fugitive air that they make vibrate; an instrument is a sort of reversed ear, after all. Paradoxically these objects can keep getting larger or more complex or demanding in the process.

The 1770s was probably the decade during which this technological maelstrom was at its most fecund, precisely when Mozart's mature keyboard style was gathering itself. His brief stay in Augsburg in the autumn of 1777 is particularly telling. It was the sort of stolid, patrician place that the composer could take against, but it was there that the great fortepiano manufacturer Johann Andreas Stein had his workshop. Mozart's excitement can be gauged by the fact that his practical joker side came out when he called on Stein; calling himself 'Trazom' there may have been a sign that a twist of identity seemed called for by these new instruments. How richly that excitement was then confirmed is suggested by the expansive list of works featured in a concert that he soon organized in the Fuggerhäuser complex; he co-opted three of the workshop's deliciously smooth products for the occasion. Stein himself and a local organist joined him in what must have been the centrepiece, his K242 triple keyboard concerto in F, a piece designed so that its soloists can be of very different standards. Mozart also played another early keyboard concerto, as well as one sonata that has come down to us and an improvisatory one that seems to have duly evanesced, and a fugue that he describes as in the style of the organ. Elated new colours must have spun from his hands as they moved. A letter from that October becomes a little hymn of praise to the craftsman, as Mozart explains how what 'distinguishes his instruments from all others is that they are built with an escapement', a mechanism that meant that the sound from each string could vanish rapidly after it was struck. After Stein has finished making a soundboard, 'he puts it outside and exposes it to the weather', to ensure robustness. He plays energetically on a new instrument himself, and 'goes on filing and fitting' until it does all that he wants. Stein's genius is summed up in the fact that 'the tone is always even' on his instruments. Evenness is at the heart of Mozart's music; balance is the ballast that his endless kinetic liberties rely on. One sonata 'sounds absolutely great' on one of the instruments produced in this little utopia of craft. The world was at Mozart's fingertips at the keyboard, and it was making itself ever more sensitive to their decisions.

The keyboard's states of technological flux and redefinition comprised a sort of training for the composer in how to live in a fluctile world. But then his own musicianship was a vital vector, forming part of what drove the culture into the piano's new world. Stein must have been reassured and stimulated by hearing his instruments extolled and sounded out by such a player, and must have learnt a lot too. Joining himself to the fortepiano meant a claim on Mozart's part that his was a pioneer art. His sometimes hectic success in Vienna around the middle of the 1780s owed a lot to some fashionable weaving together in the mind of the musical public of the power of his stylistic advances and the new worlds of sound being opened up as keyboards grew and changed. His music resounded with the most progressive, exciting momentums. Being Mozart was always a collaborative act, involving not just other musicians but machines. It was an ongoing collaboration indeed with technological change itself. His past devotion to the harpsichord and his brilliant successes on it could hardly have ceased to matter; Mozart's music can remind us that loss always scumbles the euphoria of technological change. Shifting from the tinglingly saturated soundscape of the harpsichord, and so losing the need for the trills and ornaments with which its players made up for its lack of dynamic range and sonic space, cannot have lacked ambivalence for him. Mozart's playing on the fortepiano was reportedly described by none other than Beethoven as still deeply marked by the harpsichord.

One of Mozart's crucial collaborators on the piano was a young woman called Josepha Auernhammer who was one of his earliest and most serious Viennese students, and who played so well that they could team up in concert duets. He could be critical of elements of her playing, and he joked about her 'hideously ugly' appearance and what seem to have been her matrimonial designs on him. But the music that he wrote for them to play together suggests a fruitful partnership; she was so trusted that she indeed even guided the publishing of certain works. A few months after Mozart moved to Vienna, he gave a late autumn concert alongside Auernhammer for which he wrote his K448 sonata in D for two keyboards, and the piece is a rhapsodic statement of trust both in her and in the powers of the instrument that brought them together. Its driving sense is of a fresh, sometimes giddy excitement at the pleasures of collaboration; the voices of the two instruments and of the two players respond and interconnect in a spirit of generously undulating symmetry. The whole Auernhammer family seems to have latched on to Mozart during his first months alone in Vienna, and they helped him in ways that were sincere and timely, whatever the motives. The sonata is one of Mozart's most winning, celebratory pieces; pleasure and structure alike become so shareable in it that it enacts something like a fusion between the powers of the fortepiano and the momentum of his move to Vienna.

At the fortepiano his solitude was both deepened and allayed. He was pulled into ever more singular statements of his powers, but this also gave his playing more powerful ways of reaching out into the ears of others. The new instrument's qualities of flux and raciness suited someone already pulled towards the mercurial and the unsettling, someone whose fingers were in effect already shifting. Mozart's sister-in-law Sophie Haibel has left us a nice account of his daily manner that makes him sound permanently both hyper-active and lost in thought. She is affectionate and acute as she describes how endlessly restless he was, incapable of standing still even as he washed his face in the morning, always fidgeting or crumpling a napkin while something invisible to others enthralled him. The telling detail comes when she describes his inability to stop playing with things, his hat or pockets or watch-fob but also tables and chairs, and says that it was as if they were all keyboards to him. If the keyboard was his bedrock, it brought feelings of freedom and flux that must also have diffused themselves among his life's other tasks and surfaces. As he sat at the keyboard and his fingers moved up and down it, motion and stability could blur together or interpret each other.

'Any philosophical lover of music will regard him as a remarkable man', according to an account from a Weimar journal in 1788 which goes on to describe how baffling and alien Mozart's keyboard writing could actually be. Someone who sums up the possibilities of his moment can end up all the more intricately isolated within it, and as the decade continued there was ever more wariness mixed into the headiness with which he was praised and listened to. In another ambivalent encomium published during the previous year in a magazine based in Hamburg, the critic calls him 'the most skilful and best keyboard player' that he has ever heard before lamenting that his compositions aim too high in their pursuit of novelty and sophistication. Sitting at the keyboard must have been like handling a drawn bow for Mozart, and tension must increasingly have come from how hard keyboard music could pull at once towards simple pleasures and extreme artistic vistas. According to the Hamburg writer 'feeling and heart profit little' when his works move towards the latter. But the extreme pathos in some of his highest music stems partly from how starkly it strives to align these possibilities; the lucidity that comes when it succeeds is richly tender. He was always in danger of driving himself further from others by the creative exuberance that his capacity to please them could bring on. By the middle of the decade he wanted to give an account of his own powers at the keyboard that acknowledges isolation and exuberance alike. So we can judge in any case from a work from May 1785 that imbibes so many of the instrument's ranging meanings for him that it becomes cryptically expansive. It was as much Mozart's daily rhythm to be revolving amid vaporous, often convulsive and sometimes downright dippy plans, offers and choices as it is part of the texture of his music to seem woven out of sheer possibility. But in this piece he slowly scrutinizes hyperactivity itself.

His K475 fantasia in C minor may be at once the most anomalous and the most overwhelming of all Mozart's works for solo keyboard. Now nearly halfway through his decade in Vienna, his composing had revolved around the fortepiano for so long that the older world of the harpsichord makes a strange return in the piece as a sort of floating reference point, a memory of past sounds. No other piece captures with such gnomic grandeur the sense of hovering between two worlds that would have pervaded Mozart's experience at the keyboard, the sense of brooding over alternatives and of feeling out ways of traversing the gaps between them or mapping the overlaps. In one way sitting at the keyboard sheds its repetitiveness here and reveals itself as a bottomless source of variety and change; at the same time the piece gazes back into the keyboard's past and that of the composer. In the fantasia he reaches a point of inflection where he can meditate on and play with such an array of styles and directions that the music nearly unravels. The piece rolls the ghosts of past keyboards and the promises of keyboards to come into the one that he sits at.

If the fantasy as a genre meant anything very definite towards the end of the eighteenth century, it was through its close link to improvisation. However, the fantasia in question is far from the values of dash and flashiness that the period liked in improvisatory displays; it keeps from improvisation instead its uncertainty and its sense of proliferating but suspended options. In some ways the fantasy was less a form than a licence allowing the free association of motifs. The harmonic ideas here are less developed than drawn through sequences of fluctuating prisms; a lavish hesitancy is the result. Quantities of wit, textural pleasure and expressive potential float up, but the piece commits to nothing. It is easy to imagine that years of being asked to be spontaneously dazzling at the keyboard had left charges of annoyance and resentment behind. Mozart's pride in what he could do was often winning; it might otherwise too often have been bleak. Maybe he wanted in the fantasia to hint at how much memory and disquiet remained beneath the instrument's suave surfaces.

Elements of the piece belong so vigorously to the sonic expansiveness of the 1780s fortepiano that they even seem to drive beyond it, pointing towards the dramatic intensities that the next few decades would draw from Beethoven. Passages probe away at extremes of dynamic contrast, pushing far into both the loudness and the softness with which the new instruments could resound. The fantasia often gets down into the lowest depths of sound that the fortepiano was opening up. But some deep equivocation guides this quest downwards, an oddly moving uncertainty as to whether what is sought is some further set of ranging sonic adventures or a bedrock of sound on which music can solidly rest or build. The expansiveness of the resulting sound-world throws the piece's structure further off from any clear course of development and lets the music stretch back instead towards sounds from earlier in the century. Memories seep in of the harpsichord and all its strumming or pinging textural density. The more swirlingly the fantasia explores the fortepiano's resources, the more richly allusive it becomes; hints flicker of the toccata's snappiness or of the sprawling colours of the baroque organ. A filigree likewise emerges of the cantabile melodic style which Mozart elsewhere uses the fortepiano's new dynamic directness to release. The player's fingers explore their new relationship to sound production with such crackling freedom that the music becomes both deeply singular and wildly inclusive. The future sound-world of the concert grand brims in the fantasia's background, but the further down into itself the piece dives, the more echoes it unlooses of the sense of ornamental stasis typical of late baroque keyboard music. Its restlessness is both intrepid and nostalgic.

No doubt its composer was too. An extreme psychological realism often propels Mozart's instrumental music as richly as it does his operas, and the fantasia is a self-portrait of an artist whose life could make attainment inseparable from insolidity, limned from an apex within it. He had been pushing relentlessly onwards on the keyboard and elsewhere for years, but this is a piece that opens inventiveness up to the past and lets its own style hesitate. In the harpsichord music from earlier in the century, a piece typically pumps a given set of rhythms or versions of harmony for all the variety that it can yield, rather than moving as dynamically and nimbly as Mozart and Haydn like to do. The fantasia's phrases belong to Mozart's mature style, but the fantasy genre allows it to treat them with a ruminative fervour that feels closer to that earlier world, and sometimes seems liable to lead nowhere at all. The composer's omnivorousness extends here to flashy scraps of the fantastical keyboard styles from the high baroque and the Italian renaissance, of the crunchy textures and capricious sweeps of sonority that reached back through Buxtehude and Handel, at least as far as Frescobaldi in the early seventeenth century. But there was something dissolvent about the panoramic fervency of baroque keyboard music, and no one could have been more sensitive than Mozart to how its drastic exploitations of its own conventions had ended up loosening their hold on musical sensibility. The story of how the structural imagination in keyboard music had dwindled during the eighteenth century is an intricate one; its last bursts in Sebastian Bach's feats of systematization and willpower were intense. The fantasia is a coda to this story, but one so drastic and inventive that it rewrites it. Whether he was playing or composing or teaching, sitting at the keyboard meant for Mozart decomposing himself as well as holding the strands of his artistic life together. It meant putting whatever musical materials were in hand under a relentless creative pressure that kept picking them apart but which here issues into a spirit of spiralling inclusion. The fantasia knows that the past always returns.

Mozart had written his K457 keyboard sonata in the same key a year earlier, and one possibility is that the fantasia was meant as an introductory companion for it. The two works were first published at the end of 1785 as a sort of conjoined entity, so the pairing is not without sanction. However, scholars wishing to settle such an issue once and for all may miss the amphibiousness that drenches this music, the fantasia's capacity to allude to different contexts and to move between worlds. Using it to introduce the sonata is certainly valid, and turns it into a suspenseful launchpad for the sonata's structural vim and melodic sprightliness. On the other hand publishing it in this form may have mainly been a way of getting such waywardness out into the world. How to formalize flux had been a question raised within the technological exuberance of the eighteenth-century keyboard world; moves were made towards keyboards that would transcribe whatever was improvised on them directly into some automatic notation, as if keyboard music was starting to hint at the typewriter and the laptop. One question now is whether works like this should always be played on a fortepiano of the sort that Mozart knew and loved, or should seek new resonances within that dazzling monster, the modern pianoforte.

But such music can give many different answers to any number of questions. If the keyboard was where Mozart was most himself, it was also where he was meant to be extravagantly available to others. But that availability threw him back into solitude, since listeners wanted him to do precisely what they could not. His brilliance could distance him ever further from the people that it drew towards him. The fantasia gathers in years of such feelings and turns them into a structure that gives them clarity while keeping them subtle. Mozart could wear the ruminative genre as a mask that is also a record of stylistic struggle; plangency, solitude and fervency float up while remaining quizzical. He hovers on the brink of some grand expressive gesture and then eludes it. During the nineteenth century his romantic successors tended to plunge in heroically or heedlessly; their versions of solitude became ever more exaggerated and needy too.

An account does exist of Mozart playing what seems to have been this work as a stand-alone piece in its own right, albeit in response to a prospective student who appears to have auditioned for him with it. Joseph Frank winningly reports how astonished he was when the composer was polite about his rendition, and is duly exclamatory when recalling Mozart's own playing. He describes him as turning the piano into a different instrument, and in fact the composer had literally almost done so; around the time of the piece's composition he had started using a fortepiano that had been rampantly augmented even by the standards of the day, and which Frank specifies as the one played on this occasion. During the 1790s Mozart would compose for the glass harmonica and for a mechanical organ installed in a waxworks, instruments at the furthest edges of any rubric of keyboard music. But the fantasia shows what far-flung processes the keyboard always released for him. Its deepest intimation is that it lets us hear the composer's creativity at some point before its inner ink dries, at a stage when he is still testing possibilities, is doodling or drifting or dreaming. The work can get us to fantasize about hearing Mozart fantasize. But these fantasies are filled with the nuts and bolts of the things that he played on, are made of the most real stuff of his existence. If the piece reveals a feverishness moving just beneath the surface of all his fusions of delicacy and power, maybe this is the furthest twist of Mozart's faith in what keyboard music could be.

15

Artistic Cunning

'Se vuol ballare', *Le nozze di Figaro*

Lorenzo Da Ponte was his own first great creation. He was also a monstrously representative product of the strange, wavering place that was late eighteenth-century Venice. In his *Memoirs* he says that a single recitation of a poem by himself at the seminary in the Venetian regions where he was meant to be studying Euclid and Galileo got him suddenly, at the age of twenty one, appointed to a teaching post in rhetoric. He had been surreptitiously reading the likes of Tasso while the abstruse treatises on the curriculum were expounded around him, and the story of his life as he tells it is instead an elaborate exposition of the values of artifice and invention and the adventures in the realms of the senses that he found in some of the sparklier shoots of high Italian culture. Anything encumbering or dull he jettisoned. He describes himself as having spent much of the rest of the 1770s oscillating between an increasingly chaotic impersonation of a serious ecclesiastical intellectual and rather more devoted versions of life on the hoof amid the watery city's cafes and cards parties. He becomes known as a suave verbal improviser and he slips into political difficulties as Venice's traditional compromise between republicanism and oligarchy begins to fracture; he also spends a lot of time in Padua playing draughts and ombre. Proliferating entanglements and enmities finally forced him towards the very end of the decade to flee to Dresden, but his more enduring destination became Vienna. He arrived there in the early 1780s as Joseph was tilting the city's spotlights back towards Italian opera.

In May 1783 Mozart claims in the first letter to Leopold in which he mentions Da Ponte that he has already promised to write a libretto for him. His account of Da Ponte as a possible collaborator is suavely guarded. It is not until May 1786 that the first of their three great collaborations *Le nozze di Figaro* reaches the stage; translations normally claim that the opera is about the marriage of Figaro, but 'wedding' is probably a better rendering. The depth and complexity of the affinity between them may have contributed to drawing the process out. Da Ponte's little preface to his libretto neatly shows how expansively their drives had combined, until their aim was what he calls a new type of spectacle. Modesty was seldom the librettist's style, but he leads into this claim by insisting on the grandeur of the famous comic drama that the two of them had used as their source. His excitement at what he and Mozart have done is palpable, sheathed though it is in a rueful awareness of the sheer size of the opera that they were asking audiences to embrace. Luckily it is 'a public of so refined a taste and such just understanding' that he addresses.

Venice in the eighteenth century was fecund ground for the inventive new sorts of selfhood that the likes of Da Ponte threw themselves into with desperate eagerness. The great old maritime republic no longer had much to sell the world except itself, and the aplomb with which it had once domineered in the Adriatic and beyond had started turning feverish. It resorted to being probably the first city to make itself a modern pleasure resort. The city's painters like Canaletto tried to convince the world that they were not hawking hedonism so much as civilization itself, but its public authorities responded to their shrinking geopolitical horizons by becoming draconian and fearful. Nights all around the darkly lovely canals could teem with pleasures and libertines and bouts of masquerade, but liberty itself was not to be found in the place. Da Ponte's background was in the region's often troubled Jewish enclaves, so he brought an outsider's slant to a place that was trying to reset its characteristic mixtures of the fixed and the fluid. He took from the city a sort of chancer's swagger, and it then fed into the adepts in ruse and disguise and imbroglio that populate his librettos for Mozart. Venice could teach someone like Da Ponte to love the heights of art and culture without losing a willingness to be mischievous or to wing it.

The combination was perfect for Mozart. Da Ponte arrived in the composer's circles just when the great Metastasio was ailing and about to die. In his memoir he recounts meeting the man whom he replaced as the age's defining librettist, at an evening party where the champion bestowed his approval by reciting a poem by the newcomer. But any revival of Italian opera now would want to call on new cultural bearings and juices, to go in leaner and fizzier and more openly chancy directions. The century's cunning and wit had been held as if in perfect, icy suspension within the high formal sheen of Metastasio's lyrics. Within his successor's librettos for Mozart they lose polish, but turn kinetic and flagrant and knavish. The composer loved subversive comedy and was even more subversively committed to making it seriously matter, and the librettist could find new ways of making literary Italian resound that were both gleeful and mordant. His perspective may have gained further contours from the lisp with which he spoke. A brief mention of it reaches us from an Irish tenor called Michael Kelly who was among Vienna's leading singers, and who spoofed the librettist's eccentric demeanour on stage. Da Ponte had a juggler's capacity to indulge a taste for beauty and panache while keeping it open to a sense of their possible absurdity or even violence. Social contexts were for him mutable, fragile things, as they were for many in his purview. At least since his unhappy sojourn in Paris, Mozart had known that his music belonged deeply to a culture that it also saw right through. He wanted a librettist who knew the culture's frailties as well as its strengths, and who knew where they were bonded.

Beaumarchais's plays about Figaro had been sensations, and the librettist needed a cunning worthy of his protagonist to get the project off the ground, in a city rife with musical cliques and political distrust. The Habsburg court's skittish bureaucratic apparatus was at the heart of cultural life in Vienna, and its cogs and pulleys could spin fast even while it gave so little away as to seem paralysed. Da Ponte's capacity for glee came with resources of wariness. Likewise, he was a great analyst of eighteenth-century character partly because his gleaming capacity to believe in whatever he undertook came with a ruthless readiness to leave it behind. Mozart and his librettist were both freelances who had broken away from tight institutional bearings. But part of the great city's pull for both men was the thought of grander institutional positions than they had had so far. Neither of them seems to have been attached even to the idea of detachment involved in being freelance, and both men were improvising within the hectic possibilities that Vienna opened up even while they coveted court positions; Mozart would get one before the decade was out. Ambition and rebelliousness mixed in both men's moves to the imperial capital.

We are dealing with people who were piecing together day by day what modern identity would be, probably unsure themselves whether they were renegades critiquing the established order or opportunists seeking to cut new routes through it. The frisky, searching radiance of *Le nozze di Figaro* relies on the opera's supple loyalty to the world of disorderly aristocratic order that it also teases apart and lambasts. The valet Figaro is in increasingly open rebellion against his employer. But though the character and the opera challenge, upset and mock Count Almaviva's world, the work's suppleness comes from how inventively it uses that world's own terms to do so. Its music roves among that world's styles in ways that also suggest how brilliant, various and capacious they had been all along. If *Le nozze di Figaro* is in some ways a document of imminent revolutionary fervour, it is all but rapturously conservative in others.

Da Ponte's single most important contribution to the opera may have been an odd, instinctive understanding of Joseph which helped quench any danger that the piece would be vetoed by the emperor; he ended up positively expediting it. The success of a version by Giovanni Paisiello of Beaumarchais's first Figaro play had been crucial to the emperor's turn back towards Italian comic opera. But the second play came carrying waves of scandal from its premiere in 1784 in Paris, an event delayed for at least a couple of years because of its outright criticisms of political backwardness and aristocratic immorality; it was called detestable by the king himself. As early as 1785 a German translation appeared, and it was becoming something that the whole of Europe seemed to need to have a view on. Joseph would not let it be staged in Vienna. Da Ponte claims that he undertook to finesse the emperor into allowing it to be done as an opera, and got Mozart to start composing on the assumption that he would succeed. Opera was more clearly the official artistic voice of a regime like Joseph's than theatre was, and plenty would have rated his chances beneath unlikely. An advantage of turning it into a libretto was that he could say that much had been cut. But his deeper trick was to rely on the more tricky, opaque aspects of Joseph's character. Joseph had large strains of both galumphing idealism and a certain truculent rebelliousness in him, and Da Ponte seems to have had a waggish nose for how much he could wrong-foot his own advisers and courtiers. The piece slid through the city's opera establishment on the back of some subtle manoeuvres; the librettist knew how to time an organizational intervention as smartly as the opera paces its jokes and action.

How does it feel to be a genius? A lot of it comes down to waiting, being ready for the arrival of the right thing. Mozart's mind merged extremes of hyperactivity and patience; in his letters he can be endlessly playful about prospects and schemes and failures and frustrations, no doubt because he felt ready to pounce on the liveliness of the next really creative possibility. The wedding day of Figaro and Susanna is filled with farcical mishaps, tightening deadlines and switched places; the zany rush of the action was one channel by which Mozart could pour his own life into the opera. Its music is filled with hustling narrative momentum and with a spirit of psychic acceleration, and with a sense of quicksilver responsiveness and adaptability. So too it has a deep feeling for false trails and misdirection and delayed decoding. Mozart's consuming quest for the right stage vehicle had given him a big enough batch of false starts and dead ends as he wrestled with his own intense ambition and with the gyrating factors of musical Vienna. Possible librettos and minor vocal works bustle in and out of his life during the period like characters coming and going from the scenes of a comedy. It was crucial not to commit too much energy to the wrong project. But *Le nozze di Figaro* could not have happened if his operatic style had not kept shifting and growing in the meantime, and it would not have become what it did if he had gone for a less kaleidoscopically inclusive vision of opera earlier.

Vienna's musical establishment was split during these years between the causes of German and of Italian opera, and all sorts of artistic and political and careerist aims were mixed into any one push on behalf of either. A recent phase of Joseph's reign had seemed to favour the former agenda, but in 1783 the situation switched as he boosted a new, expansive Italian company. German opera on any significant scale left the city for around two years, but then in 1785 the scene changed again as a new German company was set up under the auspices of the court, giving its first outings that autumn. Mozart was too distinctive and too versatile to fit in wholly with either faction. Of course this versatility was what made his last few operas capable of their great syntheses, and in the meantime he was not distracted by too many overly helpful suggestions or commissions. Parts of his creative psyche doubtless knew that it was biding its time over this stretch; others were providing plenty of operatic attempts for him to learn from and to absorb. Not long before leaving for Salzburg a year after the success in 1782 of his 'seraglio' opera, Mozart had been caught up in a tedious little controversy over whether he had been too eager to write insertion arias for an Italian *buffa* hit called *Il curioso indiscreto* that was being put on in Vienna. Tinkering around the edges of other people's projects or writing arias for the various purposes of specific singers were ways of keeping the grand workshop of his vocal style engaged. It is easy to imagine that his energies were sometimes released into these minor undertakings at levels that others neither expected nor wanted. His instrumental writing from these years teems with a desire for opera that comes out in large hints of storytelling or psychology as well as in singing melodic lines.

In the same 1783 letter in which Mozart first mentions Lorenzo Da Ponte, he tells his father that he has looked through probably more than a hundred librettos in search of one worth setting. Count Orsini-Rosenberg was in charge of these operatic matters in the capital; he was the official whom the manoeuvres of others had to go through or around, and Mozart seems to have had in him a fairly thoughtful admirer. He must have encouraged the composer as he trawled for something to set, driven at least as much by excitement or relief at the popularity of the revived Italian company as by any very nuanced curiosity as to what Mozart might contribute. Viennese opera was not prone to waiting for anyone during this period, and the count had other allies. It may have been hard to tell for Mozart month by month whether he was waiting to leap or being outgunned. One problem seems to have been how much input he wanted on the details of the action. After *Le nozze di Figaro* finally got off the ground, Leopold remarks sardonically in a letter to his daughter late in 1785 on how much running about and discussion will ensue before Mozart gets the libretto just right. Not much else explains how far he had earlier got with a further collaboration with the Salzburg poet Varesco who had proved so merely serviceable a librettist during their work together on *Idomeneo* for Munich, but who could reliably be cajoled into accepting the composer's demands. The general tone can be gleaned from the proposed opera's titular subject of a goose in Cairo.

Mozart may have sometimes doubted whether he would ever find the right vehicle to exploit all that he was learning and attaining, something that would let him make the most of the surrounding styles that he had been honing, and be elastic enough to feel like a release into a new creative space that could both enclose and outrun them all. Mooting projects and trying out ideas and writing arias for concerts or other people's operas may have some-times felt like being in a laboratory with no way out. Towards the end of August 1784 he went to the premiere of a new opera by Paisiello which Joseph had commissioned for the Burgtheater. He was exhausted that summer, so the occasion might have been perilous even if questions of operatic success and direction had not been so drastic for him, and the fact that he liked and admired Paisiello probably added to the event's charge. During the performance a sudden fever hit Mozart, soaking his clothes through with sweat. A severe illness followed in which fits of violent vomiting featured, and there were almost daily visits from rather a distinguished doctor.

Slowly he recovered, but the episode suggests the heady levels of need and release that opera raised in him.

The eventual opera is among other things an outpouring of what it had been like to have it waiting within him; it is densely energetic but full too of a calm determination to burnish every moment of its own unfolding. Probably only Wagner's highest fusions of grandeur with miniaturism carry musical surfaces as packed and teeming as *Le nozze di Figaro* would eventually present to the ear. The nimble richness of its orchestration and its anthological inclusiveness of vocal styles and genres, and its structural combinations of solidity and flexibility, all carry the force of years spent waiting to write a comic opera while keeping on with kaleidoscopically diverse other pieces. Rhythms and reference points come in and out of light, quick focus while instrumental colours move in bursts and patterns around the sound-world. All this almost bewildering mobility of sound and drama is inseparable from a gigantic sense of artistic purpose and formal equipoise; so what prevails is the most bizarre high-temperature fusion of anarchy and restfulness. Mozart's new opera is in effect emblazoned with the richness of the process by which he had for years worked his way towards it, one that had combined an extreme and sometimes fumbling openness to possibilities with a concentrated clarity of purpose. We get the joyful sense of an artist giving peace to himself by extending himself. One letter to Leopold from February 1784 is especially packed with the juggling of factors and choices that his artistic life involved, as a music publisher messes up a mail coach arrangement, and money is needed now and not later. But a certain uncanny high-handedness enters when he tells his father that Varesco's work on that later libretto has been too hurried, and reassures him that the music that he has been coming up with for it would make any amount of waiting and diligence worthwhile. Plenty of other operas may end up being performed by the time when this one is finished, but 'none of them will have a single idea resembling' anything from his. He guarantees it.

Purpose and resolution arise likewise in the plot of *Le nozze di Figaro* from within the most flighty twists of happenstance. Not long after it begins, the opera provides a manifesto for all the ways in which it weaves together cunning and artistry. Figaro and Susanna are preparing for their wedding, but she has just had to tell him how fully the count means to exert what he considers his erotic rights over her, controlling them both as he does as employees in his household. In response, Figaro's famous aria 'Se vuol ballare' goes far beyond any mere tirade against aristocratic vice and presumptuousness, announcing that he will make Count Almaviva dance to an altogether different music. The aria's energy comes from the way in which this valet and Mozart's music stake everything on the character's inventive intelligence as he faces up to autocratic power. He can no more confront it directly than music can change the world at a stroke or describe it point by point; but he can deflect and undermine it. Later we realize how much he must and can rely on Susanna too, as the opera's dramatization of intelligence broadens, and flows away from him. But here swirling questions of historical change and moral reform pivot momentarily on whether an aria can make a valet's cunning seem equal to a grandee's social standing. Music like this has to show how vividly it knows what cunning and acuity are. No completely clear break was ever on offer in Mozart's world from the paradigm of something close to feudal service in Salzburg to a more mobile, entrepreneurial professional lifestyle. A musician like him could mingle with starry freedom among the rich and the most powerful, while knowing that the status of a servant might still be waiting beneath it all. Figaro's aria proposes that it is precisely from a rebellious servant's perspective that this world can be grasped, and reinterpreted. Mozart's was a patchwork life now, and his opera is scrupulously frantic in its montage of styles and perspectives.

Figaro's basic metaphor in the aria is already musical. His threat to teach Almaviva a new sort of dance comes with a mocking promise to accompany him on a little guitar, and the idea is accompanied by plucking figures in the orchestral strings that mimic and amplify guitar sounds, as if the opera's musical substance is already following Figaro's imagination. The aria's freedom of shape and its sometimes prancing, sometimes nearly prosaic rhythms come from how finely its musical nerves are implicated in Figaro's search for lines of attack and mischief. Its music rises into a state of winking ardency on the crucial word 'saprò' as Figaro declares how deeply he 'knows' his world, and then it slyly hushes itself as he repeats the cautionary word 'piano', telling himself to keep quiet about how fully he sees through it. The aria moves between a sense of scheming musical bustle and sudden bright jabs of wit in the phrasing of the winds, in ways that again both mimic and energize Figaro's jabbing intelligence as he plans how he will fence with and sting and mock the count. Changes of pace and switches of phrasing almost entirely replace melody as ways of carrying expression forwards; the singer has to leap up to the odd high note as if propelled by the vividness of thought alone.

Figaro is a trickster to the second power; his adversary has his own schemes but Figaro will turn them inside out. So the music becomes a trickster itself, and teases and probes the conventions of its world as dancingly as Figaro does his employer's velleities and weaknesses. Figaro's metaphors of dancing come laden with the courtly values that he is arraigning, and the aria's playfulness is the very vehicle of its declaration of war. The aria's allusive, pastiche ceremoniousness gets mixed together with the dashing patter rhythms of comic musical style, and then the whole thing gets pumped up with a dramatic opulence redolent of *opera seria*. If Figaro's caustic assault on the count's grandeur can be heard in this richness of style, the parody flips over into something like its opposite too, because we can also hear in its copious means the aria's affirmation of just how much what he is singing about matters. All the arts of trickery, layering and decoding that Figaro summons resound in the fabric in which he and the drama have their being. We have moved into a new sphere of selfhood and agency, one where even being a person requires artistry and machination and invention. By the time oboes and bassoons join the strings for a recapitulation of the opening phrases, we know that this music is not just artful; it is setting out a new vision of art defined by subterfuge and multiplicity.

Da Ponte's sprightly, suave personality mixed wilfulness with restless charm in ways that doubtless tickled the composer. His eagerness and resilience come across in the bouncy solidity that he gives to the words of their operas. But all this both enabled and responded to the continual fate of displacement that his life seems to have invited, and in the end some uneasy underlying intuitions about their shared world must have joined the two men. Their friendship had something conspiratorial about it. Something mordant and wayward likewise criss-crosses the finesse of an aria like Figaro's. In the era of adventurers and disguises and imbroglios that his librettos did so much to crystallize, Da Ponte's own career was one of the strangest and most inventive around. He was at different times a priest, a court poet and a more or less professional gambler; early in the next century he ended up pursuing a double vocation in New York as a grocer and the first professor of Italian literature at Columbia University.

Da Ponte was an incorrigible blagger and a specialist in wild resentments as well as a brilliant talent. In his memoirs he winningly avoids imagining that anyone might have the least doubt about its runs of finely turned and casually self-mythologizing anecdotes. Maybe inviting scepticism was the key to the secret pleasure of ignoring it. Da Ponte keeps having the best lines, and the prettiest lady friends, and the most mean-spirited and tenacious enemies. The book is exuberantly sketchy, maybe because writing librettos had taught him how enlivening cursoriness can be. Few autobiographies can give as unworried a sense as his of how lightly the course of a life can change. In any case he was the right person to work alongside Mozart in changing opera, in filling it with inner variegation and an oddly light-hearted capacity to argue with itself. Mozart's three operas with him sketch a moment of uncanny historical equilibrium, in which a culture's most radiant achievements merge with its deepest critique of itself. We have been trying to recapture such equilibrium ever since. Maybe their meeting showed what the philosopher Hegel a generation or so later, as the results of the revolution in France churned around him, would call the cunning of history.

16

A Happy Change in the Nature of Lament

'Dove sono i bei momenti', Le nozze di Figaro

In the third act of *Le nozze di Figaro*, we listen again as a woman stands alone on stage and laments. But unlike Ilia in *Idomeneo*, the Countess Almaviva is all too at home in the life that is devastating her. So much hurtling comic bustle fills the later opera that it is possible to forget for stretches the amounts of expressive intensity and moral ardour undergirding the fizziness, and animating it. But then there are points when they burst through with searing clarity. The countess's aria 'Dove sono i bei momenti' draws on one of the grandest traditions of lament that poetic culture offers: those opening words translate the Latin phrase 'ubi sunt' that came to label a huge lineage of expressions of regretful memory. The question repeated by this phrase and its variants through centuries of lyric poetry is the simple, awful one of where the past has disappeared to. It keeps being asked because it has no answer, or because its answer is everywhere and nowhere. Our lives today are always filled with what by tomorrow will have become the snows of yesteryear. The countess's first consolation in this aria is in the sheer opulence with which she attaches it, and herself, to an enduring tradition of feeling and expression. But this richness is complicated by the new dimensions that Mozart adds to lament. He and the countess reiterate but also transform it, turning complaint and pathos into sources of change and action.

Questions of nationality often made the most noise in the period's operatic debates, but the status of comedy was the big artistic dilemma, one that intersected trickily with more overtly political concerns. *Opera seria* had made Italian opera a force that swept the continent. But as the vocal extravagances that *seria* style released had turned ever more exuberant and liquid, so they had contributed to the general lightening of musical texture that made *opera buffa* such a friskily appealing rival as the century continued. Vienna's tug-of-war during the early 1780s between German and Italian versions of opera was caught up in changes and uncertainties across the culture as the new comic trends challenged, in status and sheer artistic level as well as popularity, the long-standing primacy of the *seria* vision. *Seria* and *buffa* tendencies had been vying diffusely for pre-eminence in centres like Vienna for decades already, and one sign of the shifting times was how the standard of singing seems to have improved over this period among those specializing in *buffa* roles. Music had a vocation for lightness in the late eighteenth century. The intensity of their feel for this lightness was joined in Mozart and Haydn by a determination to use it to generate new sorts of heft and structure.

Joseph started calling for Italian opera to be reinstalled at the heart of his capital's culture not long after Mozart's German-language triumph in 1782 with *Die Entführung aus dem Serail*, and by this point the *buffa* mode was bound to dominate. Perhaps his taste had been loyal to Italy all along. Experts in *buffa* prevailed within the cohort of fashionable singers that Orsini-Rosenberg was tasked with wrangling, whereas the prima donna Antonia Bernasconi's famous but ageing powers were needed for the perpetually serious music of Gluck. We know how devoted to comedy as a way of life Mozart could be, and we know how vastly serious he was in pursuing *buffa* prospects for his own operatic career at this point from the piles of librettos that he looked through for sparks worth setting. All the ripened tension of the eventual opera and of arias like the countess's lament is informed by these sessions spent sifting through options, weighing attempts at jocularity and lightness of touch, and shrugging his way to the next one. It is striking in fact how much ambivalence and wavering he showed in his attitude towards comic opera during the half decade or so that led to *Le nozze di Figaro*. The idea of a hard border between serious and comic styles remained powerful; without some sympathy with the urge to keep them hygienically separate, Mozart might not have been able to hybridize them so tellingly. A more absolute *buffa* conversion would not have let him stay loyal to some idea of German opera for as long as he did. We know that *Le nozze di Figaro* was on its way, so we can see how much amplitude his take on *buffa* trends would gain from these years of oscillating between their intense appeal and variegated doubts.

The countess's aria comes at a pivotal moment in the opera's second half and may be the point in the drama where his ambivalence about comedy and his loyalty to other artistic drives surface most searingly. But the same rich ambivalence impels the richly flickering orchestration throughout, as the work fills out, slides away from and complicates its own pulsing comic rhythms. In the end this ambivalence about comedy is itself part of the highest reaches of comedy as they are discovered by the opera. Comedy here proves its reach and seriousness by proposing itself as a question to itself; it keeps seeming to have been driven beyond itself, but then whatever new place it reaches keeps turning out to be at least slightly comical too. Mozart's characters shift their understandings of one another and their ideas for what to do next in ways that are hectically funny but that also turn fun into an engine of interrogation, something with sharp edges and links to bewilderment and disaster.

The qualities of volatility and caprice that had come to suffuse Italian vocal music had pushed towards the comic not because they had nothing serious to say, but because they needed more changeable, nimble landscapes on which to extend themselves. In *Le nozze di Figaro* comedy does not just allow seriousness but drives it. Maybe one thing that feeds the opera is Mozart's reflection on his own role as an artist at this moment of attainment, and achieved powers. He was a professional entertainer whose audiences wanted music to amuse, to change, to shimmer. Becoming a freelance in Vienna had meant all the more devotedly embracing fashion, diversion and transience. Fun was a serious business partly because it was a business, but he also wanted to use its own drives to pursue new and high ideas for his art. In *Le nozze di Figaro* two elements of his identity combine, and they grow by challenging each other. As he worked on it, he could look back on what was coming close to half a decade spent in grappling with and exploiting the big city's demands and pleasures. Was he having fun or submerged in serious labour as he composed it? Pleasure is being created moment by moment as the hand pours out notes; but the stakes are large, the craft is meticulous and the concentration is intense. An urge to monumentality and flights of *sprezzatura* alike were vital to Mozart's character, and they merge in this opera. He seems to have spent several months on and off composing it, not the six weeks that Da Ponte claims. It is hard to know how old Mozart thought himself at the age of thirty, after years as a major composer famous for being young.

No one could come up with this opera's epitome of the comic who was not deadly serious about laughter. At the same time nothing could be such an epitome if its seriousness overwhelmed its comedy or blocked it. The opera was a timely project at a time when the more pushily serious forms that had traditionally hoarded moral legitimacy were buckling, though the eighteenth century generally was never sure whether it wanted comedy to undo the solidities of the past or to reinstate them in newly flexible versions that might also prove all the more tenacious. The twist at the heart of the countess's aria comes with Mozart's discovery that the dynamism within aria form could mesh with the dynamic moral drama that he wanted from comedy. Her aria asks precisely whether the comic universe of sweet moments and shared pleasures is real or enduring. Likewise, the story that the opera takes from the controversial French play was dazzlingly right as a vehicle for the composer because of how acutely it pulls at the contradictions within the machinery of comic narrative. Comedies are meant to be both happy and fun, and the trouble is that these two qualities do not fit as well as we may want to think. Mischief and mishaps may make a comedy fun while threatening its characters' happiness; the more forcefully or zanily they pursue happiness, the more elusive it may revel in being.

Comedies are of course generally light and humorous, but the essence of the genre lies in its one big narrative convention whereby a couple is brought together and reaches the presumptive haven of marriage. However *Le nozze di Figaro* does not bring Susanna and Figaro together as a couple, but is set on their wedding day, and shows how they stick together as a couple through some giddily distinctive versions of the travails of such an occasion. As Susanna is the countess's maid and confidante, Count Almaviva's preoccupation with bedding her on her wedding night trespasses especially offensively on his wife's domain. The count's desire that brought bliss to his wife's past is responsible now for her despondency in the present; the eroticism that drives comedic narrative is threatening to mangle it. Weddings are meant to resolve the plots of comedies, but the count wants to use this one to affront his own marriage. Of course this also lets it finally become an occasion that brings the count and the countess back to each other as a couple, as if they too are being married by this story. The countess and Susanna put together a plot whereby they switch identities by cover of night as the opera's deviously idyllic final act unfolds, and the wayward aristocrat is led back to his wife through the lust by which he meant to betray her. Early in 1786 Mozart reached the age of thirty; finding the right place for lament in a life may have increasingly interested him. He had been married for a smattering of years now too, enough time for continued fidelity to have come to seem at least as compelling a topic as the flying of initial erotic sparks.

The two marriages at stake in this wedding are as intimately involved with each other as the members of many a couple. It is a version of comic narrative that doubles down on the genre's meanings, and the opera's layers of musical invention respond in detail to the force of this doubling of narrative consciousness. The opera and its characters must reframe in packed detail what they think things like comedies and marriages are, and this evidently liberated Mozart to pour into its music every iota of his determination to rethink opera. He was helped here by how loosely the *buffa* genre is attached to these classical narrative conventions; its closeness to more scabrous types of satire and its sometimes pantomimic ideas of character and action feed the opera's drastic freedom of manoeuvre.

If the countess turns out to be tough and smart enough to change her life's direction, it is partly because through her aria she finds such forces in the very music that surrounds and makes her. Her determination to squeeze her situation for all its depths and possibilities makes her a stand-in for the composer. Mozart's fitful quest for the right operatic vehicle was at last issuing in momentous action, and the merger within his own creativity of extremes of reflectiveness and energy produces an aria that marries expressive force to a sort of sumptuous stillness.

Let us turn to the probing of aria form by which Mozart makes all this happen. The process is subtle and works in close conjunction with the gradients of aria form that had come to seem all but natural, because he wants to convince us that we are witnessing the inner life of an actual psyche, rather than artifice. So the whole process has three fairly pared-down units by which to achieve its effects. The countess meditates on her troubles in a brief but overwhelmingly cogent recitative before the aria itself emerges and unfurls its two singular parts; the action is given the slowness of honey in an andantino which is then precipitously followed by an urgently bubbling allegro section. Vital are the two highly geared points of transition afforded by this very simple three-part structure, first as recitative moves into aria and then as the tricklingly decelerated andantino slides into the allegro. It is at these points of formal change that moral change emerges.

Mozart had long been at the forefront of a trend towards increasing the dramatic momentum that binds recitative and aria together; we witnessed something similar in *Idomeneo*. He loads the recitative here with such forceful musical phrasing and weaving expressive heft that we are already deep within the countess's character before the aria itself quietly begins to soar out. The recitative is accompanied with full orchestration rather than on the keyboard alone, but the opulent texture points up the raggedness of her emotions as she runs through everything besetting her. It is as if some extreme musical largesse has found itself adrift in a narrow, meanly comic story. The rhythms are fitful and dominated by stops and starts that lead nowhere, and the vibrant orchestral colours feel hemmed in by the countess's search for perspective. The break into her exquisite lament does not then feel like some mere operation of the conventions, or like a way of switching between her narrative situation and the inner life responding to it. Rather, it is a dramatic aspect of her character. Escaping into memory turns out to be a feature of her soul's landscape that the form glidingly reveals.

The psychological analysis illuminates more than just the countess. As the soprano floats her vocal line over the hushed orchestration of the andantino section's opening, the reflectiveness of her sadness comes to reveal something like the psychic life of aria form itself. The revelation is acute partly because the opera keeps examining what aria form most deeply means, as if both exhilarated and baffled by the power of the procedure at its own heart. So when Cherubino sings his little poem about love in the second act, the set piece does not just delight us and describe him. It also serves as an almost hilariously acute but also tensely poignant summary of the most recycled elements from the world of Italian librettos, of their feelings of fire and ice and trembling, and their images of mountains and flowers and fountains. Finally we get the gorgeous playfulness with which Susanna's serenade in the last act treats the very question of what it means to sing to someone. She has to pretend to be enticing the count into some amorous expedition in the garden, as the opera's twists and disguises move towards their climax. She sings with a delicate ardour that is really meant for her new husband Figaro, but she is also willing for him to draw the wrong conclusion as he listens in. Mozart's music here fairly shimmers with his determination to show us in Susanna a woman whose passionate sensuousness is matched by acuity and a complex, resolute wholesomeness. Her aria is packed with slyness and misdirection because she is discovering and revealing how complex it is for a woman to have a voice at all.

The andantino section of the countess's aria shows that singing can mean pathos; it does so with singular purity and sweetness. But the next discovery for us and for her is that it can also mean power and audacity and tense moral purpose. The second transition, the one from the andantino to the aria's brisk and determined closing allegro, demonstrates that the beauty of the countess's lament has not just lulled or consoled her. Eighteenth-century opera overflowed with lamenting women, but generally their main consolation was the musical power of their sadness, at least until the conventional happy ending showered happiness around the stage just in time for the applause. The countess's andantino makes 'memoria' its keyword, but as the allegro gathers its sense of urgency and renewal, the crucial word becomes 'speranza' instead. She propels herself from memory to hope by making hope emerge from memory. Somehow the change had been secreted within the mood of lament all along; the aria's largest argument is that beauty brought to such a pitch already contains powers of psychic renewal and moral illumination. So the rich textures that bind the two sections together make her seem to have been gathering resolve to reclaim her happiness throughout her lament for its destruction. The woodwinds that multiplied the feeling of songful tone during the andantino now assume, in the allegro, a sort of chattering and pushy exuberance that upholds her renewal of purpose. It also links the aria back into the opera's overall heightening momentum. The countess is ready to rejoin her world.

New sorts of dynamism and restlessness were the motors of Mozart's style, and the sense of tension and momentum that he gives to the countess's lamenting voice helps bring her towards change. Maybe the double nature of singing is what stands before us here and sings its heart out, in the person of the countess. A vocation for pathos and lament is often linked within singing to its powers of delight and construction. The eighteenth century teems with arias in which characters sound off about woe and fragility and perdition in music that is confident, vivacious, sovereign. Blighted declarations of loss and anguish fill operas that are invitations to pleasure and psychic growth. Within the countess's gathering lament, her first listeners may have caught premonitions of the basic fact that the eighteenth century and its cornucopia of vocal music would have to end. To sing the part requires a fine and strenuous technique; it is as if the aria's broad sweeps were meant to sketch some ample experiential openness that we may all have come to need since then to aspire to.

At the start of May 1786 the Burgtheater gave the opera a glitzy opening night, as summer gathered. The packed theatre seems to have been swept by a weird mixture of spontaneous rapture, confusion at Mozart's originality and organized dislike from claques driven by the city's operatic rivalries. Connoisseurs called for many arias to be encored but, at least according to one report, louts in the uppermost gallery hissed obstreperously. Mozart's sense of creative release in the opera came from the doubled, layered, multiple perspectives on his society that it opened up. Perhaps much was apt about this mixed and intricate response. It is an opera that brings slanting mixtures of tenderness and laceration to its treatment of its own world, and one whose own insights often come in disguise. The equilibrium that it offers between fun and seriousness is so opulent because both are carried to such extremes, and it cannot have been entirely clear to Vienna whether it was witnessing the peak of Italian levity or its subtly drastic repudiation. Comedy may be meant to be a transient art, but then transience raises deep feelings. The countess's aria at once unpicks these contradictions and holds them together.

The countess may limn the composer most closely in the way in which her aria swings between a basic drive to give intense musical pleasure and the desire to revolutionize meanings. Strange things happen when a character and a creator get under each other's skin in the ways that Mozart and she do. His artistry gives her vividness and audacity which flow back into his music, powered by what he is discovering about character and morality by making the countess so alive. She is deep inside her feelings and can also turn them inside out; she is a devoted part of a stately world which she can also lacerate and transcend, and of course she is also a singer who doubtless has her own slants on these matters. An Italian soprano called Luisa Laschi with an impressive cosmopolitan reputation was the countess in the original Viennese production, and must have brought a sweeping sense of artistic power and large horizons. Mozart gives his audience what it wants more exactly and deeply than anyone else could, but he also shows the forces of revelation and change that those desires opened it to. He could have used the period's 'da capo' conventions of circular aria form and brought the andantino section back to be restated finally after the allegro. But the countess has finished lamenting; she is ready to act.

III

17

Creating Freedom

Don Giovanni

Moving to the big city in search of fortune or a decent job is one of modern culture's great, fraught stories. All the expansive enticements that take someone to the metropolis also mean that life there is churning, proliferating and uncontrollable. Mozart never completely settled in Vienna; being settled was not the point of how he lived. During his decade or so as a resident, he changed his residence more than annually on average. An especially brisk series of haphazard, or hapless, domiciles marked the period early in the 1780s when he was extracting himself from his Salzburg life and moving towards marrying Constanze. He called one of the lodgings that he fell into during these months the 'rat's cellar'. Stranger still is the frequency with which he and Constanze kept moving throughout their marriage. It can be hard to follow the logic of some of these moves, and oscillating finances and the city's unsteady economy can only explain some of the couple's restlessness.

The couple moved in April 1787 from the affluent setting of the Camesina House right in the thick of central Vienna to a house with a garden much further from the hubbub. In December they then decided to move back to the centre. Perhaps the Austrian winter brought out the drawbacks of suburban living. Mozart seems still to have been paying rent on the garden house well into the next year though, either because he was in arrears or because he had signed a lease with an unhelpful clause or two. In June 1788 they again moved out to a more suburban setting, the Alsergrund district. Six months later they moved to a flat back in the thrum of the centre, albeit one in which they did then manage to stay put for a couple of years or so. But it is hard not to conclude that restlessness itself was a big part of these shifts, as if Mozart's peripatetic past had left its residue in some indelible taste for change, a hunger for new views out of different windows. Money was an endless factor, but it is likely that his precarious finances were actually sometimes worsened by such gyrations.

Scholars and biographers argue over just how successful Mozart was throughout this period. He seems to have managed to be massively acclaimed without ceasing to be prey to constant uncertainties and setbacks. Probably he did not know whether to think of himself as successful either. In some moods renting somewhere swanky might have seemed a good investment, a way of persuading the right people that he was on the upswing; it may also have been a way of persuading himself that some nice possibilities of income were bound to become solid. The promises of success within a place like 1780s Vienna are so heady and fluid that threats of failure become their inevitable backdraught; but at the same time failure may seem ever more unbearable and grotesque, unless it starts to seem instead a possible source of relief from the cavalcade of promises. Appearing successful is often asked to come before being so. Would he get more out of the relative seclusion that would help concentrated work or the city swing that brought audiences and students and other stimulations close? Either way gyration seems to have been one of the deep laws of musical invention for Mozart; often it is what gives the large, smooth vistas of order in his works their plangency and tension. He still travelled a fair amount during these later years too, and he mulled over opportunities elsewhere that he never came close to taking up. During the last few years of his life England beckoned, burnished by Haydn's apotheoses there and indeed the general Anglomania that was oddly prominent in Vienna's landscape of fashions. A camp follower of the epochally glamorous Prince of Wales called Thomas Attwood turned up in the city and became a Mozart devotee; in 1787 the composer even embarked on improving his English skills with a teacher who was a fellow Freemason. Nothing came of it all.

A generation or so later, Beethoven seems to have been even more addicted to hopping around among Viennese residences than the dead master whose music set his templates. The restlessness that kept pointing Mozart beyond Vienna also meshed with the unsettled rhythms that life in the city was taking on. It was within the textures of the capital's urban life that an oncoming modernity began to make itself most deeply felt in the Habsburg world. Vienna's housing market was a place where the large social forces underlying the capital's busy surfaces could make them wobble and buckle; the result was a city where living conditions generally were cramped, improvisatory and fluctile. Handwritten notices advertising rooms or whatever else to rent within could be seen on the doors of many of the city's houses; the handwriting was often abominable, and doubtless this sometimes prefigured the conditions inside. Money seemed to be waiting to be made in property, either by simply packing people in, or by a few brave whirls of experiment in up-dated and luxurious design. Not long after their marriage, the couple lived for a while in the Trattner building that had just been established as a grand commercial experiment in new styles of urban living; the brilliant entrepreneur behind it was friendly with the composer and yet another fellow Freemason. We would now call its sleek spaces designer apartments, and they nestled among retail sites related to Thomas von Trattner's other schemes. Mozart kept using its smart facilities for concerts long after moving his household to less plush surroundings.

Buildings and their interiors were changing, and so were the streets outside. Mozart's appetite for amusement and novelty was suited to the ceaseless alterations and innovations among the theatres and street entertainments that formed a famously lively part of Vienna's fabric. Commercial life in the capital was going through what were sometimes flamboyant transitions. The giddy beginnings of a bourgeois business culture stimulated thoughts of big show-business profits, but they were seldom sustainably forthcoming, and the right legal frameworks had not yet developed to encourage really large-scale attempts. Faces and stories and songs came and went day by day as a result; expert types of artistry or showbusiness merged blurrily with the more highbrow ends of busking and even vagrancy. Vienna was literally buzzing with a street culture of endless and virtuosic humming and whistling, as if some ongoing act of casual mass music-making was the substance of civic togetherness. If spectacular public executions still enthralled parts of the populace, jollier and more progressive fads like the one for demonstrations of ballooning thrived too. Mozart's music stands at the edge of all this street life and listens in, sometimes chiming with its cacophonous bustle, sometimes reacting against it with its own avenues of forceful harmoniousness.

Following his alterations of fortune and opportunity over this period can feel like coming across a weirdly succinct prediction of how the modern world has proceeded to treat many of its citizens. Splendid pleasures and grand opportunities come and go for Mozart amid a nexus of complex debts, intense status insecurity and the perpetual threat of actual immiseration. His sensitivity to the latter danger seems to have been far more acute than the reality was ever imminent, but this carries its own hints of disequilibrium. Succeeding is seldom a straightforward success for anyone of much talent and ambition, and Mozart had to survive not just the disappointment when things went badly or prospects collapsed but the possibility that even his attainments would feel evanescent or vacuous. Applause is a lifeblood for performing artists that their own bodies cannot contain; it keeps draining away and never clots, all of which is one reason why the performing arts have been such signal gauges of modern experience and culture. Ceaseless volatilization has turned out to be the heart of modern living. All the big stories about political progress or industrialization or the chunky march of science and technology just get churned in.

Mozart's music can feel all but drunk on its own volatility; elsewhere it can feel so committed to finality and steadiness that every note seems to slot into a place carved by permanence itself. Contemporaries describe him flipping as he works or performs between silent states of high concentration and sudden fits of flushed impatience or merry teasing, or distracted humming, as if change was the bloodstream of his creativity. Lorenzo Da Ponte and the composer's father both stress his impulsiveness and moodiness. Friedrich Schlichtegroll's important obituary from 1793 says that even his looks were filled with mutability; the composer's expression 'changed every moment, but indicated nothing more than the pleasure or pain which he experienced at the instant'. Boldness, flightiness and unprecedentedness are again and again the impressions of those who hear him perform, as if he had ushered them into sheer possibility. The keyboard concerto that we will end up concentrating on here is one of his most far-reaching attempts to bear witness to his own creative freedom. But it is this because it knows that freedom needs to pin itself down in the end, and because it uncovers the clarity and force required to do so.

Mozart composed *Don Giovanni* in 1787 during the second period of accelerated house moves, at a time when his life teemed with questions about the success of the previous few years. In Giovanni's compulsion to seduce or to conquer women, Mozart finds a bleakly vibrant correlate to his own will to artistic power, one that shows freedom and compulsion to be sometimes less opposites than terrifyingly near neighbours. Giovanni's opera does not have much of a story, partly because he is so determined that his life should keep repeating back to him his one great aim. But it is clear from the opening action, in which he fights and kills the father of the latest object of his attentions, how fully the life of this seducer is steeped in violence. The darkly raw opening sounds of the overture said so already.

By the end of the first act efforts to track Giovanni down are becoming unsteadily mixed in with his quest for pleasure, as a party gathers at his grand residence. Giovanni sets the act's finale going with a raucously unsettling toast to liberty. He sings 'Viva la libertà' and so invokes, as authority or cover for his tumultuous pleasures, the word with which the eighteenth century sought to sum up all its vistas of emancipation and change. The seducer is becoming a quarry, and now he calls up liberty with a drastic vigour that turns febrile, since all that his cry is actually inaugurating is an aristocrat's exploitative masquerade. Was some spirit of social reinvention afoot within the mask wearing that so coloured sophisticated merriment in the eighteenth century, or did it point to destructive drives of concealment or erasure? Giovanni turns an idealistic rallying cry into a mere starting pistol for a hedonism that may just cloak pure aggression. But the music cannot help giving his toast infectious aplomb; it is as if all the ambivalence held within the century's emancipatory projects emerges in a flash of blasted clarity. The word 'liberty' breaks open and releases things that the culture's optimism strained to contain, on one hand a blaze of malicious privilege, and on the other a stark existential pathos. Mozart raises the stakes by pressing a caustically public and military flavour on the music. The politics of freedom would not find another such musical reckoning until the Sex Pistols song reinterpreted anarchy nearly two hundred years later.

Is modern freedom at root a reckless attempt to make aristocratic licence available to all? The idea of liberty danced through the eighteenth century like one of its beloved harlequins. To some it promised pleasure and to others power. To others still it promised tolerance, or free speech with all its brilliant or lacerating entailments, or a political constitution capable of generating virtue. Jefferson thought that it was what joined life to the pursuit of happiness; at the century's end the tricolour would promise liberty or death as it waved through the battlefields of the revolutionary French. Always there was the libertine standing watchfully by, ready to swallow liberty whole. Giovanni is either the dazzling, awful foretaste of a coming world of virtuosic individualism, or a blank space vampirically dependent on what surrounds him. Being tied to Salzburg had made Mozart want freedom. Now in Vienna he had to live it out day by day, and to chase ways of being tied down by deals and schedules. Sociologists describe how modern life forms itself out of the loosening or scrambling of fixed social roles, and Mozart's freelance life had to feed on bits of the versions of patronage and social and institutional hierarchy that surrounded him. The past is not abolished by modern freedoms; it gets broken up and repurposed in ways whose unpredictability can itself be oppressive. *Don Giovanni* treats its kinetic, dissolvent protagonist with music that is old-fashioned in style. Mozart's version of creative freedom never claims to come from nowhere; it scans and presses its surroundings for whatever juices of expression and structure they can yield.

Releasing *Le nozze di Figaro* into the world during the previous year must have felt like a culmination and a justification of his freelance years so far. During the carnival season early in 1786 when this first collaboration with Da Ponte was coming together, the composer presented himself at a masked ball with a brio not much less hectic than Giovanni's toast to liberty, dressing as an exotic sage and handing out a sheet featuring word games and philosophical one-liners that was eventually partly published in a newspaper in Salzburg after he sent a copy back to Leopold. His coursing eagerness is joined here as so often to something waggishly uncanny. Insight and playfulness meet in the published aphorisms as they do in his music; Mozart forever wavered between drives of provocation and charm. 'I prefer an open vice to an equivocal virtue; it shows me at least where I am.' The aphorism that says so has a nicely equivocal sense of balance itself, though. In another he says that it 'is not seemly for everybody to be modest'; it is only greatness that is up to it. Badmouthing her rivals is the 'surest and most tender' way of praising a woman, but Mozart adds that the same is true for plenty of men; the little psychology of praise here may be rooted in his own psyche. The question of what to do about rich idiots doubtless exercised him often enough, but here he just says that they should go into property. Mozart's version of free thinking here is hardly ground-breaking and sometimes vaporous, but it is mainly both merry and jumpy, and he is nicely lucid about the uses of opacity and masquerade. Puzzles may appeal most to those who are puzzles. Labelling the lines as fragments from Zoroaster linked them to the same ancient Iranian thinker whose name would inflect the figure of Sarastro in *Die Zauberflöte* a few years later. Nietzsche took his Zarathustra from the same lineage a century or so later; but then links of all sorts can suggest themselves between Mozart and that thinker devoted to music and to the lightness to be found on the far side of the tragic.

In *Le nozze di Figaro* erotic partnership is the prism through which modern freedom examines itself. The new versions of selfhood and togetherness being invented by Susanna and Figaro weave in and out of the aristocratic world that the two of them still inhabit, sometimes faithfully, often mockingly and sometimes ruefully. Mozart's music cannot settle accounts finally with the society around it; it is one reason why at its greatest it so often does not know whether to laugh or to cry. His operas are desperate to please and to succeed, while setting themselves artistic tasks that go far beyond what the culture knew how to reward. Sometimes they appear casually defiant, often serenely confident. The singer Michael Kelly had two small roles in the first production, and a few decades later recalled in a memoir a sense of giddy resplendence that suffused the composer as the premiere neared. It is as impossible to describe the presence of Mozart's genius in full action 'as it would be to paint sunbeams', according to him; of course by then it was in Kelly's interest to extract plenty of hype from having worked with the composer directly. Describing the first full orchestral rehearsal towards the end of spring, he picks out the crimson cloak and the gold-laced cockaded hat that Mozart wore as he gave the time of the music from the stage. One aria makes the musicians cry out with praise; the violinists beat their bows against the music desks in such intense applause that Kelly thinks that it might all be endless. All the tensions of Mozart's multiple psyche seem here resolved for a long moment. Being treated like a valet had been one reason for chafing so vehemently at Salzburg's reins; now he had written a masterpiece about a valet who outmanoeuvres a count, and his appearance was that of a natty dandy riffing on themes of aristocratic apparel.

The opera was immediately recognized as a masterpiece, but the broad public in Vienna only took to it later. At its first outing there were connoisseurs who loved it and claques apparently organized by operatic rivals to besmirch its reception. By early in 1787 it was clear that the real operatic smash of the period was a piece called *Una cosa rara* by one Vincente Martín y Soler. Da Ponte had written that libretto too, and some complex mutual teasing must be at work between Mozart and his collaborator when Giovanni's manservant Leporello is revealed as a big fan of the thing, as the second-act finale of *Don Giovanni* begins. The musicians hired by Giovanni to play in his dining room are running through a few hits from the *buffa* stage which finally include one from *Le nozze di Figaro* itself. Although Leporello is busily snatching food from his boss's lavish supper, he takes the trouble to remark that he is all too familiar with this number.

Mozart must often have felt uncertain whether his works had really landed in his world; but then there was pride in writing music that did not know its place. The trouble with freedom is that it can leave a person floating. During the winter between these two great operas the composer organized a small run of subscription concerts which seem to have been a bit desultory by his standards. One piece that seems to have been written for these concerts at the end of 1786 is the K503 piano concerto in C. Mozart had finally launched a major operatic statement after waiting for years to get the right chance, and then *Le nozze di Figaro* had hovered between success and failure. His new concerto mixes magnificence and slyness in ways that assert an increasingly complex argument about the place of creativity in the world. The two surrounding operas assault their audiences with dramatic and ethical challenges as well as delights. But the piano concerto has a bristling and meditative aloofness as it surveys the condition of imaginative and personal freedom that was now irreparably his. Freedom must hammer itself into the world as if through hard boards, so one side of this music is a bright, nearly brash stubbornness. It also requires quick shifts and subtle judgements, and the concerto is full of self-examination and manoeuvrability. If some of its passages hammer, elsewhere it moves in deft whispers. But this music is throughout less exuberant and pleasure-seeking than say the run of concertos that the first half of 1784 poured out, and is both more angular and more stately.

Those 1784 piano concertos had helped make the form Mozart's most consistent public vehicle in Vienna, a vessel into which he could keep pouring his artistry at its most intense and his love of giving pleasure. It was where his powers as a performer and as a composer most fluidly met. At the heart of all these factors and forces for him was the practice of improvisation, since improvisation was the slippery node that brought so many strands of his music-making together. Passages of fairly pure improvisation were typically how he most extravagantly wowed listeners, but during Mozart's century improvisational touches or adventures were also often meant to bring alive even the most carefully contrived works in performance, particularly where keyboard instruments were concerned. Musical scores were often less blueprints for exact realization than sets of suggestions, or of structures waiting to be filled out and embellished. Improvisation did not just perk up the performative moment, but was the oxygen without which much music could not be realized at all. Further, we can assume that for Mozart improvising was vital to the origins of much of his music, as well as to how it ended up being played. His was a musical culture where much was not codified and much not transcribed; sometimes all this made room for freedom and idiosyncrasy, and sometimes it just reflected or assured the unquestioned power of background norms.

Improvisation was one way in which eighteenth-century music was testing the ground for some approaching historical world of freedom. Performers who are improvising well must keep their nerves open to the promptings of freedom moment by moment, but so too to the oddly shifting requirements of clarity. At the same time improvising can bring a more biting awareness of the moods of an audience, and of how even surprising or surpassing the tastes and expectations of others may only mean meeting them all over again in the end. It can bring a sharp sense of how compulsive or limited an era's tastes and forms may be, and of how messing around with them may only confirm or refresh their constraints. An improvising musician may briefly feel as free as the sky, and then straightaway start feeling shackled by needing to incarnate freedom for others. Mozart's prowess as an improviser must have brought the most intensive education in the riptides within freedom. Did it feel like having to repeat, of all things, novelty itself?

During the year leading to the winter of the C major concerto, Mozart's great experience was composing in *Le nozze di Figaro* an opera that comprehensively enlarged the scale on which arcs of musical form could be asked to operate. It may have been this as much as any weariness with some cult of spontaneity that brought him then to write a piano concerto that seems determined to resist or to abrade the sparkly sorts of freshness of surface that his essays in the form had often relied on. The opera's second-act finale in particular weaves voices, stylistic perspectives and plot twists together into a stretch of concerted musical and dramatic action all but deliriously in excess of the period's norms. Hearing it at the time must have felt like being drawn into some new and brimmingly expansive musical space, as if the audience's ears were swelling. The finale has a catamaran's flashy strength of movement, and the point is that a catamaran's builders do not improvise. At the same time Mozart would have known better than anyone how much structural intelligence lay deep beneath the foamy surfaces thrown off by his improvisational powers, and how many hours and years of analysis and doggedness. He had turned thirty during the previous winter, so he may have been ripe to write a concerto in which music turns its back on any hope that freedom, expression or pleasure might just come all at once on the kick of the moment. Freedom now wants more durable and capacious forms and styles, structures that can both extend it and house it.

The concerto's opening movement may accordingly be the grandest structure that Mozart ever wrote for the keyboard. The grandeur of the opening bars has something coldly exciting about it, as their sense of fanfaring definition establishes a strikingly stable sound-world. Something both rousing and slightly alienating comes here from the music's rhythmic flair and the bright blazes of orchestral colour. It only gradually becomes clear what larger purposes are being served by the almost rigid simplicity of the phrases and motifs thus set up, all of them studding a steady and supple harmonic backdrop. The clue to the extravagant subtlety on its way comes when the soloist makes an entry that is both somewhat belated and almost whisperingly downbeat. Maybe Mozart wanted to try reversing the kickstarting entry that he had given the soloist in the Jenamy concerto almost exactly a decade earlier. So here the keyboard joins in with a sort of fluid echo to the end of the orchestra's large arc of opening statements, as if introducing something hesitant or uncertain into the grand proceedings, before it even thinks about setting out any material of its own. During this period, the norm was for the solo keyboard to play along during the orchestral passages as a contributor to the general instrumental texture. So the actual solo entry is here reinterpreting how concertos work in a spirit both radical and sly. The soloist comes out from the surrounding orchestral splendour not by answering or confronting it, but by swerving away or stepping back from it. The big gestures of the opening music are reframed in a vein of meditative fantasy that leaves their structural clarity in place. An entry as stealthy as this has a high drama of its own, since we know what powers this instrument has to spare.

The movement's deep aim becomes to combine extreme structural stability with a tenderly digressive freedom of treatment. It wants to show how mutual freedom and structure can be. The movement is built out of basic phrases that are so dynamic precisely because they so largely lack character, consisting in an adroit selection of rhythms and pitches that can lend themselves to multiplying revisions without ever losing their recognizable shapes, or their capacity to support the overarching aim of monumentality. No protracted tune occurs across the whole movement, because melodic vivacity is not what Mozart here wants. Rather, the music works away at combining an overarching rigour with levels of inventiveness that dart as fluidly as a swallow's flight. It is tempting to think that the solid structure is set up by the orchestra in order to provide a stable environment for the solo instrument's virtuosic thrills. Passages in the concerto do work that way round, and the effulgent romantic tradition that took off from Mozart's concerto style during the nineteenth century makes it easy to think that we know what is meant to enable what in such works. But much in this movement especially works the other way round. The keyboard writing often mimics and reinforces the movement's elemental girders, while the orchestra breaks up into groups of winds or strings that play off and absorb the soloist's free phrasing.

Freedom here does not work as we might want or expect; maybe it would not be freedom if it did. Something both provocative and slippery emerges from the mood of understatement in which the piano first surfaces. The solo entry is a charged point in a concerto, but here a negative emphasis invests it, so that its force gets mixed in with a rueful and tricksy mutedness. Whereas the orchestra had been full of bright statements and fanfaring rhythms, the keyboard has a glancing, sardonic tenderness. A spirit of guileful acceptance and tenacious rethinking emerges; it then guides the soloist through the rest of the movement, or rather releases whoever plays the solo part to find a distinctive way through its opportunities for touch and phrasing. A free life does not abscond from fact and fate but recognizes and transforms their ceaseless impacts.

In one later passage a single phrase of eight notes is put through a sequence of variations so extensive and rigorous that something like a fugue suddenly seems close. But the variations follow on from one another with a concerto's sense of open argument and freedom of texture, as if to prove that new fusions of rigour and liberty are now possible. The basic phrase is almost parodic in its simplicity and symmetry, but it also carries divisions and irregularities within it capable of sustaining all but endless reworkings. Different instrumental groupings and different layerings of the phrase's little system of rhythms link and disjoin and combine kaleidoscopically. Whoever is playing the keyboard can work through possibilities of emphasis and interpretation with a freedom that is in some ways all the more exuberant because of the tautness and repetitiveness defining it. The playing can have an acerbity that verges on bleakness, or it can have colouristic flamboyance, or analytical acumen. Maybe the performer is freer here to derive mood or to imprint gesture than anyone improvising a whole musical substance often can, because here there is so much to draw on and to be held by. The improvisational aesthetic is turned on its head in ways that also gather in its gains and strengths. Mozart has come up with a passage that is all the more surprising because its elements could scarcely surprise anyone, but maybe this only lays bare the dialectic behind much of the cleverest improvisation. The more surprising the playing here becomes, the deeper this trick reaches.

Across much of the composer's music there is a source of drama that is brought to the surface both in this passage and at the point of the soloist's entrance. Mozart's feeling for stability and symmetry within each musical phrase was so extreme that he needed all his love of drama, momentum and transformation to allay it and to vie with it. Point by point, his pieces are made up of basic bits of stylistic material that hold their own orderliness and structure, while also flowing into the surrounding musical action. Freedom cannot be all on the side of drama and fluidity and movement. Rather, a piece like this wants to know and to show how to combine these kinetic, veering drives with a strenuously ample sense of balance. It is in this fusion that Mozart's deepest energies are released. He reaches in this concerto for a version of freedom full of structure and even reality itself. If the composer was moving out of a historical world freighted with tradition and hierarchy into one that was sometimes splendidly and sometimes anxiously fluid, his music shows the uses that freedom can put structure to. Phrase by phrase in this concerto, we hear proportion and ballast at their most measured connect with vertiginous drives of animation and change. Mozart's freedom is not thin air, but a bridge joining two worlds.

Is our world more or less free now than in the eighteenth century? Grotesque negations of freedom have infected both periods. We might say that Mozart shows freedom as something that needs to be composed; it cannot just be found or left to its own devices, and it cannot just be improvised. Musical improvisation and the sexual libertinism of Giovanni's off-stage counterparts were two ways in which courtly or aristocratic cultures blurred with the rising world of the bourgeoisie. The libertine and the improviser may share amiable or grim types of scepticism towards social norms, but they both enjoy playing with those norms too much to want to sweep them away too readily. Solitude may likewise seem to be their shared destiny, but so too they share a secret need to manipulate or to yield to the pleasures of others.

Freedom turns out in the C major concerto to be something that demands large shapes, requiring them in order to achieve new fusions between originality and convention. A mere couple of days after finishing the concerto, Mozart completed his so-called 'Prague' symphony, whose own first movement may be an even more emphatic vision of the sheer structural mass that he now wanted instrumental music to be capable of. In turn writing this piece made the somehow frisky monumentality in his great final trio of symphonies possible, a year and a half or so later. But there was no repeating the precise fusion achieved in this concerto. Mozart only wrote two more keyboard concertos before his death, and they are thinner creations. In the 1786 concerto, we seem to hear him sitting in a mood that is breezily implacable and determined, maybe even a touch barbed. Music is no longer being used to get anywhere or to win over others; it has become something like the body of freedom. The 'Prague' symphony gets its moniker from the Bohemian capital because it became linked with the popularity that festooned him there early in the new year, as *Le nozze di Figaro* continued its first outing beyond Vienna. *Don Giovanni* was commissioned on the back of the same waves of applause. At a concert there in the cold middle of January as he moved towards turning thirty-one, Mozart combined the symphony with keyboard improvisations that were so fervently received that he ended up extemporizing for more than thirty minutes. He was performing in the expansive and still shinily new surroundings of the same National Theatre where his operas were put on; an early biography claims that nothing ever packed the seats there as fully as this concert. Mozart never gave up on the pleasure of others. At its heights freedom recalls the other people that it always requires.

18

Convulsive Beauty

Don Giovanni

Is Giovanni Mozart? Da Ponte's quizzical inventiveness and Mozart's often stern formal poise combine to make the opera amazingly objective; it scrutinizes its protagonist's flowing charisma as vividly as it draws on it. *Don Giovanni* has a sometimes brutal clarity along with its sweeping density, and both are powered by lines of identification that run as if electrically between the composer and his character. Mozart knows Giovanni inside out; it is how he manages to remain finally unseduced. As Leporello sashays through his catalogue number, the music's spirit of charm and variousness and conquest becomes a disturbingly apt match for the seducer's. Mozart's own hunger for experience and kaleidoscopic psychic suppleness soak into the character like liquids drunk up by a sponge. Needing to breathe life into a new batch of opera characters, or girding himself to vanquish yet another concert audience, Mozart kept being faced with questions of his own appetite for others and of their appetites for him. Giovanni and he are bonded in the enigmas and ecstasies of desire, and doubtless in its downsides. At work too in making their bonds so intense, and the opera so molten, was the high heat of the changing historical world around Mozart. He forged this sleek and awful revision of himself within a context of flux and mutation.

One marker of a modern world is its addiction to describing itself. Mozart's period was pumped full with words about itself, in the ceaseless profusion of pamphlets or the burgeoning journalism business, or in all the educational and explanatory overdrive of the enlightenment and the satires and ripostes that kept following. Since then we have had the great novels of modern urban life or of the inner corridors of the self-conscious consciousness, and then all the feverish swagger of the industrial and broadcast media of the twentieth century, and their culmination in the desperate logorrhoea of the internet. But all these words disagree with one another, so that the only thing modernity has solidly been able to say about itself is that it is indeed modern. Things have changed and the world has been disenchanted and traditions have collapsed. No one can agree on what the past was, or on whether to mourn its passing or to dance on its grave, but the present is what we are stuck with and in. Breakage and change suffuse the modern, and all its other qualities are haphazard and up for grabs, churningly fugitive. We reach towards creative artists when we seek some grip on the modern, because creativity forever shifts its terms and reinvents its grounds; it is more or less what the word means. In the great tradition of modern French poetry that emerged through the likes of Baudelaire and Rimbaud many decades after Mozart's misadventures in Paris, modernness can be a delirious promise or a spectral debacle, or it can be a sort of absolute injunction. It is somehow both implacable and placeless; descriptions and explanations get pulled towards the glare of this vacuum, but none sticks.

Music like modernity is something that constantly both entices and evades description. Music was the great obsession of eighteenth-century Europe because it was the vehicle for that culture's mad love of itself, and its most sensitive barometer for its intuitions of onrushing change. Mozart's oeuvre resonates with the great descriptions of modernity offered by the generations following his, because social commentary and literary reflection had to catch up with the premonitions that music had long been having. The modern world would be seen as a backdrop for the march of liberal progress, or a theatre for experiments in extreme subjectivity, or an arena for the illuminations of science or the vast muscles of technology and mass industry. All these visions and more already flicker within Mozart's music, within its sometimes overwhelming confidence, its slippery impishness and its often fierce pathos. Choices and possibilities faced him with all their openness and blankness whenever he sat down to play or to compose, or to weigh ideas or plans. An artistry crammed with options lays richly bare how anyone can feel as the future rushes towards us, its whole force looming even while its face stays hidden. Mozart absorbed and honed trends and styles that had themselves absorbed vast amounts of the century, and soaked up vast amounts of its fantasies about what it could become.

In a world given over to modernization, power comes to those who can capture or tap its spirit without being overwhelmed by its riddles or its crushing energies. So Marx and Engels made communism the dominant dissident movement within modern politics by writing a manifesto that featured the most acute descriptions of modernization around. Within their vision, insolidity and flux are melting down the world, while at the same time brutal combinations of force and structure are driving the process on. A creative artist who wants to be modern must pursue a similar doubleness, picking through the hectic but fugitive surfaces of a changing world in search of new routes to beauty and permanence. Something like this happens in the basic machinery of Mozart's style, as he keeps making enduring, enchanting shapes out of the ways in which musical notes move forwards in time and disappear. His music obsessively rethinks the relations between evanescence and structure, as Manet did in the fusions of lavish pleasure and icy wit that his brushwork pulled out of the complex social changes of the middle of the nineteenth century, or as Warhol did a century or so on with his tough riffs on mass-market images in all their fluidity and stubbornness. Mozart's panache is no less dazzling because it is also desperate to shore up teetering stylistic unities, or to reassert a deep connection with an audience.

It would be hard to imagine an immersion more wholesale than the composer's in the variety and volatility that some dreams and some nightmares of modernity evoke. As he played within shifting settings and milieux, he had to size up audiences and collaborators and instruments and acoustics and levels of applause and the states of his own nerves. His music became a roving set of antennae to investigate each place and the people listening or not within it. No skin separated music from its social world. Brilliant or tedious talk swung around a performer at salons; it may have been at its most distracting when it tried to be about the music. Chatter, flirtation and card games tried not to find the music too distracting in the period's opera houses. Those listening intently or hanging around at the performances of someone like Mozart would typically have been the people most plugged into the news of the world. The responses that his music got, and the sounds that it made as it moved among flickering decor and rustling dresses and grand paintings smudged from years of smoky candles, all comprised data for grasping the world.

Mozart's life was given over to being on display, and his was a period in Europe when fashions in dress and styles of design were changing at remorseless rates. It was as if the culture was drunk on cultural objects. As new materials came from China and elsewhere, trends in dress design could not stop changing. Restless new styles for laces or ribbons or ruching bubbled up; the flat planes of dresses were stressed so as to flaunt their pictorial qualities of outline and ornament. Mirrors proliferated among the rooms and halls and corridors at the high end of the social mix, and no teaspoon could escape without some quota of tinselled detailing. Paintings in the era of Boucher became desperate to be looked at. Europe's cultivated classes suddenly stressed, and stared at, their own visibility with an intentness that made fun and panic collide. The resulting rhythms have drummed through our societies ever since, as novelty tries to outrun obsolescence but then finds it waiting around every corner.

The composer was something of a dandy himself, a lover of sleek surfaces and ephemeral pleasures. A large, distinctive selection of choice garments shows up in the inventory of Mozart's possessions at his death, including two fur coats and a suit with silk embroidery shimmering amid its brown satin. Vienna was full of pleasure-seekers and followers of fashion, men and women alike driven along by curiosity, a taste for flashy clothes and gadfly movements between entertainments and visits and promenades. Milliners proliferated, and the city's two main fashion designers visited Paris at least annually to check out the latest things. Pre-empting in one letter Leopold's concern that his son's love of novelty and fun would lead him astray amid the big city's lures, Mozart claims that this would really be less of a problem than in Salzburg, because 'just to be in Vienna is entertainment enough'.

In such passages Mozart rolls Prince Hal and Falstaff into one. Early in the 1780s he was especially friendly with a certain Baroness Waldstätten, a fine keyboard player who was older than him by a couple of decades, and who was a generous and highly idiosyncratic denizen of the city's social heights. A couple of letters to her from the autumn of 1782 show off these sides of his personality with one gleaming eye on what would tickle this correspondent particularly. Their camaraderie was evidently bonded by endless drollery about dances, lavish meals and the baroness's 'exquisite coiffure'. Mozart longs for a particular 'beautiful red jacket' which his friend does eventually procure for him, but not before he has also gone on about wanting it mainly for the sake of the buttons that can complete its impact. He has seen some 'made of mother-of-pearl with several white stones around the edge and a beautiful yellow stone in the middle'. A fluid world likes to see itself crystallized in shiny little objects and gadgets, as a pearl can summarize the sea. In these two letters to the baroness, the composer dances between styles and busy references to his copious social whirl, treating her for instance to one jokey curlicue written in halting English to show off his progress in that fashionable language. A certain ruthlessness makes itself felt in the relentlessness of the charm.

Maybe the most powerful overall account of modernity that the twentieth century gave us was in the idea of the 'society of the spectacle' described in the 1960s in his book of that title by Guy Debord. Debord depicts a process in which appearances and the commercial economy driving them proliferate and accelerate until the whole of world history becomes a single spectacle, one that absorbs all human activity and annuls its most valuable qualities. It would be a terminally dark vision if such lofty ideas of history, culture and human potential did not still inhabit it; Debord's prose has a cheering haughtiness just when its diagnoses become most unhappy. One bravura passage traces the culture of the spectacle back to the baroque era that just preceded Mozart, describing its values of ceaseless theatre and festival as amounting to an art pledged to change and passage and to grasping a world with no centre. As Mozart moved through cities and drawing rooms and inns and grand courts and sprawling estates, he did indeed find an era teeming with the desire to reassess itself. In this world everything from legal codes through the grand architectural schemes underpinning communal life to the principles of design for cabinet handles was up for grabs, often remorselessly so. The period's busy hedonism and its most advanced versions of intellectual probity worked disconcertingly together in melting down certainties and pressing towards new arrangements.

Likewise Mozart's music has two impulses, one pulling towards a nearly frantic plasticity and one towards a highly stabilized sense of order and poise, whose seemingly polar opposition dissolves when they are seen as joint responses to the age's storms of redefinition. In the course of his break from Salzburg, he justifies his move to the big city to his father by playing a telling double game with its roiling proneness to fashion. Keyboard music was all the rage in Vienna, so the city was his to conquer. Yet he also claims to know how readily obsolescence preys on novelty, and he insists that his plans will transcend the trends that they will first exploit. His type of music is far too popular for him to be concerned, and besides fashions do not change all that quickly even in Vienna, and anyway he can always try his luck elsewhere. After all, 'who knows what other opportunity may come along?' However Leopold rated his son's protests, Mozart's works process these dilemmas with dazzling multifariousness; his solid structures are brought to active life by the bursts of pleasure and solicitousness on their musical surfaces.

Mozart's first couple of years in Vienna in the early 1780s coincided with a shift in policy under Joseph towards free public discourse, and with the so-called pamphlet flood that followed. Hundreds of publications gushed out in pursuit of controversies and hot takes. The emperor had an odd, telling fascination with the art of printing, and even undertook a brief apprenticeship in it. He did so under Thomas von Trattner, the wily entrepreneur who was one of the period's big winners in the imperial capital, as his paper factories and printing presses churned out the words that fed it. A flickering hiatus lit up Vienna during the 1780s in between the two vast versions of often gloomy autocracy that the Habsburgs favoured or fell into on either side of it, one reaching back into the dynasty's periods of convulsive growth, the next stretching off through the nineteenth century and all the way to Sarajevo from the regime's repressive reactions to revolutionary and Napoleonic France. Modern history has often thrown up such promises of happiness. It is easy to nod at the elements of an enlightenment program that Joseph's reign did manage; Vienna's great general hospital was built and religious tolerance grew and landowning grandees found their sway over the world slightly faltering. Harder to recapture are the effects of upheaval and disorientation spread across lives in his capital and beyond.

Modernization is grand but everywhere it brings tremors. Towards the very end of Mozart's life the journalist Johann Pezzl could give a list that is both jokey and searing of Vienna's changes in recent years. He often tracks changes and fads with as much relish as mordancy, but one entry in Pezzl's list pictures a polity so dunked in flux that it has gone from being sick with constipation to becoming sick from too many purges. 'A private individual generally lives in a completely free and easy way in Vienna today, not subject to any constraints', according to Pezzl's omnivorous chronicling. No doubt there were few for whom this was anything like the whole story, but some such fantasy can be felt flickering through Mozart's Viennese years. In Pezzl's Vienna freedom of speech whirls on amid ubiquitous police informers, and the spread of newspapers means ever more lies and trifles, and theatres stop closing during Lent even as the court spends less and less on its own pomp and spectacles. The big city is being hit by a modernity made all the more frantic by being so doubtful. Since Pezzl was a journalist, he had a great deal to gain from novelty and change. Mozart's appetite for the same shifting city powers *Don Giovanni*, but so does his richer acuity about both the city and his appetite.

Guy Debord thought that its dedication to change and artificiality made the baroque the first great modern aesthetic, one 'obliged to embody the principle of the ephemeral that it recognized in the world'. So Debord's baroque may have always had the rococo and its dashing levity in wait within it. Listening to the music of the Europe that produced Mozart does indeed suggest a culture inspired and attacked by weightlessness. Wildly pushy types of expressiveness and bejewelled technical acrobatics keep on coming in the arias of composers like say Porpora and Jommelli, or like Hasse and Leo, or like Caldara. The fierily insistent drives towards newness and display within such vocal writing made it more of a pivot between the courtly world that it came from and the worlds of spectacle and dissolvency that have ended up prevailing. It was here that Mozart's music acquired much of its gift for prophesying the future even while it was pleasing the present. Looking through the images that have come down from the eighteenth century's singers and musical spaces, we see a world of light and frothy outlines, in which performers and listeners alike merge sometimes flickeringly with their decorative surroundings. As its powers of illusionism cascade, a world like this at once flexes its confidence and empties itself out.

Numerous minor masters were pulling away at music during the century's middle decades, as baroque might splintered into its darting or merely sweet rococo successors. German has the notion of 'Zopfstil' to refer to the more placid and conformist ways in which new values of decorous surfaces and mere élan came to define the century's tastes; it means something like 'the style of the pigtail'. In French the idea of the 'style de perruque', meaning the style of the wig, makes the same diagnosis similarly visible. A composer like Luigi Boccherini could be so prolific because his immaculately creamy craftsmanship was such an elegant solution to the decline of baroque structural power, turning its break-up into nicely manipulated surface gestures. His work from around the time of Mozart's early maturity is as innovative as is needed to make a fundamental repetitiveness all too insidiously pleasant. *Sturm und Drang* trends in music might have seemed to comprise Boccherini's antitype, but expressive urgency could quickly itself seem to become a programmatically jerky obsession, pursued in the dappled shadows left behind when baroque monumentality subsided. Composers as vital as Carl Philipp Emanuel Bach and the young Joseph Haydn, however, gained much from the emphases on phrasal force and rhythmic gyration that the tendency both drew on and fed.

Examples of these drives of proliferation abound, unsurprisingly. Symphonies, suites, divertimentos, serenades, notturnos, overtures and other forms, genres and labels flooded the middle of the century with often no very clear discriminations to say why one was not another. The line of serious instrumental composition founded in Rome by Corelli around the turn of the century was never abandoned by the likes of Geminiani or Pietro Locatelli as they moved around Europe propagating revisions of their master's approach. But it was dissolved into the more flamboyant and airy styles with which they ended up wowing audiences in respectively Britain and Amsterdam. Corelli's expressive flair is matched with qualities of architectonic graft that give it piquancy, but in the later pair of composers it dissolves, leaving the violin to follow its inclinations with a freedom that is disarming but a touch insipid. By the time of his death in 1767 aged eighty-six in Hamburg, Telemann had been piecing together a mutable vision of musical progress and cosmopolitanism for decades, sucking literary allusions and folksy rhythms alike into his works. His copiousness can be wonderfully wiry as well as uncanny, but it cannot have seemed to point in any decisive direction.

Volatility and corrosion can be heard in what had happened to the mighty architecture and the gothic chutzpah of Johann Sebastian Bach's music after his death in Leipzig at the midpoint of the century. Reckoning with the music of his sons can feel like seeing different elements from a teeming cathedral break off and set out on separate aesthetic careers. In Carl Philipp Emanuel Bach their father seems to have had his most dutiful son, but of the three who became significant composers he was also the one whose work was the most guileful and idiosyncratic. He was the one most respected by Mozart, and around the middle of the century he was at the heart of one of the most relentless and complex enlightenment projects in Europe, as one of the presiding musical spirits at Frederick's court in Prussia. But his death in 1788 came many years after he had made something of a backwards step in moving to work in Hamburg, and the elements of strain within his craftsmanship and of fidgetiness within his imaginative flights can dominate his music.

The lurching fervour of Emanuel's style is one way in which the mid-century musical world measured how fissile and wobbly it had become. Others are the emaciated brightness of his brother Johann Christian's vocal music, and the blurring of conservatism and quirkiness in Wilhelm Friedemann's slight if intriguing achievement. Friedemann was the oldest of these three and had been his father's favourite; he seems to have had an intense personal connection to the mighty Sebastian's legacy, whereas Emanuel curated it with something more like zealous professionalism. The pathos of Friedemann's music comes from how yearningly it tries to animate a stylistic past that has dissolved, whereas Emanuel plunges into choppy, updated swings of style and feeling. Christian was the youngest of the trio and came the closest to throwing off his links to the family past altogether, opening his style as airily as he could to Italian influences with all their sweetness and levity, and then throwing his professional lot in with the commercial maelstrom of England. It can feel like seeing one sparkling stained glass window try to brighten an entire cathedral. All three died during the 1780s in conditions of relative neglect, but all three had been impressive sons of their appallingly impressive father. Friedemann's ambitions had foundered long before and he died in real obscurity in Berlin. Christian died in London some years after his impact there had peaked.

Mozart was a sort of genius at being a son, as none of Sebastian Bach's sons was. He was dazzlingly good at assimilating, sorting through and outdoing strands of inheritance taken from all comers; he could cut through whatever he did not need as sleekly as he could learn from whatever seemed fruitful. He loved being helped as well as helping. A genius for receiving and inheriting and passing on may be what is needed in a world engorged with changes and ruptures. The musical period of Mozart's emergence was unsure whether it wanted to inherit the baroque or to escape from its grasp. Handel went like Christian Bach from German origins to stardom in England, by way of an immersion in Italy's musical brightness. Opera had taken him to his shiniest heights, but he then moved on to the English oratorio around the middle of the century amid shifting circumstances and mutating fashions in London and all around, and found new ways of connecting German heft and Italian melodic allure. During the 1780s Mozart engaged closely with his example.

One way to understand how the rococo helped usher in a modern world is to see its entangled delicacies as halfway houses suspended between the powerful, hierarchically enshrined pleasures of the aristocratic past and some era of mass consumerism that was on its way. The music that could fit such a scheme most richly came from Domenico Scarlatti, another fluid son of a weighty father. The father this time was Alessandro Scarlatti, who defined a whole lineage of Neapolitan vocal style, but whose legacy Domenico skipped away from around the time of his death by moving during the 1720s to the relatively far-flung Portuguese court. By this time the younger Scarlatti was nearing middle age himself, but his move seems to have unchained him, and he shifted away from vocal music and into the zanily copious and almost terrifyingly original sphere of his keyboard sonatas. He traversed the arid terrains separating royal residences with his instruments strapped to the backs of mules, and his throng of short pieces reimagined the spirit of baroque comprehensiveness as if in a shaky hall of mirrors. He had spent the first half of his life mainly just perpetuating, if very skilfully, the ambient musical norms of his world. Court life on the Iberian peninsula was an odd mix of vigorous pomp and ongoing backwardness, and his music took up attitudes of piquant and poignant angularity to the European mainstream. But scholarship has made it clearer in recent years how widely disseminated his work was, and the impact of his 550 or so brief sonatas must have been breathtaking as they fizz and riff and jackknife, treating the baroque as if it had only ever been a grab-bag of fun or moody hints and tricks. Scarlatti's fingers dance on the fine lines between pluralism and vacancy, and between freedom and a sort of haunted fitfulness.

His impact was gradual but profuse, as was that of the single work that may most silkily summarize the uncertain, glitchy musical horizons of the century's middle years. *La serva padrona* was a short comic opera by Pergolesi that emerged from the same Neapolitan vocal background. It shared a certain historical arrhythmia with Scarlatti, since its composer died young of tuberculosis in 1736 long before it became a battle-cry in an intellectual war of taste of the sort that Paris enjoys. It was a fairly ramshackle revival there of this slight, rapid two-act piece in the summer of 1752 that made it the focus of the so-called 'Querelle des Bouffons', the quarrel among the comedians or comic actors. The advocates of an enlightenment version of cosmopolitan musical modernity wrangled through exchanges of pamphlets, diatribes and counter-blasts with the old-guard defenders of French opera. Any cause that could enlist Pergolesi's mighty little masterpiece was liable to prosper; it is as slenderly robust as the tail of a cat. The sharpness of his melodic contours and the lightness and responsiveness of his harmonic gearing allow him to propel a merry but freighted story with new levels of peppery realism and flair.

Upheaval is also the story's subject; we know that a maidservant will become a boss from the title's winking paradox, and Serpina arranges her rise in a patriarchal world by means of neat tricks and glinting manipulation. As she nudges and coaxes her employer into doing what he wants to do anyway in agreeing to marry her, the musical surface too is brilliantly busy with bright little motifs and shifts of weight. *La serva padrona* makes a nimble escape from a baroque world of stylistic wilfulness and laborious display. But it carries its own light, bright vision of the dynamic abundance and twisting artfulness harboured in the most advanced music before and around it. Across Pergolesi's music, swivels of texture and quick-fire phrasing lighten the burdens of the baroque in order to try to carry its expressive gains further. In this little opera we face a sliding world with a quick-fire insouciance and an almost frighteningly smooth cunning.

Mozart's operas of the 1780s advance everything from psychological complexity to sheer musical multifariousness, but Pergolesi's vision of comic style as the fluent guide to a fluctile world glistens in their background. The Parisian circles that Mozart was pitched into in the late 1770s were largely the ones that *La serva padrona* had nudged into redefining musical taste well over two decades earlier. By 1787 and the coming of *Don Giovanni*, he was ready to push as far as anyone has ever got into the ecstasies and horrors of a world pledged to redefinition, far enough to meet the elements of paralysis waiting within its changes. The opera's action moves as fast to begin with as Viennese life did during these years, as Giovanni spends the first act trying to dodge the nasty ramifications of his dealings with two of his previous targets called Anna and Elvira, while rapidly switching his sights onto Zerlina after he encounters her engaged in some prenuptial partying. Attempting to live beyond all constraint was one of many powerful fantasies that Mozart's opera was designed to weigh up. It turns out that this meant treating with sombre accuracy the realities that they traverse and change.

Giovanni is beyond all measure in his desire to live as a private individual outside constraint. He is also a character in a work whose structure comes from old morality play traditions, and this mismatch becomes one of the opera's entry points to the shifting grounds of modern selfhood. The work is lavish in its picture of pleasure. But right from the start Giovanni is being pursued by the consequences of his hedonism and cruelty; the opera's moral fervour gets going as fast as its aesthetic raptures. We are never close to being fully on the side of the seducer as he throws himself into his next pursuit, but we cannot fully identify with Anna and Elvira as they turn things around and pursue him. In effect they want to stop the opera from happening. Giovanni does not really seem to know what to do with his story himself though. He wants every day and every hour to restate with gleaming, numbing relentlessness the same pattern of pursuit and achievement; he and his manservant lurk and bicker like characters out of Beckett as his solipsism bites down into their lives. The opera puts to radical use one of the less progressive norms of eighteenth-century opera, turning the sense of depletion or vacancy that can come during the passages of recitative between arias and set-pieces into a sharply diagnostic insight. Has Giovanni's dissoluteness dissolved the world, or has he abandoned substance because he has seen the world dissolving around him? The speed of the action that his desires propel is a way for the opera to show him as being both everywhere and nowhere in its world.

It is only towards the end of the lengthy, speedy first act that we get anything like the set-piece aria from him that might be expected. Plenty of other characters have already taken their florid turns in the musical spotlight. Giovanni has mainly been in action, or manipulating others, or paired with Leporello in stretches of often rancid repartee. The aria that eventually arrives is often known as the 'champagne aria' because in it he issues crowded instructions for the party that he is suddenly planning, and hopes that the drinks that are already pouring forth will throw his guests into the party spirit that he feeds on. It is as if appetite could replace character wholesale; Giovanni bends his aria so rapidly away from introspection or even expressive depth that it becomes their violent, expressive effacement. We are ready to find out who this person really is, and what we are confronted with is voracious, cryptic momentum. If modern individuals are people liberated from the past or tradition to pursue their own desires or to fashion their own characters, the prospect for them here is bleak. Right from the start Mozart's opera has zoomed in on the violence of Giovanni's character and conduct, and here it funnels into the sheer violent pressure within his existence as a musical voice.

Don Giovanni is an opera that agglomerates elements and fuses styles at a heady rate even for Mozart. As Giovanni throws his house open to all comers with what the champagne aria shows to be hectic lavishness, the composer's musical urge towards hospitality and openness finds itself mirrored, brightly and brutally. Providing something for everyone was often a guiding concern for Mozart as he designed his pieces and programmes, but here generosity starts to buckle under the pressure of the hunger within it. Giovanni's outpouring barely keeps formal shape at all. Its haste and relentlessness mean that stunningly free phrases and melodic ideas keep being suggested, but none gets far before being made hastily obsolete. Snarls and rushes of rhythm mean that the singer's voice keeps being pulled into its next phrase, and there is no time for ornamenting the last one or bringing it to any state of conclusive finesse; his entrances bite the heads off the orchestral beats as they snap into the next musical statement. Giovanni lists the fashionable dances that he wants for his party, the minuet and the *folia* and the allemande, but he wants them delivered in a wild confusion free from regular sequence. Mozart is dreaming through him of some new vision of music beyond available structures, an all-over state of compositional fusion that his roving productivity over the preceding decade or so may have seemed to have started to sketch. The rest of the finale goes some way towards chasing such a vision down during the party itself, proliferating dances just as Giovanni demanded, and playing off the relationships between the music within the action and the opera's own level of musical existence. Who exactly is composing this opera by now? André Breton gave his surrealist movement one of its definitive, swooping sayings by declaring that modern beauty must be convulsive.

A more drastic version of musical modernity is being prospected here than anything dreamt of by those who looked to comic opera for witty and progressive dissections of social mores. Vampiric gregariousness and a haunted solipsism blend in Giovanni. The champagne aria takes the elements of melodic simplicity and rhythmic pulsation that typify *buffa* vocal writing, particularly in its 'patter' arias in which the music tracks ordinary speech with often parodic closeness, and gives them the expansive intensity of treatment typical of *opera seria*. The result combines briefness and density in ways that make it desperately demanding for singers. Harmonic richness beyond the dreams of most *seria* composers comes from the fullness of the strings writing, while a bursting textural stridency comes from the relentlessness of the horns. Combining even just the sheer volume needed amid this hubbub with the piece's sliding freedom of phrasing means that the singer is on his mettle as much as in the most extravagant baroque showpiece. Yet he is without the normal payoffs of melodic ostentation or expressive pathos. Far from opening onto decadence or lassitude, desire turns out to extort athleticism and discipline. The aria seems designed to root the character to the spot by demanding such fierce concentration of its singer. Whirlwinds of preparation and conviviality can fill the stage as obedient servants and suchlike rush around. But Giovanni can seem all but paralysed at the heart of the tumult that he unlooses.

An opera full of rhythmic variety finds at its heart someone almost crushed here by the monotonous intensity of his own need for speed and for intensity itself. Deadlines and speed and parallel processing often seem to have been the bloodstream of artistic invention for Mozart. A letter from 1782 to his sister explains a confusing reversal in order in a manuscript that he is sending her; it turns out that he has been constructing the piece's prelude in his head while copying down the fugue that he had already worked out. He could not have got to his letter to her sooner, because too many wearisome little notes needed writing. Artistic inspiration is a state in which extremes of control and loss of control come together. Giovanni thinks that he is a prince of possibility as he races through the names of dances, but in fact the single rhythm of his psyche is pulverizing the world. The zesty, fitful leanness pioneered by Scarlatti and Pergolesi had become rife across music during the decades following their deaths, but had brought its own deficits. The emphatic inventiveness that they brought to the pulse of each musical moment could erode the feeling for larger or steadier structures. Mozart's quests for structure elsewhere want to undo this without forgoing the very brightest momentary impressions. But here the aria's exaggerated sensuous impact turns out to harbour some fierce immutability of its own; an uncanny fixity tightens its grip just where the senses were finally about to have their day.

We are horrified by what we hear as Giovanni's bright pleasures turn into agitation and compulsion. The second of the opera's two acts climaxes with a smaller party. During one of their aimless interludes between exploits, Giovanni and Leporello have come across the commemorative statue of the Commendatore, who was killed at the start of the first act while trying to protect his daughter Donna Anna from the seducer. Giovanni invites the statue of the man whom he has murdered to dine with him, and at the end of the opera the statue turns up. The Commendatore is not in a party mood however; he has come instead to take Giovanni down to suffer the pains of damnation, though he first offers him a last chance to repent. It is here that the parallel between the two party scenes takes on its full and ghastly meaning, because Giovanni is stopped from repenting by precisely the ghastly fixity that the champagne aria found at the paradoxical heart of his psyche. He can only be who he endlessly is, however frightful and indeed suitably eternal the results. It is both a mythical trait and one that Mozart uses to sharpen his most acute diagnosis of modern character; an insatiable desire for change and excess at once hides and feeds a core of paralysis and fixation.

Damnation does not so much punish seduction as turn out to have been clinging to it all along, and Mozart's music summons forces of pulsation and rhythmic sweep in this passage that suddenly make terrifying sense out of the vast and turbulent stylistic array of the preceding opera. Grandeur and nervous energy fuse as the string parts darkly push the action along, as if from a place far below the three already low-lying male voices. Mozart could write this opera because he had heard more deeply than anyone else how much turbulence and opacity the century's musical pleasures could release. Somewhere beneath all its churnings, the real heart of modernity may be its ceaseless expansion of power. The heart of modern art might then be its ambivalence about power, including its own. But if *Don Giovanni* is a warning about life in a modern world, its hectic creative vitality is also a lesson in how to thrive in such conditions. Its wild absorbency of style and content and its oceanic lurches of tone show how drastic artistic play must become in order to keep up with the world that art discovers.

19

Despair

Don Giovanni

Leopold made no further forays into the great world beyond Salzburg after his stay early in 1785 with his son, though his sense of his own importance probably never faltered. His daughter had married in the summer of 1784 and did not live in Salzburg. The beloved family dog died during the same summer, and Leopold told his daughter shortly after her wedding that he was even missing hearing it snore. Reams of letters from Mozart to his father from around this point through to Leopold's death in 1787 have gone missing, though the very last letter that he sent him does survive. Their loss seems emblematic of a period when the world was fading away from the older man. His son did not need him any longer; he may have had to wonder just how necessary he had been altogether to his ascent. Mozart's extreme talent for learning and taking from others was deeply linked to his relationship with his father. But it had become a darting, partly luminous and partly violent capacity for assimilating a whole cultural world.

Leopold was seriously ill for much of early 1787 but his general indefatigability probably helped make his death at the end of May a shock nonetheless. Mozart got the news from a Salzburg family friend. It must have been hard to mourn someone whom he had moved beyond so trenchantly years earlier. His letters to his sister following their shared loss have an oddly arch formality and even something close to curtness, and turn rapidly to practical matters. The composer treats the potentially vexing subject of Leopold's estate with an almost bristling coolness, and seems uninterested in inheriting much from their father, though he is keen to retrieve a little wooden box containing his own scores as quickly as possible. It was in his music that he would continue receiving what he was from his father; his creative life was as immersed in his patrimony as Giovanni's voice is vivified by the Commendatore's ghostly arrival, as his opera rushes towards its end.

Of course, it was Giovanni who killed the old man at the start of the opera's action. Mozart had already consigned Leopold to a sort of afterlife when he broke from Salzburg, or so he may have thought. His final letter to Leopold comes from early in April, and it is touchingly aware of how 'really ill' his father was. Their relationship had long featured a heavy strain of duelling versions of wisdom and sententious advice, and Mozart is keen here to expound on sagacity in the face of death, and to explain that 'it holds much that is soothing and consoling'. A hint of farce enters as it becomes apparent that he had already written one such letter to Leopold; it has gone missing 'because of a stupid carelessness' on the part of the friend tasked with delivering it. Happily he can give his thoughts this further airing. He seems to want to signpost one last time how fully he had outdistanced his father already, in a language that was Leopold's own. Can someone commit patricide by smothering the father with wisdom? Mozart was preparing to survive someone whom he had already eaten alive, in his music at least.

Giovanni would not have been capable of composing this opera about him. The seducer's awful acuity can only grasp certain highly specific sides of Anna and Elvira and Zerlina. His desirousness is a hunger for the real but it burns up the reality of the women that it fixes on; the vicious circuit that results drives his solitude and inconsolability at the opera's end. But this is no simple morality lesson, and the sense of pallor and emptiness that pervades the other characters there is not just a further reflection of how badly they have been treated by him, not just a final result of his malign reductions. The opera does not stint on either Giovanni's attractions or his loathsomeness, and its extremes of stylistic dash and brio are ways of straining to maintain its sinuous ethical implacability. The world of the other characters really is reduced by losing him, and the opera must mark and mourn its own loss of the desirous vividness which even their enmity towards him drew on. Despair has been waiting all along within the opera's virulent panache.

Composing these scenes over the middle of 1787 and then conducting and indeed listening to them over several nights in October and November must have been thrilling and frightening. In the *Prager Oberpostamtszeitung* connoisseurs and musicians are cited as saying that the city had never before heard the like of it. Mozart's feel for Italian vocal music was joined to a stenographic sensitivity to what its explosive charms said about the culture that loved them so deeply. Because music and musicians live so close to the nerves of their audience's reactions, musical styles become intensely responsive to a culture's desire for new pleasures, or more exaggerated or jolting types of expression. Mozart could probably not have survived his immersion in this responsiveness if his talent for analytical distance had not also been extreme. But then *Don Giovanni* is partly about the costs of lucidity itself.

The opera is so ambiguous that it gets two endings. Giovanni's descent into hell is the story's climax, and as he and the Commendatore's spectral statue sing together the passages that bring him to damnation, their duet becomes more fiercely impassioned than anything else in this opera devoted to erotic power. Giovanni's voice has found its deep match, and the right ambit in which to proclaim its final meaning. But all this is followed by the almost painfully undramatic coda in which the remaining characters join in a final round of exclamations against him, and make some mainly unengaging announcements of their future plans. The narrative comedown is discomforting even as these people go about arranging happier versions of their lives. We yearn for the intensity of the first ending almost as soon as it has torn Giovanni down into the bowels of the stage; the smoothness with which the others celebrate his downfall sticks in our throats, not least because we know how largely they are right. Mozart fiddled around with many aspects of the opera in the months after it was unveiled in Prague, and he seems to have been especially unhappy with the ending. So Vienna first saw a version in May 1788 with the second of these two endings lopped off. The opera then closes on Giovanni's damnation, as if he had persuaded it that nothing else mattered. Directors still sometimes do some version of this ending; it can bring gains in dramatic impact, and make the opera's complexities more jagged and strident.

As he wrote the opera, Leopold's death meant that questions of what it means to survive someone were hitting Mozart with intimate urgency. Giovanni would not have cared; it is one reason why he could not have written the opera. One reason why Mozart could write it was the cascading complexity of the ways in which he cared. The darkly flaring chords with which the overture opens turn out to have been setting the whole opera's sound-world on course for their recapitulations as the Commendatore reappears; it is as if the whole drama had been suspended within their uncertainty as to whether to be thrilled or appalled by what it describes. Throughout, the music must both exploit and explore its links to Giovanni's kaleidoscopic psychic fluency. But it must also finally get outside him. In the Vienna version the opera dies alongside him. But the unsteady, winded pathos of the earlier, larger Prague version may more hauntingly elaborate the opera's doubts as to whether eighteenth-century culture can survive him. Can a culture bear knowing that it produces people like Giovanni, and can it bear knowing that it must condemn him and move on?

Towards the end of 1787 Mozart returned to Vienna from the complex raptures of launching *Don Giovanni* in Prague to face more questions of succession. He may have got back just in time for the ceremonious funeral of the great Gluck, whose spirit had already been both conjured and outdone in the new opera's dramatic sweep and orchestral density. Gluck had long been sitting on one of the greatest and best rewarded positions anywhere, in his role as official composer at the imperial court. Joseph seems to have been unsure what to do about Mozart's claims to advancement, and the composer's forays into Prague counted both for and against him, reminding the court of how unbiddable he was but also of how many options could stir for him across the continent. The emperor elevated him in December, but to a lesser title than Gluck's, and with a much lower salary. Mozart must have been grateful for what he got, and relieved, but he knew that he had more than proved himself the deceased master's successor. Being pulled at last into anything even very mildly resembling his past in Salzburg would not have been without doubts and resentment, however rueful.

The court appointment that he had wanted and which his father had craved for him came too late to please Leopold. The conclusion to a vast story of years of ambition fell into place at a moment both nearly right and utterly wrong. Death may have only seemed to heighten Leopold's insatiability; he also happens to have especially distrusted Gluck. Mozart had not attended any of his father's obsequies, and everything involved in losing him had been swept into the momentum of creating *Don Giovanni*. Prague also gave the composer a busy social circle which was full of both admiration for him and glamorous energy of the sort that he fed on. He wrapped himself determinedly into the convivial life of the city's taverns, or the fun at the suburban villa Bertramka where two old musical friends idyllically lived. Games of skittles and evening bouts of strong black coffee seem to have been big parts of his Bohemian autumn. No opera is more honest about both the charm and the awfulness of all social whirls than *Don Giovanni*; feelings of loss and a sense of his own isolated immersion in his music must have shimmered around him like ghosts over his many weeks there of composing and launching the opera. The nights were long by the time of his return to Vienna. Whether he got back in time for Gluck's funeral or found its aftermath waiting, the ways in which he had or had not mourned his father must have been hard to face and hard to ignore.

Mozart had just unveiled an opera that both consummated the promises of eighteenth-century culture and analysed them to destruction. Being appointed to the court represented perhaps his firmest arrival yet on that culture's heights. In such rarefied air ambiguities and mixed feelings can become starker. In fact the opulent fuss that the city made over bidding Gluck farewell was a high-water mark of Vienna's attempts at some ambitious confluence between civic pride and musical culture. Gluck's music has a plush rigour that could make boldly updated ideas and the most orderly visions of imperial harmony overlap. The Habsburg empire was by this point one of the world's more wobbly political composites, an array of shiftingly resentful or rebellious bits and pieces which spread jumpily over the map of Europe. Its haphazardness and languor must have helped the Habsburg world to endure. But Mozart's appointment was badly timed by the political clock too. Peasant uprisings in the empire's muddled east and more focused political disquiet in the western territories of the Austrian lowlands were darkening what would turn out to be the emperor's last years. Joseph was far from alone in thinking that reform and authoritarian monarchy were not just compatible but mutually supportive. But the latter was so far prevailing and as the decade drove on that authoritarianism was starting to seem not just reform's brutal ally but its secret heartbeat. As early as December 1785 new regulations imposing state supervision on the Freemasons were proclaimed; the emperor sympathized with the movement's progressive humanitarianism, but secretive structures of authority running outside the empire's norms were beginning to seem unacceptable. Vienna was a city of factions and grouplets, and the outlook was murky for the various, vague circles hoping for some version of liberal progress to which the composer vaguely belonged.

Acclaim of the sorts that Prague gave him cuts two ways for an artist's sense of belonging. Was he a man of the people with his finger on the age's pulse, or an isolated star surveying adulation from his mountaintop? Giovanni himself is a virtuoso of social connection condemned to solitude; his seductiveness separates him from the people with whom it should link him. The difference for Mozart was that he had music by which to survive both the depth of his knowledge of his society and his intense isolation within it, in fact to survive having written this opera. But this meant that the stakes for his music were constantly being raised. A slight but distinct creative lull set in during the dark days of the early months of 1788 as he digested what he had done in the opera, and Leopold's death, and the changes that Gluck's death had helped to bring. But his drives of curiosity and comprehensiveness were also available to push him towards making music out of whatever he experienced and out of the fullest range of emotions, including despair. Early that spring Mozart composed his K540 adagio in B minor for solo keyboard, and it is a piece that brings right into the searching flesh of its notes the questions of artistic and professional direction that confronted him, and those of how to represent ranging emotions and how to face the nihilism lurking at the heights of achievement. In the adagio everything that might threaten artistic paralysis is pulled down into the substance of musical creation.

The piece consists of a single adagio movement whose fundamentals would suit it nicely to sitting in the middle of a three-movement sonata; the word 'adagio' just tells us that it is to be taken slowly. A slow movement would typically have formed the central column of such a sonata, exploiting what could emerge between the desire for a high-energy opening and that for a happy ending. But this piece's music has grown too large for such a role and has isolated itself, broken itself loose from succession. At the same time it seeks a structure that will make communication possible, and this will mean showing that isolation and breakdown can be overcome, or in any case survived. So the adagio tests how an adagio movement can work in the absence of a larger sequence, and the first discovery is that such a movement on its own cannot support anything resembling the lengthy, languid melodies that Mozart's slow movements often revel in. Without outer movements to give definition and contrast, it turns out that such lyrical wanderings would simply feel too shapeless and unmotivated; their qualities of rapture or effulgence need bracing against more punchy or rectangular surroundings. We cannot ask an adagio to be punchy, but this one must find its own ways of giving context and tension to its deep feelings. It does so by making terseness itself become expansive; the paradox is that the piece's stretching length requires it to be tight in its phrasing, as if its task was to survive impoverishment by bearing with it.

The straining, widely spaced harmonies of its opening chords set an agenda for the piece's desire to combine a large scale with pithy means. But their halting and opaque texture also casts doubt on any sense of inauguration, let alone momentum. At the heart of all music there is a basic need to keep its disparate sonic materials moving forwards, and the sounds within these chords pull in such different directions that this need becomes suddenly and desperately clear. The resulting suspense becomes the piece's basic interpretation of what slow music amounts to, of what the simple fact of being an adagio movement means. Slowness here is not lyrical or languid or mellow, but reveals something very different; it becomes a way for music to wonder whether it wants to keep going at all. As the music's stark textures continue, two distinct thematic ideas wander on in the scorched landscape that results. But both are designed to pre-empt any great development of their basic melodic profiles, and instead put themselves through harmonic shifts that are repetitive to the point of stubbornness. A haunting sense of resilience emerges.

The piece's blocky chords reiterate and probe and fray themselves, but the expansiveness that ensues is paradoxical. The further it extends these delvings, the more cloistral and introverted it sounds. As its textures go on pulling and straining, the pianist's hands keep crossing as they play it. Needing to cross hands is rare in the neat sphere of Mozart's keyboard writing, and here it means that the left hand has broken loose from merely accompanying melodies that happen further up the keyboard. Phrases that had seemed to have melodic significance slide into an accompanimental role instead, as the left hand stretches up the keyboard to recalibrate them differently from above; it is like being faced with a painting in which two different systems of perspective dispute the same vista. The piece fragments and recombines its themes in a trance that is both sombre and audacious. We find ourselves deep within the stylistic machinery by which Mozart's music normally progresses, so deep that progress seems to vanish.

A piece that isolates itself from any larger musical statement, and keeps invoking thematic development without really developing its themes, has given itself a dilemma when it comes to ending. Its overall starkness of statement cries out for a conclusive conclusion, an ending that will not just bring formal finish, but give a larger idea of the finality that an adagio can generate. At the same time its lack of argumentative momentum works against such effects. It is here that Mozart gives the adagio its masterstroke, by giving it two very different endings. The first ending provides such an unbudgingly satisfactory conclusion to the basic sonata pattern that the ambiguities only tighten. No extra qualities of embroidery or tension are found within the musical materials to convince us that some final statement of their meaning or shape has arrived. Rather, dramatic satisfaction leaks away from the formal tidiness that it is meant to bolster. It is only for a moment that this first ending prevails. But it is briefly as though satisfaction itself has been made unsatisfying.

The second ending proceeds by a gentle but cogent change in the soundscape. A series of brief downward runs on the keyboard allows this to happen; it does not break with the harsh and misty landscape of the preceding music, but the piece's timbres are suddenly freer and lighter. The phrasing becomes brighter and riper now that there is a momentary firmness underfoot. The coda is over quickly, because it does not want to erase what has gone before, but just to sketch a flickering way out of it. Its abruptness is part of its uncanny sense of alleviation; different performers can give highly distinct emphases either to the break between the two endings or to their continuities. No doubt the two endings of *Don Giovanni* were on the composer's mind when he came up with this solution; the adagio arrived about halfway between the initial runs of the opera. Maybe ending any great musical work means trying to consummate its spell while releasing us from it, and the smaller piece can sum up this reconciliation with a trenchant neatness that is beyond the opera's overspilling reach. The coda's appeal for the composer probably also lay in how neatly it rethinks what keyboard virtuosity is all about. Anyone listening to him playing the piece may have wondered where the snap and flow of his style had got to. Mozart's more gracious timbres resurface in the coda briefly, but this may partly be to reassure us or him that it has been worth going so far. Not much comes even here to distract us from asking whether we believe what this music is saying. The piece keeps shifting throughout between loud and soft motifs, and the dynamic contrasts are so rugged and fixated that all a good player's normal tricks of elegant phrasing or interpretative finesse are progressively emptied out. Musicians instead have to commit the nerves of their fingers to the piece's jagged bareness.

Finally what emerges is a degree zero of classical style. The adagio weighs what might happen if all that style's powers of development stopped believing in themselves, looked for their own freezing point. One of Mozart's regular publishers was trying to develop a market for short or single-movement pieces, and the troubles that the composer was having with his own business schemes by the later part of the decade made this an appealing avenue. It is often hard to know where to draw any line between commercial expediency and Mozart's creative needs and juices. But here they may well have come together to power a work that absorbs all its culture's drives of change, and reveals their links to states of separation and singularity. The strange, singular works for exotic instruments like the glass harmonica that pop up during the composer's final years can likewise feel like investigations of uniqueness itself. The sound-world of the adagio is in a way all the more unique for coming from a standard instrument, as the notes probe or shape or summon the silences that they break. We find here someone navigating within his mind's most opaque zones.

The lack of developmental ingenuity describes what it is like to live in a world where timings, links and plans fall away or misfire. The composer's new appointment could have suggested that courtliness, dance steps and pleasantry should be the stuff of his music; he never lacked sympathy for such values. But his adagio is truculent and still and austere. It seems likely that the wait to see a Viennese staging of *Don Giovanni* was getting on Mozart's nerves by this point, but the adagio mines frustration and stasis themselves for their distinctive creative minerals. He throws himself down into the essence of his life in music, the freighted encounter with the keyboard and its sounds. Music is in search of a place where it no longer matters what is pleasure and what is sadness.

20

Symphonic Largesse

Symphonies in E flat, G minor and C

Pleasure and sadness are not the only opposites that can blur at the heights of art, or turn out not to be opposites after all. The same can happen with success and failure, and the odd ways in which they fused during Mozart's final years have made it hard for biographers to settle how he ended up. His life around the time of the B minor adagio was dominated by the first public outing in Vienna of *Don Giovanni* around the beginning of May. Creating the piece for Prague in the first place had been a liberating decision, but the momentum of his popularity there did not immediately power it into a rapturous reception in Vienna. The imperial capital was good at disappointing him, and the layers of factional complexity within operatic life there were always likely to impress themselves on a bold new masterpiece created by Vienna's most complex star for the place that was its main rival within the empire. Mozart's official and nicely salaried court appointment should have helped; it doubtless made his new opera's fate there a more raw concern for him. But the court's atmosphere of rivalry and jealousy intensified when opera was involved, and Joseph's personal interest in the new piece cut in two directions at least, ensuring that it did at length reach the stage but also strengthening the reluctance of others to aid its progress. By the time it was eventually put on, the emperor had departed to oversee the small war simmering in his Balkan domains, leaving behind him in the capital lumps of unease as to how the court's musical life would continue.

On top of quantities of organization and institutional finagling, the new staging required a lot of musical work from the composer. Hefty amounts of new writing and structural rethinking were needed, all for a cast that was less enthusiastic than the one in Prague and less committed to Mozart's idiom and to the opera as a project, though it may have been a bit more professionally regimented instead. Vienna's audiences were more guarded too, cross-hatched as they were by the court's vectors of intrigue, and affected too no doubt by the military unrest not far off in the south-east of the empire. While the story may have struck the sophisticated Viennese as overfamiliar and a bit hokey, the music's extravagances of invention and intensity continue to pull apart anyone's claims to sophistication to this day. '*Don Giovanni* did not please', according to its librettist's pithy summary of its initial fate in Vienna. Da Ponte hints at disputes behind the scenes centring on Mozart's reluctance to make too many changes for its new outings. His memoir is as vivid as ever on the opera's reception, but reliably unreliable and confusing too, and it is unclear when he can have got private feedback from an emperor who was off at the wars when the opera made its Viennese bow. But the line that he attributes to Joseph sounds telling; he has the emperor say that such an opera is food too tough for the teeth of the Viennese. Joseph's rule was darkening as the opera emerged, and he may have intuited analogies with the doubtful fate of his capital's most radiant talent. Da Ponte adds that he told Mozart of the emperor's little review, and that the composer quietly replied that they could chew on it.

The opera did get a decent number of performances over the next few months. It hovered between success and failure. But outright failures or even scandalous debacles can be easier to process than the unveiling of an outrageous and bizarre masterpiece that garners respect but which no one can fully grasp. *Don Giovanni* combines as comprehensively as anyone has ever managed a sleek cultural entertainment with a driving excavation of that culture's most drastic truths, so mixed feelings in response must always have been on the cards. No major review of it seems to have been published, a silence that Mozart may have hoped came less from indifference than from bafflement or even awe; we may wonder what conceivable response could have struck him as adequate. Count Karl von Zinzendorf in his diary initially finds the music agreeable and very varied, but a few days later he reports the verdict of a certain Madame de la Lippe who thinks it excessively learned and little suited to the voice; he still turns up to performances some weeks later in June but gets very bored. Da Ponte claims that the reverse is true and that the opera gradually won the grudging admiration of Vienna. *Don Giovanni* was recognized from the start as a decisive contribution to musical culture, but exactly what it contributed or indeed decided seems to have been exceedingly uncertain, and consternation rippled throughout all the admiration that it garnered during its early years of performance in the imperial capital and across the German-speaking world. It disconcerted as many as it overwhelmed; it was leaping into the musical future, but at the same time its storytelling was folkloric or even crudely populist. Its Viennese debut in any case galvanized no further operatic prospects for the composer. The commission that led to *Così fan tutte* emerged only after a revival of *Le nozze di Figaro* a year or so later in which Susanna was sung by a starry and demanding new soprano.

Mozart spent the summer of 1788 in a state that was neither peak nor trough but somehow both together. He had a defining work of the culture playing at the heart of the great capital, and he had had enough acclaim to be fairly certain of what he had achieved; but he was now less sure of who was really listening. The richer the reaches of his artistry became, the more surely they opened themselves up to split energies and ambiguous ramifications, and a shadowy sense of the different artists and selves that he could become. Mixed, confusing and unsatisfactory responses are endemic to such careers. If something is too clearly right or gets acclaimed too easily, it has probably not been pushed far enough, or has stayed too much like its precedents. The last few years of Mozart's life were full of a grand creativity that was also eclectic and spotty, marked more by incomplete or one-off projects than resolute trends. Their achievements are teemingly various, but it is hard to know whether this is because he was casting around desperately for new avenues, or brimming with ideas and directions of travel. His letters during these years often swing between heartbreaking complaint or disarray and attitudes full of reassurance or merriment.

Those summer months seem to have been empty ones for Mozart. Since his return from Prague late in 1787 he had composed little music, as the travails and implications of getting *Don Giovanni* to Vienna preoccupied him. He was also still incorporating his new court role into his working rhythms. Fairly trivial dance music for the capital's array of parties was what it exacted, so the role was not too onerous; but it cannot have been greatly stimulating either. Towards the end of June Mozart made a rather sad little announcement in the musical news section of the *Wiener Zeitung*, postponing publication of the set of quintets that was meant to have amounted to one of his more artistically ambitious enterprises of the period; too few subscribers had come on board. He had turned thirty-two during the winter, and was far beyond any capacity for youth and promise to dazzle on their own account. The fact that he now had some very solid achievements under his belt may have been both reassuring and unnerving; one problem with a talent so expansive is that it is hard to say what could count as fulfilling it. He had pushed far down three major routes of musical and professional advance in Vienna, as a keyboard artist and as a writer of serious instrumental chamber music and as an opera composer. He had ended up at a place both zenith and impasse, one where his headiest position yet as an official part of the Viennese court apparatus could seem to come down to pressing out potboiler tunes for partygoers to wheel around to. It is easy to imagine why he slightly fudges the nature of his appointment when writing to his sister at the start of August, particularly if we recall that such letters had in the past been written mainly to his father. Living people were not the only ones whom he hated to disappoint.

Yet this summer also finds him in a spate of dense creativity centred on the three great final symphonies that he wrote more or less in sequence over these months. Whether the three of them end up amounting to a coherent whole is a key question, because they work by turning the ebbtide in his life inside out, and finding within it a heightened urge towards creative fullness. A desperate urge to comprehensiveness within his personal artistic trajectory combined over the summer of the symphonies with a grasp of the drives of scope and wholeness that symphonic form had waiting within it. It was during this time that he downgraded his family's living arrangements by moving to the Alsergrund district. No doubt the summer heat was best enjoyed away from the city's heart, and the less addled and interrupted atmosphere amid the suburb's gardens ventilated what became a startling creative burst. Mozart's move seems to have fed him with a sense of expansive creative space.

The whole city would have been largely cleared of grand culture and high society for the summer months, and a foreboding edge would have attended this year's version of the annual lassitude. No one could be sure when Vienna would return to functioning at full musical tilt or even whether it ever would. Mozart's court appointment had come at a time of general economic downturn in the Habsburg heartlands. Joseph had instigated enough reform to create uncertainty and disruption, but not enough to bring really systematic economic change, or even a rationally functional tax system. The composer had been clasped to the ship of state just as it began taking on water, and the sharp Russian empress Catherine was pulling Joseph into deepening, expensive military entanglements with the Ottomans. Russia had been extending its holdings along the north coast of the Black Sea, and Joseph's keenness to throw in his lot with Catherine probably involved some mixture of nervousness as to where her expansions might end up and a desire to get in on the action. He seems to have underestimated how firmly the Ottomans would push back against this pair of enlightened despots and their condescending schemes. Yet another grotty little war between Austria and Turkey dug in, and the emperor spent much of 1788 on the front line. His health never really recovered, and his reign lost more momentum than it gained territory or prestige; in Vienna prices shot despondently up. All over the city private orchestras were being cut back and disbanded, and aristocratic patrons were eyeing their coffers nervously. Morale across the musical world drooped, as unhappy rumours surrounded the future of the Italian opera itself; the flagship of Viennese cultural life was wholly reliant on the flow of the court's coffers. In the end the cash did keep coming, but some notable singers seem to have received notice that they would no longer be needed, and they may not have reacted quietly.

During this summer the composer wrote the first of the twenty or so unhappy letters that he would send during his last few years to a friendly, wealthy music-lover by the name of Michael Puchberg, endlessly bewailing his debts and poverty while importuning loans and relief. One result of the war was some fairly draconian reform of the laws governing debt and borrowing, and these changes were probably part of what blighted Mozart's finances from the late 1780s on. He may not have been very clear himself sometimes whether these letters were more credible when they bemoaned his nearness to disaster or emphasized the glories still patiently awaiting him just around the corner. He was living in ways that made these two possibilities densely coexist. Neither scenario suggested hard confidence in the version of success that he had reached over the preceding years; in one it vaporized while the other seemed set to dwarf it. Elements of volatility and strain fired his grand hopes and his grand fears alike, and made them inflame one another.

Creative false starts began to dot themselves increasingly across his work from around 1788 on; pieces kept going nowhere after being promised or started, or only reached completion by unusually winding routes. The number of such projects suggests that creative exuberance never left him, or never for long anyhow. But he seems to have become less sure which channels to throw his creativity into and why, or more aware of his plethora of options, and the limitations of any given one. Maybe being uncertain was a skill that Mozart had to learn; maybe getting older made it clearer that some possibilities in a creative life just have to be left behind. *Don Giovanni* had given the culture a prodigious extrapolation of itself, one pitched with virtuosic ambiguity between the most flighty celebration and the most hard-bitten and rigorous critique. It left the composer at once striding into the future and twisting on deeply unsure terrain.

Viennese audiences seem to have been at once amazed by the opera's power and sure that there was something wrong with it; in some ways *Don Giovanni* led its composer nowhere.

Mozart's leap into the symphony over this summer was a way of processing musically this stand-off between excitement and the uncertain. To do this he needed a form that was still not wholly defined, and brimmed over with lines of inquiry and directions of travel. As a composer of symphonies he had been at best brilliantly haphazard so far; his symphonic output would seem patchy if these three had not come along to cap it so definitively. Haydn's work in the form was so clearly higher in general inventiveness as well as more abundant that it was probably the one area in the musical landscape where he would have known himself comprehensively outgunned. Symphonic writing had never been meant to loom large on his Viennese agenda. The dozens that he had already composed here or there were mainly either outright apprentice pieces or more or less adroit responses to various commissions or opportunities. Of course some few do contain great and original music, but they are too scattergun to add up to much of an oeuvre. His most recent essay was the D major symphony elicited by his popularity in Prague, and it is exemplary for both good and ill. Its orchestral writing is so rich as to ally the most ornate elegance with the plainest vigour. But the singular extravagance of its first movement throws the piece out of proportion, and the absence of a dance movement or equivalent means that it lacks variety and comprehensiveness. No other work shows him so clearly right on the cusp of a transformative new grasp of a whole sphere of creation. Maybe its link to his happiness and popularity in the Bohemian capital increased the appeal of the symphonic genre during the lull after *Don Giovanni* finally got to Vienna.

The three symphonies have the exuberant stability that variety gains from comprehensiveness. Symphonies were things that Mozart was still having to stretch to reach, and these three carry the marks of highly objective, richly impersonal efforts of construction. But then the symphony itself was still inchoate at this point, was still a form stretching to become itself. The word 'symphony' only tells us that some sounds are going to be joined together, and the emptiness of the promise has been matched in the symphonic tradition by the agglomerative looseness with which it has been carried out. It was still the norm during the 1780s to break a symphony up into its different movements over a concert, so that each was played separately and scattered among other items. Any large artistic unity on a symphony's part had to take its chances within the throng of the evening's sounds, and the general urge towards such unity was only spasmodically growing. The classical symphony's main origins were in the opera overture, and it never ceased drawing on the links to the worlds of drama and action that overtures unloose. But as it moved away from anything much more than formal memories of these origins, so the desire for expositional drama and expansive impact became attached to new types of eclectic stylistic breadth. The symphony listened to and plundered neighbouring musical zones like the different types of dance suites that swished across Europe, or the Viennese fashion for technically expansive wind groups. It took from the former their loose and contrastive sequencing but made it dynamic; it took from the latter their adventurous soundscapes but gave them dramatic purposes.

Mozart's stints in Mannheim and Paris a decade earlier had immersed him in the two centres where the symphony was being most broadly pushed along. The loss of the bright world of operatic storytelling never ceased to beat at the heart of the eighteenth-century symphony, and the tough swivels of texture and the rampancy of sonic surface that mark symphonies of the Mannheim school were its ways of trying to get over it, of trying to whip up its own versions of drama and pathos. Social music genres like the divertimento and the serenade were crunched into the symphony. In fact its blurring with the divertimento over the middle decades of the century produced a feature that finally lifted the symphony away from the overture's ternary shape; an extra movement started coming between the slow movement and the finale, often taking the form of a minuet. Overtures went from a fast section through a slow one to another fast section, but now the spirit of dance was messing deliciously with that efficient pattern. All the rhythms of late eighteenth-century social life flow and jostle in the period's symphonies.

Maybe Mozart wanted new bearings away from the volatility of the opera world, as he turned towards a form that was establishing its own distance from operatic origins. The symphony was a place where volatility could be thought through, a forum for both exploring stylistic multiplicity and holding it steady. It was not a fashionable form or a conspicuously plausible route to success at this time in Vienna. Rather, Mozart seems to have responded to his ambiguous situation by reaching towards a version of music that was itself beset with multiple drives and had its own problems of reception. The nearest thing to a really dynamic, popular trend in symphonic writing then in Vienna appears to have been a fitful revival of descriptive or characteristic styles approaching what came to be called 'programme music'. But such genres could only have offered arbitrary definitions and a superficial ease of response. Mozart's hunches were driving him elsewhere. In his hands the symphony does not exit the concrete world of opera in order to embrace new limits on its descriptive terrain, any more than it aspires to some separate zone of pure aesthetic reflection. His three symphonies from that summer have qualities of urgency, colour and imaginative extremity that traverse and test innumerable flickering ideas about the world, and they grab hold of their listeners with veering aplomb. The so-called 'Jupiter' symphony that completes the set opens with a fanfaring phrasal burst charged with as much narrative imminence as the sound of the starting pistol in a hushed stadium.

The paradox is stark in retrospect; the symphony would have seemed a woozy and inchoate genre just when what we now consider to be the great Viennese symphonic tradition was approaching full articulation. Mozart's great ally Haydn had done more than anyone else to gather the form's resources and to push it towards the epochal status that was imminent. The symphony turned out to be the form capable of making most sense out of stylistic openness itself, and Haydn's musical personality combined cosmopolitan geniality with a burly artisanal forcefulness in ways that suited him

ideally to again and again performing this pivot. His actual personality combined the same qualities. During the 1780s especially the
older composer was a living embodiment of the paradox of the
symphony. Working for so many years out in the sweeping seclusion
of the Hungarian countryside, and now developing such a wide
reputation that he could in effect bypass Vienna, he had long
been both inside and outside the city's main musical currents. His
so-called 'Paris' symphonies appeared around the time of Mozart's
symphonic summer, and writing them for the French capital enabled
him to use the grand porousness of the symphony form to find a
voice for a large idea of European music. But it was his spending
much of the year at the remote new Esterházy court from 1766
on that had flung him into the endlessly experimental, fiercely
mischievous musical attitudes that made this synthesis possible.

Haydn had his own musicians there to play with and to dictate
to, but he was also nicely removed from many of the pressures of
commentary and rivalry that larger centres packed into themselves.
The palace at Esterháza was far enough away to feel cut off, but its
wealth and prestige meant that it was not really so. Instead it was a
microcosm of European cultural headiness over these decades, an
anxiously luxuriant hothouse that pulled in trends and entertainments and impresarios from all around. Living there gave Haydn
a wide-angled lens through which to survey the buccaneering
spread of eighteenth-century musical culture. His seclusion turned
into a source of violently absorbent liberty, and by the late 1780s
the symphony had become the melting pot into which he could tip
wheeling quantities of genres and sounds and reference points.
Gilded dance rhythms, almost naively pastoral landscape illustrations
and ribald structural jesting all get stirred in; so do a grinding
structural turbulence taken from the *Sturm und Drang* world and a
shimmering oscillation of instrumental colours. The symphony for
Haydn was a dazzlingly open ear.

Mozart was able to find in this form something like a toolkit that
let him engage with his culture with new sorts of dense but joyful
amplitude. Haydn is especially palpable in the very opening music
of this trio of works, the slow introduction of the K543 E-flat

symphony. At the heart of the piece is the overwhelming sensuous charge with which it meditates on orchestral scale itself, as if arguing for it as a more primordial factor than form or style in what a symphony could be. Haydn had pioneered the use of slow introductions in allegro first movements, and Mozart's use of one here must have been in part a gesture of allegiance; no doubt it also signalled his desire for the large cosmopolitan audiences that Haydn had won. Using a slow introduction like this means that the sonata argument of this first movement does not start until the first allegro theme enters, and this allows Mozart to keep the opening from needing to be tied too entirely to this particular movement's subsequent lines of argument. Instead we get a massively impending sense of sheer orchestral scope. Mozart wants to concentrate for a while with a certain luxuriant earnestness on the basic question of what it means to begin a symphonic argument, a question that pulls him into a newly imposing treatment of orchestral scale itself.

Haydn would use this sort of slow introduction to give both ballast and a certain glancingly contrastive emphasis to the relatively slight thematic bases of many of his allegros. Mozart has very different ideas. He goes on next to smooth the transition between his introduction and the ensuing allegro, throwing the sweeping introductory mass forwards so that it imbues the rest of the movement. A rich pulse of orchestral texture is maintained across the two sections, and an intermediary passage avoids attaching itself entirely to either, instead blurring the large sonic gestures of the opening with the allegro's clearer melodic shapes. Perhaps no other symphonic movement by Mozart puts such emphasis on large-scale unison writing; the grand unity of the orchestra accrues a mountainous clarity. Around him as well as in his own music, the symphony was in the slow and complex act of being revealed, and here he draws the fullest consequences from the most basic set of facts about it. The gradual flowering of the form over the century came alongside the gradual resolution of the orchestra itself, its gelling within broadly predictable parameters on which composers could rely across the culture. The first movement of this symphony serves as a new introduction to orchestral composition itself.

Mozart thus responds to the conundrums of his situation by throwing himself into symphonic form with all its clamorous, unsteady openness, and symphonic form then throws him into the sheer material heft of composing orchestral music. His hand dashes among the staves, and emptiness turns into fullness. The summer was full of warm hours to write in; it stretched like a symphony around him. If we dart forwards to the start of the following K550 symphony in G minor, we find another route into the largest symphonic questions. Critical writing from the time takes vocal music as the basis for all musical style and meaning, but it is clearer in retrospect that specifically orchestral styles had gained eminence from around the middle of the century, and were more and more able to dispute the priority of the voice. Mozart's turn to the symphony over this summer was inseparable from his fate as an opera composer, and the mixtures of elation and frustration that it brought. But gauging the form's potential might always have brought a reckoning with opera that would go beyond links to the overture, right into the melodic heart of vocal style. The opening of the G minor symphony has always struck commentators as deeply baffling as well as deeply moving and impressive, fusing as it does a quality of quick grace with a terse and inward intensity of feeling. Pulsing within the symphony's opening theme is a rhythmic signature that unmistakably recalls the great first-act aria 'Non so più' from *Le nozze di Figaro*, in which Cherubino describes the intensities brought on by women. His mood is so deliriously flighty that the aria becomes a quick anthology of motifs of amorous ardour, and skips through echoes of the reams of Italian vocal music that were defined by such images, reaching back at least to Monteverdi's madrigals. Europe's sound waves had been filled for centuries with feats of burning with longing or freezing with awe, of desperate ecstasy or delicious despair. In the opera Mozart summarily packs them all into this one aria's crystalline fervour, and from there he uploads them into this symphony's opening statements a couple of years later.

So Cherubino's aria is not just a great example of lyrical vocal writing; it forms a crammed and giddy meditation on what vocal lyricism means. Sampling it in the later symphony turns the question of how symphonies relate to vocal music at all into the topic. The central role of the concerto in Mozart's output made him especially sensitive to this question, because a concerto's solo part can allude to singing or turn itself into something close to it, and so mediate between vocal and orchestral styles. The opening of the G minor symphony works by flattening out the melodic profile of Cherubino's phrases, keeping their rhythm and their basic arc, but using far fewer different pitches. One result is a feeling of something withheld, of a passionate intensity that will unfurl by way of reticence. At the same time simplifying the motif's basic rhythmic and harmonic properties fits it to the more systematic unfurling of developments and rephrasing that symphonic form thrives on. The motif no longer kickstarts a vocal line that carries its own drama of expression, but generates enough expressive and structural potential to power a large-scale instrumental argument; the symphony turns Cherubino's breathless lyrical outpouring into a protracted investigation of the meaning of such passion. In the aria Cherubino does not know just what he is feeling, because the emotional life that he is discovering is so full of different images and possibilities, different flickering versions of wishfulness or dismay. It was some basic expressive fluidity that Mozart reached back into when thinking through what the symphony could become; no single way of expressing mood has indeed ever been enough to give emotional life to ambitious symphonies, to the qualities of comprehensiveness and scope that they need and generate. Symphonic passions are constantly shaded and structured by other possibilities, constantly transformed from within by shifting processes of harmony and rephrasing. The mazy lyricism of this symphony has kept attracting and baffling listeners so headily because the piece gets beneath the skin of symphonic expressiveness itself, and reveals the bloodstream of enigma that pervades it.

We can guess that this all gives us a fairly accurate vision of Mozart's own shifting emotional terrain during this summer. A multicoloured inclusiveness spins through the three symphonies, climaxing in the festival of finality that the last movement of the third unleashes. The unhappy fact that this K551 symphony in C was the last that the composer ever wrote has been a distraction over the years from what fuels this movement's kaleidoscopic account of what it means to end something. Haydn had yet again been the pioneer, having shown especially in some quartet finales how convincingly fugal style could bring complex, propulsive music to an end. The question for ambitious final movements at the time was how to combine the simplicity needed for a clear sense of ending with the complexity needed to ensure that this ending satisfies, after the complex movements preceding it; fugal technique turned out to be a good answer because it pulls simple phrases into systems of layering and reiteration. Mozart's favourite solution elsewhere was to fuse the dramatic push of sonata form with the rondo's relative simplicity of shape. But this finale needed something more drastic, and what he achieved was an exuberant braiding of dynamic drama with elements of fugue that not even Haydn could match.

Using fugue in this way makes the movement into a reverse image of the opening of the E-flat symphony. The finale uses the stylistic traits of fugal writing with a dashing freedom that never loses imprints of structural rigour, but that threatens and promises to turn the movement into a teeming centrifuge for orchestral phrases. If the earlier symphony's opening movement threw its weight into showing off unisonal orchestral substance, the fugal texture of this finale splits the orchestra again and again into its component voices and noises, as if orchestral composition was searching for a new, intricate foundation. Different instruments and combinations and sequences of instruments take up the phrases that have set the fugal machine in motion, and each instrument's voice yields its own spinning meditation on how the instruments differ from and resemble one another. The flute's flighty sound treats the fugal phrases with the rushing decorative flourishes that suit it, while the writing for horns plays no real role in passing them around, but gives the process grainy punctuation and flaring texture. Mozart seems determined to lay bare the extravagant inner life of the compositional process, the ways in which it works by just ceaselessly combining notes and sounds, making them play off one another and support or undo or remake one another. He seems fuelled by some vast mixture of joy and anger at all that writing music had come to involve, and at how it kept leading to further achievements and further losses and impasses. The C major symphony is filled with phrases that are both chunkily assertive and swimmingly fluid, and its kinetic harmonic landscape becomes an attempt to describe how things ever fit together at all. The orchestra keeps picking itself apart in the finale because it is fascinated by how it also keeps holding together; it will not fall silent until it has got unity and splitting to coincide.

The finale is dazzlingly powerful, but it is powered by a deep equivocation. Right at the heart of the composer's brilliance is a fertile uncertainty as to whether his music lived more by show-business panache or technical rectitude. The music that shoots out of this finale does not escape this dilemma; it turns it into a flexing and brightly articulated abundance. Mozart may have been the most original of the great composers, and he may have been the most unoriginal too. Originality and unoriginality were linked in his music, joined by how avidly it knew how to learn from the music around it. Using fugal style as trenchantly and freely as he does here was a way of broadcasting, at a moment when he had been thrown back into his aloneness with his art, how vast an access it gave him to expanses of his century's music. His fanatical fan George Bernard Shaw went so far as to argue that Mozart concluded an entire arc of musical civilization, and played no real part in initiating a new one. Writing in 1891 to mark the centenary of the composer's death, he claims that what he nicely calls 'Mozart's finality' is the key to his achievement. But Mozart's voracity towards the past of the art, and also its present possibilities, powers the openness that threw his music into the future. His oeuvre bulges with ways of being both brilliantly and creatively unoriginal, of adapting or siphoning or twisting the music or projects of others; it can feel as if we were listening to hearing itself taken to a maximum level of hunger and creativity.

During the middle part of the decade he had become preoccupied with Sebastian Bach and made some resonant arrangements for string quartet of some fugues by the old master. The speed with which Mozart moved forwards during these years was part of what drove him towards the past too, in a dialectic that would recur across the arts as they hit the modern world. Because fugues keep restating the materials that get them started, the form's intimate machinery is suffused with a sense of the past and of repetition or recursion. However, in the K551 finale the form's stylistic traits pull hard in two directions, as if Mozart wanted to find ever more compelling ways of binding the past to the future. The movement feeds on the baroque past in all its glory, but it also shreds any hope of pretending that the past has not ended. The styles of the past may be ransacked and its vigour recycled, but this music turns fugal style into a source of all but cascading freedom. In the thick of this restlessly productive summer, music must have been an endless task and an endless release. Whether he was restless or vibrant was possibly not a question that Mozart asked. While working on the third act of *Idomeneo* a few years earlier, he had told his father that his head and his hands were so full of it that it was a wonder that he was not turning into a third act himself. In these three symphonies and in this closing movement above all, we get a portrait of the artist as the incarnation of music.

All this may make the movement sound like a finale to end all finales, and it becomes hard to know whether to take it as the last of four movements or of twelve, as the climax of the K551 symphony alone or of all three symphonies as a set. We must face our strange ignorance as to exactly why these vastly deliberate works were written, an ignorance that may or may not reflect some underlying uncertainty on Mozart's part as to his intentions for the batch. Thinking of them as a sequence conceived by him as some sort of package, or at least grasped by him as such while they were emerging, is encouraged by how avidly the opening movement of the first of the three launches such a large argument about how symphonies should begin. The fine intimacy of the G minor symphony likewise has something of the slow middle movement about it. No clear template existed for a sequence of symphonies like these to be received or performed as a single entity, however, and there is no evidence that they ever were played together under Mozart's auspices. Certainly no one can doubt how distinctive their separate impacts are. On the other hand their lavishness flows from how ambitiously they rethink symphonic form in all its elements, and no evidence exists to establish some specific purpose that any one of them was separately tied to.

Mozart may never have heard the symphonies. Numerous accounts have been given of plans for them that he may have had, or even realized. He may have meant them for performances later in the year at a series of subscription concerts, and their expansiveness and mutual synchronicity could have been driven by wanting to rethink what such occasions could amount to. He may have thought publication as a trio to be their best route to a public, rather than being performed either separately or together, or alongside performance in whatever configuration fitted. Issuing his recent symphonies as two groups of three had been the route to the international market for Haydn, and Mozart may well have wanted not just to emulate his commercially successful friend, but to construe a new artistic logic capable of justifying and animating some such grouping. We cannot answer the question unequivocally, and that is part of the point; the abundance of supposition and piecemeal evidence around the symphonies shows how unsettlingly they were related to the surrounding norms and opportunities. If it was unclear whether *Don Giovanni* was a success or a failure, the uncertainty seems to issue here in works that both yearn for a large, supportive audience and overflow the grounds on which such listeners might be appealed to. Mozart may have been less sure of what he was doing in them or what he meant them to be than scholars have wanted to think possible. His immersion in opera may have made him prone to thinking on an ever larger scale, without entirely knowing how symphonies could inhabit it. He may have got carried away by how creative these three symphonies were making him.

It is clear that their abundance of craft and constructive force is driven partly by the hesitancy and frailty drifting through Mozart's life that summer. He did not know where his life was heading, but his music could create purposes and fulfilments endlessly. The symphonies are not just about extending or indulging feelings of potency, however, but about withstanding them and reconciling them to loss and chaos. During the century or so of symphonic tradition that followed, a will to cosmic inflation set in that would culminate in Gustav Mahler and his more fulsome, sprawling manifestations in Freud's Vienna of some idea of the symphony as a world in itself. Within the finale of the third of these symphonies, Mozart shows how intimately linked he now knew construction and unmaking to be. Creativity meant letting them join hands as they proceeded; a creative life can mean letting success and failure do so too. As the composer's world wavered around him, he wanted music to be so many different things that these works would feel crammed, if his structural intelligence was not so aerated. He wanted the symphonies to be ravishing and austere, intellectually cogent and wildly sensuous, and radiantly charming and deftly witty and wheelingly bombastic. The eighteenth century was turning the symphony into the form charged most directly with expressing a will to experiential abundance. But no value or feeling or stylistic parameter can stay still for long in works that grasp this project; the minds of such symphonies must keep changing. No one can teach the finale of the 'Jupiter' anything about the vulnerability of worlds, or the constant need to create new structures.

Two actors visiting Vienna from the Danish Theatre Royal wrote up in their diaries what they found when they called on Mozart out in the suburbs on a Sunday afternoon near the end of that summer. One of them was a true devotee of the century's musical cult who described hearing Mozart at the keyboard that day as the happiest hour of music that ever fell to him. He added that everything that surrounded the composer was musical. Mozart had completed the last of the three symphonies a couple of weeks earlier, and his streak of productivity lasted a little while into the autumn. He may or may not have organized a batch of subscription concerts before the year ended, but if so they made little impression and had no sequels. He ended up moving back to the heart of the city soon enough, maybe partly in order to reconnect with whatever re-mained of its cultural bustle. The lavishness of his runs of such concerts only a handful of years earlier must have felt distant. At the same time composing these three symphonies meant attaining a freestyle overview of the gamut of artistic and social data that Vienna had brought, a conspectus in which exuberance and serenity and a buccaneering creative rage mix.

After this he wrote no more symphonies, and only one further concerto, projecting his own instrument of the keyboard onto an orchestral scale. During the last years of the decade his comic operas were taken up across musical centres from Brunswick to Florence. Mixed receptions and mixed feelings met them everywhere though; sometimes they pleased connoisseurs but not the broad public, and sometimes their play of attitudes and their narrative exuberance disoriented those trying to concentrate on their musical brilliance. The three 1788 symphonies exist in the historical record over the next few years only in hints and scraps, as if their world could not cope with their desire to give a total account of it, to make it extravagantly audible. Mainly they stayed as mute and abundant as the summer in which they were written. In December Joseph returned to Vienna from his chaotic war against the Ottomans, some days before the last outing that *Don Giovanni* would have there while the composer was alive. The emperor was exhausted and unwell, and probably did not make the performance. It may be no coincidence that his military fortunes improved while ongoing illness kept him from the front line during the following summer. Joseph's authority was now slumping, and rebellions pocked his empire during the summer of the fall of the Bastille in France. Early in 1790 a fever killed him. He was not yet fifty years of age; plenty thought it a good thing for the future of the Habsburgs. The following year brought Mozart's death. The three symphonies knew their world so well that they had already gone beyond it and ahead of him into the future.

21

Gamblers

Divertimento for string trio in E flat

Vienna during the 1780s saw a vogue for musical dice games, but the version sold under the composer's name in the years following his death seems to have lacked any solid connection with him. It was published in 1793 by the firm of Johann Julius Hummel in Amsterdam and Berlin, and consisted of instructions for using dice throws to construct dance music. Mozart's commercial reputation was leaping forwards after his death, and he had left his affairs in a chaotic state that made it hard to be entirely sure what he had written, and hard to know who was meant to have any say or control. A draft eventually turned up of a genuine dabble on his part at a similar confection; so whoever came up with this wheeze was working at least on a good instinct. The composer only got as far as some preliminary sketches which bear no great resemblance to the game eventually released. But he loved everything playful and novel, and this attempt at exploitation might have amused him. During the later 1780s Mozart made attempts to shift the thrust of his chamber music from the string quartet to the quintet, but this ploy to refresh its market appeal foundered on the scale and intensity of the quintets that he composed. It was among the sketches for one of them from early 1787 that his draft for a dice game turned up, so perhaps he had felt one day like pulling against his grandest artistic drives. Games like these could make composing seem hilariously easy or appallingly so, and this had a wry charge for Mozart more than anyone.

Games of chance obsessed Mozart's period, and at the peak of his world's obsessions was gambling. The composer's own propensities or otherwise to gamble have become a hoary biographical question, one unlikely to be resolved. Since there are no solid records to show that he took any large interest in the pursuit, the safest course will continue for many to be to assume that he did not. But those captivated by images of the composer spinning away his nights accumulating losses can reply that gambling shrouds itself in secrecy and evades evidence. Something was amiss in the composer's financial life for long periods, and the issues involved are too murky to be attributed entirely to Vienna's general economic and cultural downturn. Recent scholarship has tended to dissolve any idea that his financial dealings were merely feckless; his earnings were often impressive, and he kept trying astutely enough to advance his position. If this can make it harder to imagine him frittering money away at the gaming tables, it also makes it hard to see exactly how he kept ending up in financial travails. Mozart combined savvy success with chaos and debt in ways that may have had to turn on some opaque, slippery factor. Maybe it was tempting to transfer the talents that he had honed so drastically within music to the card table or games of chance, to the varieties of mathematical nimbleness, psychological assessment and feeling for the rhythm of events that they involve. Certainly Mozart could be carried away by the inner logic of some undertaking or by some social event's exhilarations.

It was a manically golden age of gambling across Europe. Mozart's contemporaries took the redistribution of wealth by chance to new heights, as if they could not think of anything better to do with it. His circles of friends were full of gamblers, and the opera houses and dance parties and drawing rooms around him were among the locales where the hobby most addictively flowed. During a visit to Munich in the 1770s Leopold recorded that gambling tables were included in the set-up of the hall where comic operas were staged. Da Ponte emerged from a Venetian milieu of often ruinously obsessive gamblers, and betting and other sorts of financial chicanery recur throughout his *Memoirs*. Perhaps an even more devoted gambler was that other great literary adventurer Beaumarchais, the author of the 'Figaro' plays. Beaumarchais worked as a spy for the French monarchy, published an ambitious edition of Voltaire and found fame as a propagandist for the losing side in a vast legal battle, whirling through the world of eighteenth-century cosmopolitanism and grift at a rate that made it implausible that he would not be hit hard by gambling. He seems never to have visited the city of Seville where he set his most famous character up as a barber, but his time pursuing exotic entrepreneurial schemes elsewhere in Spain pulled him into grand circles of gamblers, and bouts of extreme financial peril. Beaumarchais played for such high stakes that it became a high-society spectacle to watch him in action. A key explanation offered for Scarlatti's extended time at the Spanish court has likewise always been Queen Maria Barbara's willingness to take care of his gambling debts. Figures like these were people drawn alongside Mozart to experiment with the newest forms of life and the most adventurous versions of selfhood offered by their world. Gambling is one of the great siren songs with which modernity has beset such characters with lures of changed fortunes and experiential enlargement.

The mighty world often could not resist assaulting even its own foundations as its denizens chased the fun proffered by gambling. But all these games and bets were at the same time full of hints about the then onrushing world of commercial wealth creation and its basis in endless churn. Freedom, as its modern versions spread, could not help revealing some inner coil joining it to luck at its sheerest. If gambling was often improvisatory or surreptitious or involved with mischief and crime, the period also saw the organization of a state lottery in Vienna itself, and various spa towns and resorts were making moves towards the glitzy casino culture that would set the ambiguous tone of high bourgeois capitalism during the nineteenth century. The roulette wheel was being perfected during Mozart's lifetime, and his music finds a sharp parallel in the quest for a wheel whose action would be entirely even and hence reliably random. The ancient image of the wheel of fortune was assuming a literal new guise. In England horse racing was starting to take its modern form as a sport in which speed and privilege come together to produce spectacle, obsession and above all wagers.

Gambling and music were two key forms of experimental social life offered by this accelerating period. The gambler and the musician both go in search of patterns and openings that will release transformation and splendour; musicians can feel that they are riding waves of chance and serendipity, and gamblers that they are practising a cuttingly fine art. Pleasure and playfulness run amok in a world as devoted to gambling as this one, eating into the ease of social life or the solidity of livelihoods, and all this will raise the stakes for music too. Mozart oscillated between splendour and hardship in ways that typified the world spinning around him. He pursued his large capacities for both earning and spending within a financial world that brimmed with elaborate credit schemes and new types of currency, and with con tricks and speculations in cascading variants. As circuits of trade and investment widened and internationalized, and commercial adventurers of all sorts swam up from place to place, it became indecipherable who was on the level or where some chain of credit was meant to find solid ground. Gambling forced such factors into view with lurid emphasis. In the period's opera houses, those in charge of the finances had to improvise as fervently as the singers, as credit notes flew around and debts stamped their feet and promises of profits whistled emptily. In these circles money was gambled with only as ardently as it was also being spent or lent or lost to prodigious graphs of interest. Wealth may have seemed so capricious that it was best to get rid of it sooner rather than later. Crowds of composers and musicians were blasted in their later years by bankruptcy or immiseration. Vivaldi composed the works that brought him such success so fast that it only seems logical that his wealth and prestige slid away at breakneck speed too. However imminent or not any actual prospect, the thought of bankruptcy must have been visceral for Mozart, whose life meant monetizing day by day a talent full of fluidity and metamorphosis. Poverty may sometimes be the one thing that a society pledged to wealth has faith in.

Mozart rails against the difficulties of relying on irregular bursts of income in one of three financially woebegone letters that he wrote early in the summer of 1788 to Michael Puchberg. He wants his friend to set him up with a dollop of capital sufficient for him to get his payments in order and to protect himself from constant financial insecurity; he neatly claims that he would then earn more too, because he would be able to work more freely. Puchberg carried on assisting him through to the year of his death, but his help stayed disappointingly piecemeal. Through much of the middle of the decade Mozart's earnings had been high and steady, and his court appointment now brought a solid salary. But something in the matrix of factors that could buoy the finances of someone like Mozart was rendering them leaky too; wealth looked to be perpetually within reach, but seems to have then shot away from him ever more shyly during his final years. His financial life had often been a sort of gamble, because daily life was so expensive in the places that were rich enough to be worth travelling to. Ambitious musicians had to be capable of seeming to belong to the world of high spending that they wanted to exploit. Mozart's talent had opened a world of shiny aristocratic pleasures to him, but that world was proving fragile or destructive for plenty of its insiders. The same forces that propelled the rising man of the eighteenth century were dissolving the heights that he aspired to; it is a vortex that has caught many since. Since loans are only likely if the future looks bright, Mozart's letters often flicker with optimism as he continues writing to Puchberg, among their complaints about landlords or Constanze's medical bills or the decline in musical audiences in Vienna. But they are stalked by multiplying bills and the beckoning figure of the pawnbroker, and shadowy debts already incurred at high interest elsewhere.

Puchberg was a civic grandee and a dealer in luxuries, but he was no aristocrat himself; the letters that he got from Mozart bulge with grand requests, but he marked them up punctiliously with the often much smaller quantities that he disbursed. Because he was a fellow Freemason, Mozart could address him in a spirit of sympathetic intimacy and with guaranteed secrecy. The letters are by turns plangent and wheedling, enraged and defiant, conspiratorial and businesslike and rather slyly casual. Something of the composer's feel for dramatic aplomb can be felt in their recitations of lament and misfortune as they conjure the 'black thoughts' that beset him, the 'true philosophical equanimity' with which his wife faces her proliferating ailments, or the 'sheer grief' at his situation that means that he can neither go out nor compose. By the summer of 1789 he is offering to pay whatever interest his friend wishes to charge while also pleading for 'advice and consolation' if funds do not arrive. During the following spring he calls on Puchberg 'once more and for the last time in this most desperate moment'. It would not be the last time though.

All this makes grim reading. But loving the composer's music means grasping a style that knows loss inside out, knows how to recover from it and how to thrive on it. As that summer of 1788 cooled into autumn, Mozart produced what may be his single finest and strangest piece for a small ensemble, the K563 divertimento for string trio in E flat. Fairly strong evidence suggests that he wrote the piece for Puchberg, though the crucial reference in a letter from the following year is only to a trio for unspecified instruments, and recent scholars have pencilled question marks next to what used to be a solid assumption. No more might be implied there in any case than that the piece had a first or early performance at some salon evening hosted by Puchberg, although it could also mean that it was somehow dedicated to him. Maybe the piece had served as a gleaming compensation for Mozart's burgeoning neediness. The divertimento's drastic elegance and its sharp grasp of both fun and structure make it a work capable of coolly surveying and deflecting any number of ambiguous circumstances and complex attitudes.

Biographical accounts tend to seek the ways in which the troubled elements of his later life are reflected in his music, or inflect or infect his artistic decisions. No one will want to be insensitive to such patterns. But a different psychic possibility sketches itself at this point. It must be likely that deep aspects of his creativity were released by his dissolving or unsure material position, whether pronged by feelings of rejection, kicked into gear by sheer financial need or liberated by feelings of independence and recklessness. Maybe the fear of failure helped the nerves of his talent stay as sharp as a gambler's eye for the next hand of cards. No doubt his court position mitigated prospects of disaster, and acclaim and success never came close to abandoning him completely. But he had struck out earlier in the decade as a solitary artist, and maybe he liked the feeling of freefall that this could bring, and was relieved to find it still tangible after his elevation by Joseph. Mozart liked luxury; maybe he liked being in need too. A life filled with such polarities certainly seems to have encouraged his music to seek expressive range and comprehensive perspectives.

Mozart was getting older now, a strange enough fate even for those who have not been singled out for a renown defined by youth. He was a perpetual son who now lacked a father; he threw himself into grand compositional projects as if time was suddenly chasing him. The divertimento came late enough in the resulting spate for him to have known what impressive fruits it was bringing. The piece reopens his imagination with renewed, limber tenderness to the world of manners and amusement that the divertimento genre conjures. But it does so with a certain curt freedom that comes from having traversed the vast territories of the summer's symphonies. It must have been hard to step away from the architectural vigour of the symphonies and their sense of ramifying scale; writing them would have been both exhausting and addictive. The divertimento makes the great sideways move of pouring the momentum from those works into a vessel that claims delicacy and charm as its idioms, rather than into some more self-evidently serious genre of chamber music. The divertimento treats its own slightness with expansiveness and fervour, but it does stay relentlessly slight. Choosing such a small ensemble has sharply ambiguous consequences in this context; the sound-world can seem somehow both harshly pared down and deliciously light.

Maybe writing the piece was Mozart's way of coming back down into a shared, pleasant social world after his weeks of exalted clambering on the heights of the symphonies. It does then still carry the charge of their mountainous air. But the divertimento seems to know just how hard it would be for the symphonies to find routes into the world that they also so richly grasped; it encodes Mozart's fierce desire for formal reach within more modest and manoeuvrable shapes and attitudes. The ambitious styles of classical chamber music or of Haydn's symphonies retain blurry links to the divertimento genre's more arbitrary and skittish musical world. But a slipperiness of style and purpose is exactly what Mozart now exploits by using the label of divertimento for the first time in years; the strenuousness of the symphonies can be cast off, but the gains that it brought are flexibly retained. The composer gives the piece the six movements characteristic of divertimentos, and includes the two usual minuets; by this point much of his chamber music did not call for any dance movement at all. Its feel for the bodily and social rhythms and angles of eighteenth-century dance baits the divertimento with allusions to an entire historical world, one filled with elegant dance halls and shiny decor and flowing flesh. A fine work might have resulted if Mozart had wanted just to reconnect the progressive ardour of his 1780s chamber music style to this vision's smooth flights and sparkly choreography. The crucial prism here comes instead from using the string trio as a group, a choice that turns out to reach far further than we might guess if we simply see it as a quartet that has lost a violin.

String instruments cannot easily harmonize their own lines or phrases as keyboard instruments can; the two hands of a violinist can only produce one note at a time except by the dramatic and often cumbersome expedient of double stopping, whereby the bow pulls across two strings in the same gesture. One result is that dropping from four to three string instruments in a group makes a massive difference to how richly or otherwise they can harmonize one another. The divertimento finds itself thrown onto a terrain of sonorities that has been emptied out, as if poverty and curtailment lurk deep within the social loveliness that nevertheless keeps bubbling up. Mozart's trio of instruments gambles on making restriction and exposure work in its favour; the piece matches its tense harmonies with melodic lines that are themselves highly idiosyncratic and exposed, and its players face not so much grand interpretative choices as teeming opportunities for intricate and intimate touches and nuances. Instead of making the cello run through basic accompanimental motifs to fill out the group's harmonic textures, the piece gets it to oscillate with an often quick-fire flexibility between accompaniment and soloistic excursions of its own. The violin and the viola must consequently work out their relations to each other on their own terms, a task complicated by how high in its range the viola plays, as its sonorities touch and tangle with the violin's. The three instruments use rhythms and phrase lengths that are often drastically different, as the musical flow seeks waveringly singular ways of locking itself together.

The divertimento's meditations on togetherness logically enough extend to patches of counterpoint; after all, the term refers to the most traditionally attested set of means for binding musical lines together into coherent textures. Counterpoint is used here in ways that are renowned for their elegance but that can be bitingly curt too, as the precision-tooled rigour that it brings bursts out of these wavering relationships before slipping back into their more playfully melodic gambits. Mozart merges a distinctively tight harmonic vision with the capaciousness of older genres like the baroque suite. The divertimento contains two allegros as well as the two minuets, creating a more relaxed and digressive sense of musical space than the composer's more recent quartets or symphonies do. If listeners did not like one minuet, another would be along in a minute. But the minuet was also the one great dance form that was thriving within the high vistas of the classical symphony, so its deployments here help turn the piece into a bridge between the broad musical past and the insistent present.

During 1788 he was often busy writing the society dance music exacted by his court appointment; maybe the mixture of duress with relief involved in this elevation prodded him towards this piece that is somehow simultaneously reductionist and expansive. Writing all this dance music was in some ways an artistic move backwards, but there was also much to energize Mozart's liberal, progressive sides in the seasonal balls in which many strands of Viennese society were meant to weave together. The sides of him that just loved fun and spectacle were involved too; the opulent Redoutensaal was the setting for balls during each carnival season, and it must have been exhilarating to see his music streaming through so many moving, finely encased bodies. The task and its pleasures loomed as autumn began and the winter's balls approached, while he was working on the divertimento's mixtures of charmed curiosity and steely incision. At the same time the piece casts its cool mind back through the forcefully sociable wind serenades from earlier in the decade and through his ambitious and sometimes outright experimental divertimentos and society music from the later 1770s in Salzburg, all the way to the maelstrom of occasional and social genres and categories that had crowded the musical world during the century's middle decades. Serenades, nocturnes and divertimentos had poured through that world often indiscriminately, but had fertilized the soil for the classical symphony in the process. In this divertimento Mozart returns to that profusion from the other side of the stylistic advances that had emerged from it. The dance music that he wrote now thronged with fairly short pieces of no great structural ingenuity, but bursting with fulsome orchestration or rich rhythms. It is probably no coincidence that the divertimento is the opposite; a pared-down delicacy here extends and complicates itself. Eighteenth-century culture finds itself un-housed, and so seeks a new and expansive knowledge of itself. It is as if a mask was removed to reveal another mask beneath, one that is more starkly elegant. In this work masking has no end; it can seem to show its own true face though.

No other string trio of similar stature was composed until Schoenberg's massive, acerbic piece about a century and a half later, itself a thrillingly strange meditation on historical loss and personal vulnerability. In the divertimento elegance comes not from refusing complex experience but from inviting and subsuming it. No one with no love for them could pass through as many salons and parties as Mozart had, but no one could develop such a feel for them without having often enough been sick at the thought of the next one. Whatever raw ambivalence he must often have felt towards success and its hinterland turns here into refinement, as artistic seriousness and social levity remake each other, and dance. The divertimento still resounds with the swish of fine dresses and the gleam of bodies dancing beneath gilt ceilings, and the flutter of cards being shuffled. But the piece has a gambler's lucidity about its world, and a gambler's ruefulness about how far such lucidity gets anyone. Nothing is more ambivalent than watching the roulette wheel as it flies; a gambler's winnings come laced with fear and contempt, while losses savour of near misses and the awful likelihood that hope will soon return. In both music and gambling, the eighteenth century told the truth about itself in the form of yet more distraction.

Mozart's divertimento ends with an allegro movement whose spirit of wiry melodic release speaks of a certain relief at having moved over such highly contoured ground and emerged. Are liberalism and democracy and republicanism gambles too? No society can sanely seek their realization without a large tolerance for uncertainty of outcome. A society throws itself into gambling when it no longer finds its own values and bases compelling. In the decades following Mozart's death, the greatest music extended itself to extremes of subjectivity, inwardness and wilfulness in its attempts to balance itself against a world addicted to crises. But the E flat divertimento advocates coolness, refinement, tolerance, curiosity, a certain almost violently winnowed tenderness, and a lightness full of trenchancy. Perhaps Tchaikovsky's *The Queen Of Spades* is the work that makes the ecstasies of music and of gambling interpret each other most openly and acutely. Composed more or less exactly a century later, it focuses all the rampancy of nineteenth-century opera on the tale of a man obsessed with a particular trick for winning at cards, a man for whom gambling reveals the full horror of its version of pleasure and desire. At its heart are dazzling and trenchant passages of pastiche Mozart.

22

Reconciliations

Le nozze di Figaro

After he drags his wife's chambermaid from the bushes, the count's refusal to forgive her is full of the pride of a great seigneur. But of course he thinks that he is refusing forgiveness to the countess. We are in the last act of Mozart's *Le nozze di Figaro*, the garden is wrapped in night-time and promises of pleasure, and Susanna and the countess are disguised as each other. It is with his wife herself that the count has been trying so hard to be unfaithful to her. Likewise, it is really Susanna whom he ends up berating when he catches her with Figaro, to whom she has just got married. It is a tangled and glinting web, and even the newlyweds become confused about whether anyone is actually being betrayed. Figaro is sent reeling into an aria powered by sheer moral panic, as he sings to men in general that they need to open their eyes to the weaknesses of women. It is a terrifying passage packed with its own version of farcical doubleness, because it takes the opera's deep obsession with getting us to open our eyes to one another and gives it an obscenely wrong-headed revision.

The community of servants and revellers implores the count to show his wife forgiveness. But he is resolved to be stern, and yet more doubleness is involved when the actual countess comes back into the garden to confront him. She decides to forgive not just his wrongdoing, but his refusal to forgive what he had thought was hers too. The reversal is full of both wit and what might be called ethical largesse. It turns out here that forgiveness is the answer to living in a world both animated and ravaged by desire, one capable of using precisely artistry and disguise and creative playfulness. We may not believe that this marital harmony will endure; we have learnt too much about these people and their desires. But we come to see forgiveness as an enduring possibility packed within their lives, and the key to perceiving those lives in their fullness. The quest is to find the places where moral injunctions and experiential gains concur. Music can be such a place. A renewed relationship to the past and to the movements of time itself is the aim within drives of forgiveness or reconciliation, and time is something that all music is immersed in, driven by.

The deepest subject of this opera is its own process of turning artistic power into playfulness, pathos and a heightened idea of pure conviviality. Creativity is always having to choose between revenging itself on the world and forgiving it. In this meltingly brief exchange between the countess and her husband, the opera becomes capable of resolving its plot in a spirit of celebratory, relieved joy. But this only works because the music at this crucial juncture breaks up the last act's restless comic rhythms and changes their meaning. Mozart slows the tempo down as these two people finally face each other in all truthfulness; it is this moment that expunges what had become the twitching and finally agonized nervous intensity of the opera's rhythms as the narrative imbroglio tied them in its knots. At the same time forgiveness must be shown to relate realistically to whatever it is forgiveness of, and hence there must be devices here to bind the exchange in to the action that has led to it. The awful thing about forgiveness is that it must measure more precisely than anything else the awful thing that it wants to overcome. Mozart here gets the hugely varying dynamic levels of the music to change in ways that blur across the points where the sense of tempo or rhythm changes. The moment of forgiving floats up from within the streaming, troubled momentum that it also ruptures and transfigures.

An artistry as powerful as Mozart's will need to cultivate drives of forgiveness and repentance, if its own acuity and freedom are not to undo it. The spirit of intense reconciliation as the opera ends is charged by all the hectic multifariousness that has preceded it, and this is often how musical form more widely works for the composer. The movements of his sonatas, concertos and symphonies stream forwards through sometimes teeming, sometimes tense and sometimes precarious structures. But the dynamism of these structures is inseparable from the sense of homecoming and reconciliation that their harmonic actions and their drives of shape alike sculpt. It is this that makes the classical style inherently comedic, and makes forgiveness the secret ethical force at its heart; a movement's elements of impishness or metamorphosis or expressive depth are defined by the resolution that eventually folds them back into itself. Mozart's operas more generally pursue forgiveness obsessively. In *La clemenza di Tito* the emperor Titus survives the assassination plot that gives the first act its climax, and spends the second act in what is nearly a paroxysm of magnanimity as he relentlessly pardons the plotters. *Don Giovanni* enacts something like the opposite of Titus's ballooning clemency; the story climaxes with the protagonist preferring hell to having to repent, as if refusing forgiveness constituted some final kernel of his psyche. Mozart's operas know how right being forgiving is, and they know what a complex fact about the world this is, and what complex fates it engages. Mozart knows how existentially rich forgiveness is, how it leads to more contact with the world and more knowledge of others. Invention cries out for reconciliation and then becomes one of its rewards.

During the spring and early summer of 1789 Mozart went with his smart friend Prince Lichnowsky up to northern Germany and Berlin; it would prove his last major period of travel. Vienna seemed barren, and Lichnowsky offered to pay the costs of travel and accommodation, though the composer also took out a loan before they left in early April. The prince had been taught by Mozart, and he was a thoughtful participant in the whirring of musical progress in Vienna, an amiable grandee around whom musicians and aristocrats mixed freely. Mozart's main target was the Prussian court, since the Hohenzollern dynasty was still renowned for its musical commitments, the current king being an excellent cellist. But the composer's encounters in the north and especially in Berlin and the court's other base of Potsdam soon replicated familiar patterns, as garlands of praise and dangled possibilities mingled with airiness and gridlock. The esteem that Mozart was now held in probably worsened his annoyance and confusion; straight rejection from the

Prussians might have been more helpful than yet more combinations of polite welcome and prolonged vagueness. He might have been an easier fit for advancement if he had been less grandly, bewilderingly talented; plenty of merely proficient composers were thriving wherever anyone looked. Outright hostility from potential rivals may have been involved, and the composer seems to have got along badly with the influential French cellist with whom the king had studied. Early in April he had boasted in a letter to his wife about how good his prospects were in Berlin, but he and Lichnowsky were then still in Prague. A few erratic weeks later he writes that he is about to play for Queen Friederike, but immediately and rather loftily dismisses possible outcomes; he had only informed the court that he was in the capital to avoid offence. The writer Ludwig Tieck was a huge fan, but failed to recognize Mozart when they spoke by chance around the time of this letter to Constanze, during the preamble to a performance in Berlin. As he explained in a memoir many years later, the great Mozart was 'an unprepossessing figure in a grey overcoat'.

The whole journey parodies Mozart's restlessness, and the ambiguous outcomes that it kept bringing. In the same letter from late May he reminds Constanze that he has written to her from Budwitz and Prague and Dresden and Potsdam and Leipzig and Berlin. He describes life on the road with a resigned drollness that threatens to become mordant, rather than with expansive curiosity. Doubtless he had had enough of ragged roads and dodgy postal systems and rushed or evanescent deals; he is going through the motions of being in motion. He seems to end up lending money to Prince Lichnowsky, though he may be wanting to muddy his wife's impression of his actual financial arrangements. Around the same time he sums up one major attempt to rally an audience in Leipzig; 'the concert was a splendid success as far as applause and honours go, but it was all the more disappointing in terms of income'. Possible plans and unclear consequences spill in split directions. In Prague Mozart and the producer Domenico Guardasoni hastily concoct a deal for a further opera, but they do not seal it, and indeed they never would. The Prussian king eventually slips him some money, but he still needs to dampen Constanze's financial hopes for his return. His eventual plan to write two sets of half a dozen string quartets and keyboard sonatas for the Prussians was a nugatory outcome, and it is not clear that they were even officially commissioned. He may have acted on more or less blatant or misleading hints, or have undertaken the sets off his own bat, desperate to pin fruitful consequences onto at least some of his northern efforts.

He was back in Vienna for the meat of the summer, as ever a difficult time of year to gather reassurance or momentum. Constanze was ill and often away getting expensive treatment; a foot injury had become a dangerous infection. Mozart's venture north had meant weeks of worrying about money in pricey inns or arranging haphazard lodgings with friends, and making weary conversation with the latter or with supercilious officials, though at least the little circles of fans who beset him with reverence were different. Now he had returned to the same old problems and the same old admirers. The journey had reiterated the issues facing him, but being back in Vienna opened flashes of deeper despondency and protest. Returning to the great capital may have started to bring feelings all too similar to those set off by the prospect of Salzburg many years earlier. The way to forgive his life was by artistry; but remarkably little music came over the next eighteen months or so. His final Da Ponte collaboration *Così fan tutte* was Mozart's grandest undertaking over this stretch, and it makes sense that his most densely intimate opera defines this period of scepticism and retrenchment. On the other hand the finest instrumental piece that he composed over this stretch came fairly soon after his return from the Prussian journey, and it carries at its heart such a forceful response to the sense of impasse that he had been left with that it ends up turning it into resolution and resolve.

A genius leaves behind family and friends and entailments, and then has to make amends by being a genius. The K581 clarinet quintet in A is exhilaratingly open both about his continual need for adventure or even transgression, and about the need for reconciliation that accompanies it. He had spent some of the summer writing two of the quartets for the Prussian monarch, and we can assume that he nebulously intended to continue the set. But the undertaking lapsed about a year later with only one more added, and the three so-called 'Prussian' quartets add few unique vistas to his chamber music. Plenty of their music is suave and some is radiant, but they lack the charge of argument or the spring-loaded sensuous energy of the quartets dedicated to Haydn. The summer of the burgeoning revolution in France may not have been the right time to orient the future of music around the stringent and stiff-necked versions of power installed in Berlin. Mozart followed current affairs keenly; he may have been waiting for a way to give creative vent to whatever mixtures of eagerness and reflection came from the exciting, unsettling news from around his old Parisian haunts. By early autumn his instrumental imagination had been fired by someone who tallied with the more wayward and unofficial elements of his sensibility, the great clarinettist Anton Stadler.

In the quintet the clarinet throws new possibilities of both chaos and order into his chamber music style, and hence new and much needed possibilities of regeneration. Stadler may have been the single most talented representative of the great Viennese boom in wind playing, and dropping him and his clarinet into the skeins of the quartet form was a way of keeping faith with some of the decade's most deliciously progressive trends, while also insisting that new tasks and pleasures were needed. A progressive style stays progressive by messing with itself. The clarinettist's messy personality was formative for the quintet, and he and Mozart shared a rich and complex history of friendship and collaboration that by now stretched back over many years. Stadler was part of the rambunctious travelling party that went with the composer at the very start of 1787 on his first trip to Prague. His nickname of Nàtschibinìtschibi was the most elaborate of all those doled out by Mozart on the journey; being called Schamanuzky probably struck the composer's dog Gauckerl as getting off lightly. Within the two men's shared past the vast and extravagantly pretty K361 wind serenade loomed large; Stadler was a key participant in the first public performance of sections from it, but his drastically gifted presence on the scene must have been crucial to making its grand mellifluousness even thinkable. One listener was so impressed by this music as starred in by Stadler that he nearly ran out of adjectives, announcing that it was 'glorious and grand, excellent and sublime'. Mozart's wind pieces from earlier in the decade had already probed and transfigured the world of garden entertainments and their twilit delights, and great flickers of the ambience of those works return in the quintet's lyrical colours. But the intricate calibrations and the sometimes nearly shattering speed with which they move around on the later piece's canvas owe even more to Mozart's faith in this musician, and doubtless too to some high-wire, mischievous desire to challenge him. The wind instrument's fusions of grainy mellowness and flighty agility pull against how the string group might otherwise proceed, but they thereby bring the veering amplitude of style and sound that makes the work so almost graspingly inclusive.

Stadler was a difficult character, something of a grifter and at best evasive, and he was especially untrustworthy in financial affairs. The mercurial and tricky virtuoso seems to have been a sort of alter ego in whom Mozart could contemplate aspects of his own waywardness; he was unsteady enough in his habits that the composer ended up lending him money. The quintet is one of Mozart's great essays in reconciliation, and much of this must stem from how much Stadler provoked in him the drives that make forms sway and curve and buckle. The same drives make the more forgiving sides of his formal imagination all the more compelling. Audience members would have known that they were in for something inventive from the sheer ungainly bulk of Stadler's instrument. Another woodwind aficionado named Theodor Lotz had been involved with the composer and the clarinettist for a few years, and the favoured product of their collaborations was a new version of the clarinet with an augmented sound box to extend its range of low notes. The quintet opens up an audacious tension between a tight chamber music style and the sorts of expressive largesse and blippy, flaring brio that this instrument thrived on, and needed if its presence was to make sense. All that we know about Stadler suggests that his playing would have doubled down on these qualities, but that he was also vastly capable of dramatizing their roles within a larger effort of coherence. The more mischief there is, the more richly it will be resolved. It is something like the basic law of Mozart's structural imagination, but in a piece like this atonement is made to feel how closely involved it thus is with the transgressions that it constantly chases. The quintet is not just musically inventive; the very sounds that it makes must be unprecedented as it fathoms what it has to say. Of course this increases the premium on resolution too.

The clarinet teases and disrupts the strings as much by its sometimes basking vocal ebullience as by its jolting plastic vividness. Maybe moving back to engage with the quartet form for a possibly rather indifferent Prussian king had made Mozart impatient with how rapidly even his own chamber music style could feel merely polished. Stadler released his need to do something different. The little twists of asymmetry that give Mozart's orderliness its grist and sparkle are pushed towards incoherence throughout the quintet by the mismatches among the instruments. Surges of highly vocal melody from the clarinet threaten to break searingly away from the structural tension that unequal phrase lengths are normally meant to impart, but the physique of Stadler's instrument also lets the piece pull downwards into regions of blurting innovation that the other parts strain to encompass. Two worlds collide in this music, the world of dense structural argument that Mozart had taught the strings to thrive on and the clarinet's world of variously languid and chirping melodic fluency. Instead of undoing each other in this collision, the two worlds overlap and merge and indeed reinforce each other. It is a piece voluminously aware of mismatch and disorder, but it learns to turn them into sources of structural attainment and surface lustre. In the second movement the clarinet's most melodic impulses are given space to sing out in, while the strings come as close to an accompanimental role as any allegiance to chamber music can let happen. By contrast, in the finale Mozart uses the theme and variations form to downplay both the mellifluousness of the clarinet and any need for thematic extension, sending the five instruments into a copiously jumpy range of often textural options for relating to one another. Throughout the work the clarinet keeps breaking away from the world of the string parts and then rejoining it and being forgiven by it, and in turn stirringly enriching it.

Was Mozart ever liable to feel a need to be forgiven for his own mastery? The first recorded performance of the quintet was, aptly enough for a work so preoccupied with the morality of music, as part of a charity concert held by Vienna's official society of musicians. It was a vast occasion organized to raise funds for the families of musicians who had died in poverty, a possibility often close to Mozart's heart. The splendid decor of the Burgtheater set the scene for the concert, and the poster promised that over 180 performers would be participating; the audience would have included many of the city's residents who were most attuned to the questions animating the quintet. Having a piece so ostensibly small in scale at the heart of such a grand event could only have made sense because the quintet is in so many ways rivetingly grand itself, and suspense may have been generated in the first place by the very fact that a chamber music work was going to try to impose itself. A starry violinist called Joseph Zistler was engaged to lead the strings, so the clarinet may have been able to provoke the right sorts of sometimes suave, sometimes volatile skill in its player's colleagues. Mozart probably played the viola himself in a private performance not long afterwards. A further twist of context comes with the fact that the composer never succeeded in joining the society himself. A few years earlier he seems to have tried fairly hard to do so, but the bureaucratic process defeated him. Maybe some flickering reluctance to belong among a broad mass of musicians intervened too.

Constanze thus could not rely on the society's assistance after his death a couple of years after this concert. Already in 1789 Mozart may not have known whether to be grateful to Vienna for the achievements that it continued to make possible, or to forgive it for not making more of him. The Bastille had been stormed in France that summer, and the whole culture's powers of critique, polemic and blame went into arcs of proliferation that only sometimes clarified anything. The rights of man were leaping out from the pages and conversations that had endlessly disputed such matters, falling onto the hard ground of history. As Joseph's reign wound down with shaky inexorability, Vienna was a richly dubious vantage point from which to assess what was happening; it is worth recalling that Marie Antoinette was the sister of the Habsburg emperor. Mozart told Puchberg during that summer that 'sheer grief' kept him from composing at all, as his wife's health dangerously gyrated. While Constanze tried to recover in Baden, he mainly stayed in Vienna, and a letter that he wrote to her sometime in August suggests that the separation was troubled. Mozart emphasizes that she has no need to be jealous as he carries on with musical life in the capital, but then cautions her rather cryptically against being overfamiliar with others herself, while insisting that he likes it when she has fun. He asks her to forgive him for being so frank.

Mozart was writing on the eve of departing to visit her in Baden. But what is interesting is the reason that he gives for why he will need to be back soon in Vienna. A revival of *Le nozze di Figaro* was coming at the end of the summer, and a changing cast meant that he was writing some new music and would have to attend rehearsals. So his major musical experience over the rest of that moody and unclear summer was to engage anew with an opera that was deeply caught up with Parisian political debate and disquiet, and which makes forgiveness its crucial hinge. The concert at which Stadler unveiled the quintet to the world did not happen until the festive season in late December. But the composer finished the work around the end of September, recording its completion exactly a month after the start of the opera's new run. The quintet thus emerged out of a period of renewed immersion in a work where forgiveness is both the key to and the only possible exit from a world of frenetic, revolutionary multiplicity. Reconciliation is the bedrock faith and the formal endpoint that the whole drama's multifarious twists on everything from psychology to style depend on; it gives the characters their freedom by allowing them ways back towards one another. The same energies play out in the intense interest that the quintet takes in its own wild varieties of expression, shape and sound. In the finale, the clarinet dares the surrounding strings to keep up with its impudent, riffing shifts between moods and rhythms. But the ways in which they do so give the movement the sense of order and balance that resolves its tumult into charm, and grace. Mozart died a couple of years later, without Stadler having repaid the money that he had borrowed with impressive insouciance from his financially beleaguered friend. Not long afterwards, the composer's estate would be sued by none other than Prince Lichnowsky. The three 'Prussian' quartets that Mozart did complete were published commercially after his death with no dedication to the king who may never have had any real interest in them at all.

23

Couples

Così fan tutte

Listening to two sisters languidly discussing love in an idyllic but maybe sultry garden, we suddenly hear something extraordinary happen to the word 'amore'. The duet near the start of *Così fan tutte* is known by the tender words between the sisters with which it opens, 'Ah guarda, sorella'. Fiordiligi and Dorabella are gazing at the portraits of their respective suitors in their lockets, and wondering whether proposals of marriage are in the air. But what they do not know is that the opera has begun a few minutes earlier with a different deal involving them being struck. Their two suitors have got into an argument with the philosophically inclined old libertine Don Alfonso, and his insistence on the fickleness of women has so affronted them that they have ended up wagering on the fidelity of these beloved sisters. 'È la fede delle femmine / come l'araba fenice'; Alfonso believes that the faithfulness of women is as impossible to pin down as the Arabian phoenix. In the wager each of the younger men must try in disguise to sweep away the fidelity of his friend's beloved. The open question must be whether the older man's argument has somewhat titillated them too; the merriment surrounding the bet feels tinged with excitement at the thought of losing it. So the opera's title comes from Alfonso's conviction that all women act as he believes. It means that they all do the same thing. The work's beautiful sting will be that it ends up not exactly proving him wrong, but making his rightness about the sisters seem pointless. The opera redraws the perspectives from which questions of fidelity and infidelity and wooing and trusting and being in a couple and so endlessly on are even imagined.

The seething musical extrapolation that takes hold of the word 'amore' as the two sisters sing is an early clue to the opera's larger purposes, its interest precisely in finding love to be stranger and wider than its characters have grasped. The duet is full of the svelte and winsome romantic clichés scattered across Mozart's century, as the sisters catalogue the sweet mouths, noble countenances and combinations of martial fieriness and graceful sweetness that distinguish their beloveds as surely as they did many others. But Da Ponte's libretto has already begun shifting the ground beneath the feet of such notions, as the context packs the word for love with frisky narrative tension. The sisters are not just singing love's praises as the word floats and stretches in the air, but calling for its punishments to be heaped upon them if they should ever prove unfaithful. The playful lavishness with which the word is treated, as these two melismatic voices embrace it and each other so elaborately, already pulls in ambiguous emotional directions. Maybe the sisters already guess that more possibilities are rolled into its appeal for them than their current states of idyllic confidence can contain. Because the men are motivated at least superficially by the wager, the women are the characters who most entirely carry the pulses of erotic desire in this opera, in one of its many nice twists on the normal machinery of amorous narrative.

No other opera may be so aware that every couple is indeed an ambiguity, and is so not least because the erotic forces that bring it together can also violently or subtly disjoin it. No other opera may reveal what a churning, depersonalizing machinery for the transformation of desire musical drama can contain, yet insist so strenuously and movingly on humanizing that process after all. The syllables of the word for love hover and dilate here because they are already full of the switches of mind and mood and all the expansions of meaning that the drama will so intimately track. A set of orchestral lines that are rich enough already is joined by a sequence of deftly shivering little blurts in the horn writing, and the effect is to give momentary sonic form to the incessant appetite for further meaning, suggestion and resonance that moves through the opera. Lurking menace and panicky farce alike start to hint at their presence in such sounds. Elements of sensuous overspill within the garden's idyllic mood and gleams of vocal rivalry between the sisters are all pulled into simmering focus by this slow musical zoom in on the word 'amore'. Ferrando has a recitative much later where he tells us 'in qual disordine / Di pensieri e di affetti' he now finds himself, but the chaos of thoughts and feelings that he describes was waiting within the erotic all along.

An appetite for layers and ambiguities is good to have within a world where desires are becoming complex, jagged and frenetic, and prone too to the types of paralysis or entropy that live on the obverse of too much excitement. The opera is a landmark in the lineage that carried Europe from eighteenth-century libertinism to Flaubert's vehement take on bourgeois marriage and passion in *Madame Bovary* and beyond, but Mozart and Da Ponte keep more interpretations of desire in play than others generally managed. The complex, slightly ragged reinvention of his emotional life that getting married had meant for Mozart had transpired by routes that must have made composing the opera voraciously charged. A pair of sisters and some tricky questions concerning the transfer of affections had come to dominate his own erotic life and marriage over the decade or so before he wrote it. Of course, the sisters who croon so richly about love in *Così fan tutte* do not correspond in any simple way to Mozart's pair of Weber sisters. The composer's vision here of the reshaping of emotions and identities is far too broad for such equations. Rather, the opera itself prismatically reshapes parts of his own erotic identity and marital story.

The composer fell idyllically in love with Aloysia Weber around his twenty-second birthday, during the months of 1778 that he spent in Mannheim as part of the tour with his mother that took them through southern Germany to Paris. She was the elder of the two Weber sisters with whom we are concerned, not just beautiful but a terrifically talented young singer. Vocal music was at the heart of her entanglement with Mozart, as was Mannheim's sophisticated musical milieu, in which her family was nicely nestled. The sisters' father seems to have been something of an intellectual highbrow, but at this time was mainly working as a bass singer at the court theatre. The Weber household must have carried engrossing echoes of Mozart's own family, and its paterfamilias may have re-called Leopold's combinations of attachment to prestige with cultural sophistication; the young composer may have liked him all the more because his hints of mordant bohemianism were closer to the surface. Mozart's first letter back to his own father about Aloysia in January 1778 is touchingly strategic; he tries to bring her up casually but also to make the best possible impression on her behalf. He is not sure whether he has mentioned the daughter of a 'certain Herr Weber' before, but 'she sings superbly and has a beautifully clear voice'. In fact she sings 'exceedingly well' even some of Mozart's most 'horrific' music, and is 'well respected' at least by all 'kindly thinking people' too. Furthermore 'she is allowed to visit the Electress' at all times of day 'because of her excellent manners'. Leopold responds with 'amazement and horror' in one letter back as he realizes how lavishly this young singer could derail his plans. Mozart was meant to be scouting Europe tenaciously for the openings that would fulfil his destiny of achievement, renown and not least income. He was not meant to be falling in love with a lovely throat.

The young man's infatuation meant that Aloysia got not just training and advice but bespoke compositions from the greatest musical figure of her or any era; but we should consider the situation the other way round too. In many ways Aloysia Weber may have seemed in 1778 a better proposition for future success than her staggeringly gifted but sometimes plainly hapless suitor. Her talent was raw and conventional, but it was large and its conventionality promised money; the waning of the era of the castrato meant that female singers were increasingly unchallenged for commercial tug. Mozart's own talent pointed grandly in all too many directions, any number of which he would doubtless emphatically but rather changeably describe. He will in any case have gained immensely from the ardent match that occurred between his passion for Italian vocal styles and his erotic response to this excellent young woman. One of the uncanny things about a talent like his is how often it ends up learning more from others than they do from it, no matter how utterly it ought to be the other way round. Surges of vista and possibility power the flurry of letters back to Salzburg where he sets out his new, unlicensed vision of a future with her, featuring tours to Italy and Holland and Switzerland in an itinerary not guaranteed to convince his steely father. Doubtless finding something that could complicate and stretch his relationship with Leopold was part of this period's fraught joy.

The capacity of its composers and audiences to learn from female voices was one large way in which the eighteenth century learnt to pay at least some attention to the experiences and authority of women. But much of what Mozart ended up getting from Aloysia was in the needling creative charge left when she eventually rejected him. He went to stay with the Weber family in Munich at the end of the year on his way back to Salzburg from Paris, but whatever reciprocity there had been in the erotic sparkle between them had dampened. The most vivid account that we have of what ensued must originate from Constanze herself, the younger sister of Aloysia whom the composer would marry a few years later, and whose second husband would become his biographer many years in the future. In Georg Nikolaus von Nissen's telling Mozart returns to the Weber family circle after his time in Paris, attired in a smart French costume signifying his mourning for his mother, to be greeted barely even with recognition from the young singer. Mozart is rejected in this account so quickly and thoroughly that he merely catches his breath before going to the nearest keyboard, and launching into what may have been a rather meanly sardonic little song about leaving behind the person who rejects him.

Mozart did leave her behind too, equably enough, before finding her reinvented before his eyes in the person of Constanze when he reconnected with the family in Vienna a couple of years later. Something almost farcical tinges the letters in which Leopold hears the results; not only is he again considering what his father would consider a premature marriage, but a further Weber daughter is the target. His strategy this time is to play up the differences between the two sisters. So Aloysia is now revealed as a 'false, malicious person' and a mere coquette, while Constanze 'knows all about householding and has the kindest heart in the world'. In fact 'she does her own hair every day', a detail that does not seem to have placated Leopold. We may recall how ceaselessly Mozart's music makes its patterns and ideas reappear in new guises, so that sameness and difference are kneaded into each other.

Mozart and Aloysia worked closely together at various points in the years after he married her sister. She became one of Vienna's star sopranos, after all. But such collaboration is only the most obvious way in which his musical life had to become capable of bearing and transforming the pain of this rejection. Erotic passion comprises a central food of the Italian vocal styles that were in turn the basic nutrients of Mozart's music. But the voice whose feel for those styles he had most rapturously cared about had ejected him. No doubt the experience sensitized him to the places that loss and rejection and insatiability had always held within this music's vision of the passions. The freight of Aloysia's memory and presence was something that the composer and his wife both had to make their marriage capable of bearing; it is impressive and a bit uncanny how imperturbably they largely seem to have done so. Their marriage seems to have been a fraught, delicate improvisation that was also often enough delicious. During his travels in 1789 before he started composing this new opera, Mozart wrote a run of letters to Constanze that veers conspiratorially from careful reassurance to kooky shared humour, or from practical solicitude to playful sensuous yearning. In the summer of 1784 Mozart's sister had got married just over two years after his nuptials, and the little poem of teasing advice for married life that he sent her suggests some frisky confidence that he and Constanze were fairly good at it. Discharging them with delight can banish any fright that marital duties may contain, or so the ditty claims; besides, mastery of the situation will shift from husband to wife as day becomes night. Mozart's music can be so alive to the complexities of coupledom because it shares with couples the drive to make forms of order out of giddying mixtures of desire and freedom. It is like a couple in needing to make shapely sense out of the facts of sensuous intensity itself. Sometimes his operas feel close to being derailed by the sharpness of their attraction to states of eroticism and desire; but each time they use this threat to deepen their investigations.

In *Così fan tutte* Mozart found a story that gave a set of richly fluid metaphors to his own failures and transformations in the erotic sphere. The opera's two sisters are only partial doubles of the Weber sisters, and there are two men swivelling between them in this story. Don Alfonso adds another shadowy level of doubling to the men's psychic lives, giving voice from without to their doubts about their sweethearts, and in the end about themselves. Their own unfaithful urges do not fully belong to the men, but stream back to them under the unsteady cover of Alfonso's thesis of female faithlessness. A parallel role for the sisters is played by their maidservant Despina, whose chirpy erotic worldliness needles and channels their more wayward urges. Alfonso finds a sort of accomplice in her, and the original cast in fact featured two married singers in these parts. The opera cannot stop doubling; the two men assume disguises to test Alfonso's argument, and agree to switch the two sisters between them for the purposes of their false pursuits. Ferrando and Guglielmo spend much of the action as doubled versions of themselves that also represent aspects of their truest selves, as they pursue with apparent ardency a proposition that they claim to resent. We know that they will succeed, but not because we believe Alfonso, or because we think that the opera believes him. Rather, the success of his thesis is something more like the raw material that the opera wants to use in order to work up its own account of what love is, and what being in a couple means.

Mozart seems to have shifted his affections fairly expeditiously between the Weber sisters. He must have wondered what mutability on his own part made this possible, and then whether some equally unsettling loyalty to the first sister might have underpinned it instead. The sleek conviction with which the men can woo the switched sisters is one metaphor for what he had gone through and what he feared in himself. The agonized yet impetuous speed with which the sisters do indeed switch their affections is a second metaphor, but it also refracts and changes the meaning of the first, suggesting an unmooring of desire whose breadth and painfulness define how full of possibility it is. The opera obsessively makes perspectives slide. Nothing in the music either confirms or denies the different pulsations that seem to hover by the time Ferrando follows his friend's success by winning over his target. Maybe he succeeds because women really are fickle, or maybe these two were always waiting to be right for each other. Maybe by this point deep in the opera's second act Fiordiligi has begun to feel that something strange is going on, and that her sister's infidelity with the disguised Guglielmo has more implications than she has yet grasped. Mozart's music does not exactly say, and it will not confirm whether we should be taking all this in a spirit of fun or of plangent regret or shrugging philosophical acceptance, or of satirical or moral disdain.

Across the arts and especially in opera and theatre, the enlightenment spirit had brought polemical or didactic strains, and the ways in which Alfonso sets the opera up to test his thesis show him to be an enlightenment man. The spirit of the enlightenment is as much part of the opera as Alfonso himself. But Mozart's relationship to any simple vision of enlightenment lucidity and proof is as labyrinthine as the enlightenment became, and it is tempting to say that the opera tests testing itself, and finds that it does not want enough from the world. The music perpetually says that more is happening than these characters and even we in the audience can grasp; phrases move around among different instruments in rhythms that shift more swiftly and amply than the characters' desires. Responses to the opera have often been baffled as to why Mozart wanted to throw its musical riches into such a nakedly schematic narrative. But this mismatch is the point. Mozart's idea is that the story's thinness comes exactly from the diminished view taken by Alfonso of the ways in which humans do and do not belong to one another. Alfonso does win his bet; but his success seems grimly fatuous. His diminished philosophy of human affairs diminishes him, and he ends the drama a marginal figure. The opera's story proves his isolated point, but its wider forces of revelation and largesse contradict the terms of his perspective, and overrun his dramatic presence. Its rippling, probing music is the opera's way of keeping such contradictions in prismatic motion.

The word 'amore' in the sisters' duet is a trapdoor that swings open and draws the characters down and in, pulling them into discovering the real nature of their emotions. Mozart's music opens up here too, setting out with new amplitude the opera's world of brightly dreamy sound. It is the first number scored in the wind parts for the combination of two clarinets, two bassoons and two horns that ends up colouring much of the opera, a subtly dark-hued grouping that is ideally suited to painting layers of sonority and suggestion. Dilation and suspended time ooze out of this early passage into what follows. A sense of engorged stasis sometimes all but wholly displaces action, suffusing both the idyllic reveries of the characters at their most confident, and their states of confusion when their visions of themselves teeter. The writing for wind instruments is sometimes finely supple and sometimes all but overweening as it tells the characters that their desires are not what they think, almost becoming an extra protagonist in the story. A searing oboe melody windingly transfigures Ferrando and Fiordiligi in the second act just as she finally begins to succumb to him.

The sister whom Mozart married was a fine singer herself, though Constanze missed out on the high-octane rightness of her older sister's talent. She may also have been without the high-octane temperament that the age's star singers seldom lacked. We can assume that the composer would have heard the two of them sing together, and hence that the sound of the opera's sisters as their voices join is instilled with some dream version of memories of such occasions. It is worth pondering just how many musical settings of the word 'amore' had floated and gushed and whispered through the eighteenth century. We can imagine how many times Mozart had heard the word sung by this point, and wonder how often the experience had been tedious, sickening or icy. The opera does not want to abandon the word 'amore', but is unsure how solid it remains. We hear Dorabella learning to call love a 'ladroncello' and a 'serpentello' in one acutely nifty aria late on in the story; it is a little thief and a little snake rather than any sort of bland ideal. Further complex and delicious keywords from the century's opera and culture pour through the drama too, words like 'dolcezza' and 'fedeltà' and 'cor' and 'pietà' and 'voglia' and 'costanza', sweetness and fidelity and heart and pity and desire and constancy. The characters are often working out themselves whether they are using them sincerely or quoting them cleverly or brandishing them manipulatively.

If the two sisters turn out to be fickle, it is not in the end through deficiencies of love or loyalty or even moral passion. Rather, it comes from having so much of all these things. Psychological richness is one of the basic forms of Mozart's creative largesse, and the sisters must learn how to enlarge their takes on what the word 'amore' contains, how to get their lives to resound with more of their own capacities for responsiveness and change. The exquisite density of the opera's sound-world makes abundance light; the work has an adamantine silkiness. Of all Mozart's major operas, it has by far the most consistent overall sense of rhythmic pulse, and it is by far the most generically and stylistically stable of his major comic operas. All this gives it an enhanced holism of impact, bringing it across in a single, honeyed flow of music onto the hearing. Mozart's singular feel for what was, ambiguously, at stake in the disputes between comic and serious versions of opera was crucial to how he became the decisive operatic composer during this decisive period for the art. Elsewhere he oscillates rapidly between comedy and seriousness or throws them into stark juxtapositions, whereas here they are much more fully fused. In some arias he uses the bravura conventions of *seria* style to show how his characters cling to ideas of love or of themselves that are no longer fully meaningful; his parodies are so vivid and so full of psychic need that they verge on homage. But in the great second-act rondo that he eventually gives Fiordiligi, all the tides of grandeur and poignancy still waiting within *seria* style become sincerely and sumptuously available to her. No one has pursued further than Mozart a vision of operatic seriousness that can swallow frivolity whole.

Da Ponte may or may not have had a third collaboration with Mozart in mind when writing the libretto. External evidence strongly suggests that he did not, as Salieri apparently had a go at scoring the piece first. But the librettist may have been bargaining on some failure on the older composer's part to make headway; the whirling machinations and factors of precedence that made Vienna's operatic functionings so opaque never found a sharper diagnostician. The piece's supple psychological reaches certainly seem to call out for Mozart's amplitude and flexibility, rather than for Salieri's brand of thinner, choppier friskiness. Of course, Mozart's affinity with the libretto could have been highlighted for him if it became his by happenstance; the ways in which its substance spoke to him and its structures seemed ready for him may only have been giddily sharpened. The action works as an algorithm for producing different ensemble groupings out of its few characters, and Mozart's music can thus make itself a laboratory for investigating whether and how people and voices belong together.

Mozart was working on the piece during the later months of 1789 when his Figaro opera was successfully revived in Vienna, and around the same time he was producing on and off a spate of occasional or insertion arias in parallel comic veins. A fizzy inundation of versions of comic style had been driven across the music of the later eighteenth century by the light, bright brio of their outlines and contours. But the results were in constant danger of becoming insipid or merely skittish, or of sometimes veering off too far in the opposite direction, towards over-engineered attempts at force or novelty. In *Così fan tutte* Mozart digs deep into the inner life of a style whose reach he has already more buccaneeringly expanded. Comedy here no longer zooms endlessly outwards in search of new excitements; it turns in on itself in search of its centre of gravity. Mozart and Italian comic form by now comprise an established couple, and they must find possibilities of renewal deep within a relationship that has its own dense history. The opera has swagger and a lissome sense of fun, but it also ruminates and slows down and murmurs to itself. Its rich scoring shows Mozart probing and lingering over the flesh of the sound of comic style, as if some new reach of curiosity had opened in him towards something that he had already loved for years. By this point he and Da Ponte were an established couple too, and we can assume that their ongoing negotiations over structure or nuance fed the opera's intricate account of what bearing with other people requires.

Coupling and erotic life loomed so urgently within the eighteenth century partly because conviction and credibility were leaking away out of many of the larger institutions of public meaning. The diffuseness with which the enlightenment's critical ideas about the church and society and material reality itself spread and were understood across Europe created moods of scepticism that were all the more pervasive because they were so vague. The figure of the libertine took off because it could incarnate both the scepticism and the aimlessness; someone like Casanova did not even really need to disbelieve in anything. Creating *Don Giovanni* must have convinced the composer how pivotal libertinism was becoming, but *Così fan tutte* is then partly a way of dispelling its predecessor's allure. *Don Giovanni* had nearly spun apart under the pressure of its protagonist's deeds and meanings. In *Così fan tutte* Mozart returns to opera as if from the other side of the libertine adventure; the new piece traverses it more equably on our behalf, but it also moves smoothly beyond it. Its structural simplicity and its holism of style and sound are markers of this reversal. Ferrando and Guglielmo play at being libertines while seeming to themselves to stay faithful, and their numbers oscillate between a wayward seductiveness and an idealism that is sometimes mawkish and sometimes desperate. Their understanding of both these poles is gradually chastened. The libertine's taste for licence and instability could seem to be the century's best way of anticipating and surviving within the historical dissolutions that were emerging; at the same time he relied on the past models of structure and behaviour for which he felt contempt, being addicted to both privilege and repetition itself. Mozart's new opera was more slidingly responsive to the flux of desire than libertine literature could end up being, but it was also inventively committed to reaffirming integrity and structure. Music had already taught him more than anyone else has ever known about turning fluctuation into structure.

The characters are making efforts at understanding and forgiveness as the story closes, but there is a notorious ambiguity too. The libretto does not spell out whether the lovers return to their pairings from the opening, or make their promises to the vibrant couplings that the action has brought. Stagings need to make decisions, and the default has been the first option. But the other option at least ghosts it, as if the opera cannot stop opening up possibilities. A couple, in this rendition, is less a fact than a question. The sumptuous flexibility of the opera's music summarizes a century of erotic experiments across European culture, and limns a way of living in the world of restless, fraught coupling that was on its way. Alfonso turns out to be right that the initial couples can be disjoined, but the opera's deeper story is that these people are endlessly fated to versions of conjoining. Vital to the weight and steadiness that the work exudes, despite its speedy scale and flimsy story, is the fact that these insights are generated out of the basic stuff of the operatic art. Opera brings characters together on stage in endless acts of conjoining, endless different dispositions of togetherness and response, endless permutations of vocal alliance or juxtaposition. An aria is a slice of artifice that is also meant to overflow with sincerity and passion, and these characters discover how far their emotions and desires pour into conventional patterns, but also how restlessly liquid those patterns turn out to be. Cavalcades of lovers in love with the wrong people sing their ways through the century's operas, often in disguise, often confused by the disguises of others. The scenario let Mozart write an opera that is both a compendium and a distillation of its culture, one that brings eighteenth-century psychology to its furthest fruition and the brink of collapse. Its ending shows these characters far out at sea within the flux of their lives, unsure of who they are, and whether unsureness is paralysis or enchantment. Rimbaud wrote that a wise music is missing from our desires.

Mozart's life with Constanze was seldom straightforward; he was hardly a simple husband. A stony compulsiveness lurked within his sense of what his life was about, yet in other ways could be flighty, wacky or elusive. In 1790 he pawned the couple's silverware to finance a trip to Frankfurt for the coronation of the new emperor Leopold, showing his single-mindedness and ambition in ways that might have both maddened and impressed his spouse. Yet once the trip was underway, he met the opportunities that it brought with mixtures of wilfulness and irresolution that made the whole enterprise seem baffling. As Constanze fretted in Vienna, her husband was flitting between addresses after failing to organize proper accommodation, while being all but brushed off by the royal circles. He finally performed at a single concert that was yet another 'splendid success from the standpoint of honour but a failure as far as money is concerned'. Attendance was low, owing to such rival attractions as displays of manoeuvres by the Hessian troops and some prince's lunch party. One count who did go recorded that the last piece was left out, because everyone got too hungry.

We can imagine Constanze's frustration and disbelief. But a dense intimacy drenches the letters in which Mozart notates these episodes for her. He tells her when his mood is as 'cold as ice'; another time he tells her that he would like to give a kiss to a particularly nice carriage that he finds himself travelling in. He tells her how ugly he finds medieval Nuremberg, as a man with enlightenment tastes should; but he is pleased that during his initial journey north only one innkeeper thoroughly fleeced his party. The letters jerk from stark effusions about how much he misses her, through mordant complaints about skinflints, to intensely mundane financial details. A comprehensive and flexible version of coupledom emerges; his constant psychic volatility runs through the endless reports like an electric current earthed in her. In one letter he tells her how one tear after another had fallen on the previous page that he had written, but then describes the 'amazing number of kisses flying about' as he starts another. He catches three of them and they taste delicious.

Couples must carry more of their own meanings when the public sphere buckles or blackens. The trip to Frankfurt came during the same year of 1790 as the first staging of this great opera of erotic togetherness and distance, and the composer appears to be relying ever more on Constanze; he seems ever more immersed in the rhythms of their marriage. Classical comedies of all sorts are so keen on getting couples together that the ongoing flows and tussles of actually being in a couple can seem left out. The density and holism of the opera may finally suggest that this is what really interests it; the action's brevity and speed fill the piece with a paradoxical sense of duration. Its story wheels through motifs of seduction, courtship and weddings, but its fusions of steadiness and flexibility make it feel like the work of someone captivated by his own capacity to stay in a couple. He had known the Weber sisters for about a dozen years by the opera's first performance, and he had poured that span into its music. The links between the two pairs of sisters form a node of access by which his actual emotional life could swim into this opera with new directness, revealing itself more fully in the work's dream vision than open articulation could have allowed. At the same time a snappy analytical acumen fills the opera.

As these characters resume the original pairings that may now seem so capricious, or push on into the new forms that may seem even more so, the opera holds proliferation in balance with containment just as any coupling of lively modern psyches must try to do. Constanze's life had already immersed her in a world of artistic talents and freethinking sensibilities; possibly only someone deeply sympathetic to such drives and capable of sometimes shrugging off their claims could have survived life beside Mozart. Their life together was itself a shared artistic creation. One friend visited the pair during these years of financial confusion, and oscillating illness on both their parts, and found them dancing together to keep warm in the absence of money to buy firewood. Playfulness and deep need come together here as for Mozart they often did.

A couple for Mozart is a complex and composite thing. It is full of disparate and erratic elements of memory and fantasy, and fragments of lost aspects of the self or of the beloved. It teems with metamorphoses of itself and of the two people within it, and of people from the world outside it too, who turn up deep within its inner world. The man whom Aloysia married not too long after she rejected Mozart started a painting of him later; the portrait was not finished, but appears to be the most telling likeness that exists. Joseph Lange was mainly an actor, and his intimacy with drives of performance may have helped him to see his brother-in-law clearly. But perhaps his closeness to some of the deeper vectors of Mozart's life helped the picture combine breezy intimacy with a certain tender restraint. Mozart is not wearing a wig, so we can assume that he is portrayed in a domestic setting, working away at some musical task which the unfilled lower portion of the canvas should have revealed. Its lack of finish may in fact help the image; it is an informal glance at someone elusive, someone whose intensity of concentration is overlaid by a steely pleasantness. Mozart does not look up from his invisible task of, or joy in, music. Constanze must have had such a sight often enough. The otherness of other people is one of the best things about them and one of the worst.

24

Unsure Fun

Die Zauberflöte

Eighteenth-century culture was rocked by the suicide of a young man who was splendidly talented and rather oddly attired. His death could scarcely have shocked Europe more if he had been a real person. In fact he was the title character in *The Sorrows Of Young Werther*, the short, tenderly explosive novel published in 1774 with which Johann Wolfgang Goethe threw his name to the front of the culture. The book is as good a candidate as any work across the arts to mark the shift, or the explosion, of that culture into a modern version of itself. Werther's clothing may seem a finicky detail to fix on, but the novel makes it an emphatic key to the expansively strange new strains of sensibility that he embodies, and it was vital to the craze for the book which saw its imagery reproduced in all sorts of knick-knacks and porcelain. He is in his signature outfit when his body is found, 'wearing a blue dress coat with a yellow waistcoat' to the end, and it has accompanied him into his peculiarly mortal version of immortality.

Werther's death resounded so shockingly partly because he inhabits the same doubleness in the period's culture as Mozart's music. Clothes matter here because courtly display and aristocratic finery were losing their grip during the period; no longer was a figure like Marie Antoinette able to sway public conviction by the glamour of her costuming. No reliable codes for fashion had yet replaced these fading ideals, but Europe was beginning to feel its way towards the necessary reinvention of style that a figure like Beau Brummel would crystallize, a generation or so later in England. Werther's outfit is a colourful but finally intensely sad flare pointing to his combinations of promise and lostness. Mozart and his father often discussed enhancing his impact with stylish outfitting, and having to dress in the cheaply smart regalia of a liveried servant had been one of the aspects of a court career that he most vividly resented. Joseph's unstinting efforts of economizing and reform made the aesthetics and the meanings of clothes especially loaded in 1780s Vienna, accelerating moves away from courtly lavishness, but also making those moves seem ways of according with official values. The city was awash with tailors and milliners, so we can assume that these factors were fought out with hyperactive visibility. Men were already starting to dress more in the stripped-back English style, though women still looked restlessly to Paris. Mozart's insistent dapperness seems to have hovered between a yearning for some new version of sartorial panache and a sometimes almost exaggerated loyalty to the recent past with all its glitz and swagger. Perhaps the exaggerations with which he cut a dash gave him an odd sort of balance, endowing his need to sell himself and indeed his real attachment to some vision of courtly élan with stretchy or parodic hints of other attitudes. New possibilities of selfhood often show up on the outsides of people first.

Goethe's book arrived in a hectic burst; maybe writing it took a bit longer than the six weeks later recalled by the great man, but a sense of passionate immediacy scorches the novel. He was still living at the time back with his family in Frankfurt, and the work is charged with the combinations of drifting uncertainty and creative abundance that beset him, in a milieu that thronged with literary ideas but gave them no clear direction or place. Werther is drifting when we meet him between careers as an artist and as a diplomat in the service of a minor German court, a young man whose culture has filled him with charm and ambition that it then cannot use. His reaches of mind and sensibility are really as much the vehicles of his downfall as the disastrous infatuation with the eventually married Lotte that becomes the novel's story. His unmoored situation drives his passion for her, and that passion eats up the world, deteriorating into obsession and the despair that brings his suicide. Beneath the pathos of the novel's stark narrative, another story was vibrating about the violent forces within the cultural landscape.

Goethe's novel sets itself among the idyllic homes, gardens and landscapes of rural Germany, but this radiantly backwards world becomes suffused with loss and phantasmagoria. The book is a farewell to eighteenth-century culture which is full of its levity and emotional freedom; the pathos partly comes from the novel's knowledge of how fragile they are. Werther's passion for Lotte is powered by her immersion in rural rhythms; we famously see her all but transfigured in his eyes as she prepares bread and butter for her family. So he falls for the very qualities that mean that she will not break this world apart for him. In Goethe's vision idyllic simplicity and the paradoxes of desire haunt one another. The possibility of happiness besets as much as it animates Werther and the novel alike, as if the eighteenth century could madden itself by the promises that it held out.

Links of all sorts trace between the novel and Mozart. In one central episode Werther parallels the composer by fairly scandalously disentangling himself from the humiliating restrictions of a career at court when it fails to help him forget his infatuation. He lacks a credible world to act in; his downfall moved readers so intensely because the lurking frailty of their entire world was thus hinting at itself. Mozart's music found ways of giving expressive shape to the same predicament and so of staying drastically alive. Werther gives himself only his impossible love for Lotte to orientate himself by, until finally only suicide remains. The novel balances the fate of an entire symbolic order on the shoulders of this young man, and gains its stealthy heft as a result. It can feel unclear whether the book is about narcissism or is overrun by it. Werther could not achieve a creative act but Goethe did; writing the novel turned him into who he would be, and he thrived tenaciously for most of the rest of his life as a celebrity grandee ensconced at the little court in Weimar.

Music plays a subtly central part in Werther's story, and Lotte's connection to it resonates through her character. She appeals to Werther not just as an idyllic exponent of the kitchen and the hearth, but as a soulmate and a cultivated equal. The set piece that brings them together uses the ambiguous place of music in this social world to open up the fissures within that world that make their story lethal. Werther goes to a seasonal dance as part of Lotte's party, while her fiancé is away on a journey. He describes how the talk on the way there already turned to dancing, and how he 'feasted on her black eyes' while she spoke of her passion for it. The atmosphere of whirling sensuous intensity that takes hold of the pair when the dancing kicks in drives the rest of the novel. Dancing transfigures Lotte and makes 'her whole body one harmony'. Other couples fall away as the simpler dances give way to the complex lures of waltzing. Werther has crossed over into a passion that will kill him, but while waltzing with Lotte he 'was no longer a mere mortal'.

Goethe makes his character a sacrificial victim to the death drive spinning within his culture, but he gives him all the pleasures of culture and its death drive first. Among the cultural questions pulling across the later eighteenth century in German domains was the status of the boisterous, unruly rural dances that had increasingly displaced the hierarchical rhythms of French styles. The historical career of the waltz is large enough to suggest the vast vistas involved; the free contact that waltzing couples spun into was not just a bracing rebellion against French cultural constraints, but an opening onto social chaos. The novel finds in dancing an image of this society's attempts to make new patterns of experience for itself, but also of the perilousness and frailty of such attempts. A thunderstorm is summoned by the novel's febrile tension to break up the dancing, and Werther and Lotte are pulled into further intimacy as they shelter. A rush of warm scented air strikes them and he kisses her hands. In this episode, music both binds the social world together and reveals factors of destruction glaring within it. Giovanni's ambiguous cry of 'liberty', proclaimed at another dangerous dance party, can be heard lurking within this thunder. The different consequences of their different interpretations of their desires make Werther and Giovanni mutually eclipsing brothers.

The period in which Mozart and Goethe worked threw them into bewilderingly expanded flows and tides of cultural impact; anyone who could stand the bewilderment could reap the expansion. Goethe's novel has an imaginative intensity that both delighted and shocked a society bent on cultural ingestion, one filled with readers and amateur musicians and with debates on aesthetic taste or on the meaning of the enlightenment or the future of theological study. If Mozart's music synthesizes styles and inheritances with an ease that can be disquieting itself, Werther shows more clearly the weariness or disdain that polyglot cultural receptiveness can harbour, as he inveighs against the shallow controversies by which the educated distract themselves. His mutating states of mind turn the book into a quick, unsettled anthology of eighteenth-century attitudes, rather as Mozart's symphonies seek to incorporate emotional variousness itself into their workings. The novel then became such a success within this world of engrossed cultural appetite that it was thought to have brought a spate of imitation suicides. The Habsburg regime briefly banned it.

The rest of Goethe's life was fuelled by a protracted argument with himself as well as his culture about what he had done in writing it. The novel is often associated with the *Sturm und Drang* tendency in German culture that the young Mozart's music dipped towards during the 1770s too. But Goethe's writing no more settled into any cult of unruly fervour than Mozart's music did, and the book analyses its culture's restless forces too acutely to be part of any campaign that they were sprawling towards. Bringing his protagonist to suicide let Goethe delay deciding whether the job of culture was to announce or to repudiate the maelstrom of mood and critique that propels Werther. His novel's renown did bring him to perhaps the most splendidly odd scene that the whole history of literary criticism offers, the meeting with Napoleon decades later when that avatar of the spirit of historical convulsion claimed to have read it seven times. He insisted that Werther's motivation was not properly thought through; the great author discovered that an emperor too can combine fandom and nitpicking. But then Goethe's novel was also the favourite book of the monster in Mary Shelley's *Frankenstein*.

The art of the novel was richly suited to this veering period and its packed, fraught culture. A novel is not a novel for the sorts of reasons that make a sonnet a sonnet; it does not have to contain a certain number of lines or to rhyme according to some fixed scheme. Rather, novels have at their disposal a loose and fluctuating mass of formal and stylistic options that they can grab hold of, discard or reconstrue as they go about making themselves up. Mozart and Haydn likewise made sonata form yield vertiginously various ways of deploying and exploiting some general principles about how tonal organization could suggest musical argument, or delineate it or be played off against it. Porousness, flexibility and an often amused distrust of fixed schemes were the markers of the novel and of sonata form alike; loosely defined but urgently conveyed processes of impetus and development and sheer forward momentum drive interest and conviction. Haydn's symphonies describe the eighteenth century as keenly and hungrily as *Tom Jones*. The novel grabbed hold of European literature over this period because as a form it was both satisfyingly monumental and tensely sceptical, and sonata form met the same need in music. No one got to tell the novel in this period what a novel was, and the likes of Sterne and Laclos then discovered that this matches the experiences of their characters, as they are dunked into enigmatic worlds as adventurers or victims or investigators. Character is not destiny in this period; it is a way of navigating a world from which destiny has vanished. Mozart's music likewise sends its themes and patterns out to seek their fortunes in a fluctile world, and they are both changed and revealed by what they undergo.

Werther's elusion of the fixed narrative markers that marriage, surrounding community or public career would provide means that he carries with special, princely clarity the psychic freedom that novels purvey. He is a character in a novel, and he is an emanation of some basic novelistic ethos. He seeks to invent himself out of a larger and more turbulent idea of what selfhood and culture can be, but the turbulence heightens into deadlock. Sacredness has fled from the containers that gave lives their shapes and meanings, notably the institution of wedlock, and begun to flood out into the reckless territories that romanticism would wander around in. Goethe constructed an experimental shadow self in Werther, pouring much of his own psychic darkness into the vessel of the character before moving on to the career of cultural omnipotence that the book launched. Something uncanny invested the radiance of his fame from the beginning; the book pulled into focus an entire historical landscape of change and uprooting from which he then held himself aloof with cerulean haughtiness. Whether or not there really was some epidemic of imitation suicides, the stories persist. The book can feel like a cultural monument and like a raw wound.

Right to the end of his life Goethe vastly admired Mozart, and he seems to have realized early that the composer was defining their epoch. He settled in Weimar after the place's eccentric, pensive ruler Duke Karl August offered him an exalted role in his little fiefdom, and a lot of his fitful efforts there to weld together the arts with large political purposes centred on the court theatre. The dash that Mozart's 1782 'seraglio' opera cut as it began to be staged all around impressed him mightily, after he had overcome some resistance to what can seem cartoonish in its vigour. In January 1794 Goethe opened a staging of *Die Zauberflöte* that became the most performed production during his volatile directorship of the theatre. He even set out later in the decade to provide the opera with a sequel. But his progress as a writer for the theatre was beset by a mania for fragmentary attempts and unrealized projects that swallowed up this instance.

Why were these two artistic titans thus aligned by such a veering amalgam as *Die Zauberflöte* offers of high musical artifice and low theatrical spectacle, of lofty didactic fervour and deliriously popular comedy? One answer is that the opera's extravagant mishmash of styles and drives represents with whirling precision just how complex and unlikely the basic projects of both men had become by the last decade of the century, as they both sought ever more inclusive, agglomerative versions of their different aesthetic endeavours. Perhaps getting *Così fan tutte* to the stage in 1790 had already made Mozart feel that his dazzling, fraught partnership with Lorenzo Da Ponte had run its course; the opera's smooth engineering has the feel of a richly final achievement. But the emperor Joseph's death and the accession of his gnarlier brother Leopold were unpromising for Da Ponte, in whose memoirs the new emperor takes against him with efficient briskness. Orsini-Rosenberg was soon enough dismissed from his position, after having been at the organizational heart of Viennese opera throughout the pair's collaborative glory years. The librettist suggested that he and Mozart should go to London together, but his friend had already embarked on this vastly new operatic project. Da Ponte claims that Mozart asked if he could think about it for six months; it is true that he hated letting people down point blank.

The composer had known and admired the great impresario and comic actor Emanuel Schikaneder for many years, and they had worked together tangentially over a decade earlier, a little while before Mozart's move to Vienna. In the meantime away from Vienna Schikaneder had put on his own production of *Die Entführung aus dem Serail*. But choosing him was still a surprising swerve, and suggests just how richly or maybe chaotically open the cultural field must have seemed to the composer at this point. Choosing him brought a return to the German 'Singspiel' tradition, and this meant interspersing the music with spoken dialogue, rather than using sung recitatives to link the major numbers. The shift was momentous for Mozart, because he and Da Ponte had worked so hard to achieve an effect of continuously unfolding musical drama in their operas, an aim that the quality of all-over compositional consistency in *Così fan tutte* had brought to a climax. He was faced with two choices, and characteristically he took the more drastic one of working with the grain of the dilemma. Instead of masking this loss of consistency by building musical ensemble numbers up to be as large and homogenous as possible, or by simply minimizing the amount of spoken dialogue, he wrote an opera that revels in its own gaps and veerings. Different musical styles at vastly different levels of sophistication flow through the score, turning disparity into a new and giddily charming principle; tender ariettas and full-throated blasts of Italianate vocal stylization jostle with stringently sober chorale references and clever bursts of counterpoint. An extreme concision in the treatment of each idea or passage becomes the necessary complement of this cornucopian energy, and its impact on Goethe must have been driven partly by the virtuosic virtue that the opera makes out of fragmentation and stylistic change. Its spoken dialogues extend sometimes to impressively discursive lengths. The fairy-tale elements of quest and initiation that dominate the plot are so familiar and broadly based that they can be pushed and pulled around with a centrifugal goofiness.

Goethe's novel had seemed fairly literally revolutionary, and during the period of its reception he was himself caught up in some of the inchoate but prodigious strains of revolutionary opinion that pushed through many artistic and philosophical circles. By the early 1790s the ongoing and ever more complex thunder of the actual revolution in France was enthralling and horrifying the culture, and Mozart's response was to write an opera that is itself full of shock, breakage and reversal. In fact *Die Zauberflöte* turns these forces into drivers of nimbleness, jocularity and an extravagant imaginative generosity. France's revolution was an apogee for some enlightenment hopes and drives, but it also entrenched and strengthened advocates of reaction and mystique across Europe; the extravagant deftness of Mozart's opera lets it incorporate aspects of both sides of this fissure. The work carries a strident openness to popular experience at its heart, and this means for one thing finding voluble nutrition in the real circumstances of its nature as a work of theatre. Working with Schikaneder meant moving away from the gilt-edged world of official or even high bourgeois Viennese culture, and works like this were not staged in the city itself. His version of culture was based in life on the road with its unpredictable perils and needs and its glib shifts from place to place; he often must have had to match behind the scenes his renowned improvisations on stage. The new types of audience afforded by Vienna appealed to him, but his shows were done in the suburban theatres which were exempt from the licensing, censorship and taxation in the city's official precincts. Mozart's opera is exuberantly determined to open itself at every point to the actual life of this sort of populist theatre, to the rowdiness and silliness of the sort of troupe that Schikaneder helmed. So even the earnestness of Tamino's trials by fire and water in the second act is invested with popular, lurid theatrical delight, and the scene exploited the expensive new types of stage machinery that such theatres ran to for their most whizzbang effects.

The Freihaustheater that Schikaneder ran was less elaborately decorative than court opera houses and their imitators normally aimed to be, but it was pragmatically geared for novel types of spectacle, and it suited a rambunctious and unpredictable theatricality. Tickets could be cheap and performances crammed, and it could get hot and sweaty even before the show started. Performers get chances to unleash their own traits or routines from all the toing and froing between speech and singing in this opera; we can all but hear embedded in the music's veering rhythms the whirring of cumbersome stage effects or the conspiratorial laughter of bit players watching from the wings. Mozart scored a risky success in the middle of October when he arranged for a carriage to take two of the grandees of official Viennese music to a performance of this radiantly bizarre opera, a pair that was made up of Salieri and the singer Caterina Cavalieri who was his mistress as well as his favourite soprano. She was a veteran of Mozart's Viennese productions, but the two of them may have baulked at going out to a show in the suburbs, teasingly or otherwise. Getting them there a few weeks into its run and recording Salieri's fulsome approval must have been very pleasing, and helped Mozart to feel that he really could piece the drives and loyalties of his art and his life into one flexible and bold mosaic. *Die Zauberflöte* overthrows official Viennese music but carries off its highest and most delicious spoils. Modern culture often makes progress by way of a rage at culture.

In the three Da Ponte operas libertinism is the great threat that spurs morality on to reinvent itself as a more copious and vivid enterprise. But the intensities of individualism and scepticism flung up by this investigation were hard to control. By the end of his opera Giovanni's solipsism has rendered him all but incomprehensible as a dramatic character, while the gyrations of desire in *Così fan tutte* produce a work that merges the most acute psychological realism and the most delirious improbability. In *Die Zauberflöte* the composer wanted a different sort of amplitude, a generosity of reach that would extend from its packed stylistic pluralism to its frantic determination to entertain. Mozart had liked the work of Schikaneder and his troupe for years, so collaborating with him meant engaging with a broader sense of his own past and its pleasures and involvements. The Freihaus was one of Vienna's more venturesome attempts at a new vision of modern urban living. It was a sprawling complex of buildings and houses, featuring its own church and inn along with workshops; a pleasure garden lay alongside the theatre. Since Schikaneder and many of his troupe had apartments within it, their lives of rehearsals and performances and showbusiness bohemianism must have spilt over into the surrounding communal world. Working out there seems to have brought Mozart a wider, bendier sense of connection to the cultural possibilities around him. The intensity with which his works of the later 1780s often probe their relationships with the audience and their own techniques gives way in the opera to something loosely porous to the general life around it.

It feels as if Mozart wanted to fling greasepaint right onto the notes of the score as he wrote. Lingering attachments on Da Ponte's part to correctness of taste may have subdued this side of him. But the ribald imaginative vitality of *Die Zauberflöte* has another aim too, one that in some ways may seem to contradict the opera's waywardness, but in others intensifies it. Throwing itself into broad spectacle and silly humour allows the whole thing to pull hard towards a more didactic moral earnestness than Mozart's previous dramas claimed. The farcically endearing birdcatcher Papageno would be too loopy to survive in any other Mozart opera, and Sarastro's stately homilies would be too relentlessly noble. *Die Zauberflöte* does not just get disparate forces to coexist, but makes them all need one another. Breadth and mixture had always been keys to the love of the real in Mozart's great dramas. But here they have been exaggerated so that the most downmarket slapstick and the most high-minded speechifying offset and irradiate each other, and at every turn the music exacerbates the starkness of the drama's disjunctions. The imaginative leap is intense even by the composer's standards. He must have looked at Schikaneder and resolved, not just to make the most of the chance to create a more popular confection, but to get the great entertainer's exuberant vulgarity to license and to fuel an equally exuberant moral fervour.

Two anxieties plague opera fans particularly, though they can bounce around within lovers of the arts more widely. One is the anxiety that the whole enterprise is simply too frivolous; the other is that it is too pompously serious. Mozart had spent the 1780s engaged with every flicker of possibility and experiment that opera could offer him, and *Die Zauberflöte* in effect at once absorbs and defies both these worries; the result is something both hilariously silly and lapidary in its moral injunctions. Rather than seeking a style of its own that can pour its elements of popular song and contrapuntal learnedness and so on into a streaming fusion, the opera reaches for something broader and stranger, a distinctive sound-world that all these switching facets end up mapping. No one who loves the opera can fail to recognize this sonic world; its resonance comes from building itself out of such inconsistent particles. It is sparse, voluble, intensely coloured, speedy, capable of bursts of sweeping orchestral grandeur, but often nimbly minimal in its use of its resources, as well as full of bouncy echo effects between voice and instrumentation, and often given to soloistic playing in ways that now depart from Italian obbligato style.

The story too is famously full of inconsistencies, one of which supplies the title of the opera. Tamino's magic flute gets him through his ordeals, but it was given to him by the followers of the Queen of the Night too early on in the narrative for her to have emerged as the real villain. One temptation is to turn this into some subtle philosophical argument about the relationship between goodness and her sphere of evil and illusion, but the temptation must be resisted. *Die Zauberflöte* is indeed philosophically acute, but its acuity goes far beyond allegorical niceties, taking us instead into a sphere of rampant mutation. A lot of what we find there is conceptually ragged and capricious, or dramaturgically untidy, and some of it is repugnant; the treatment of the villainous Monostatos indulges racist stereotyping in ways that the giddy vitality of his characterization feeds off but cannot efface. Mozart shows the eighteenth century at the end of its tether in this opera. It turns out to be a place where his imagination can thrive, by taking skill weirdly close to heedlessness and frenzy. A cartoonish velocity pulls the opera onwards, but the characters keep nearly losing themselves in the sheer fulsomeness with which the musical numbers plumb their own distinct modes.

Stark lament and exuberant delight and expository sobriety come and go. It is a work in which fun turns out to contain unsureness and hence succeeds in bringing a renewal of earnestness. Its leaping textures keep it open to its own extreme compositional freedom, and to the exuberant ethical freedom of at least its main characters.

Its skittish compendiousness allows Mozart to be surgingly original while also broadcasting his love of conventions. 'Welch' unbekannter Ort' is Tamino's exclamation early on, as he recovers from a fainting fit to find himself in a strange place, and sees that the monstrous serpent that had been pursuing him has been killed. But the really strange place that we all find ourselves in is opera itself. Mountains part to reveal celestial thrones, magic bells force troupes of villains to dance, and two men in black armour with fire burning in their helmets explain how to reach heaven. Mozart's music shifts and gleams and hesitates by turns, is itself sometimes celestial and sometimes bristling with armour and sometimes earthily fun. His hand moves across the paper as he composes as if it could hear his whole culture flickering in the sound of writing. The playbill that survives from the first performance at the end of September 1791 makes a point of mentioning that the composer would conduct it that evening, no doubt playing keyboard continuo in the midst of the big orchestra that Schikaneder's version of showbusiness ran to. Perhaps Mozart's presence was needed to guarantee some unity amid the piece's teeming sounds. Around twenty performances followed in October, and even in November the noted Viennese music lover Count Zinzendorf remarked on the huge audience, though his diary entry then calls it an 'incredible farce'. He should have meant it as praise, but he would have had to grasp all the other things that the opera was.

A strangely costumed character in *Die Zauberflöte* is rendered suicidal by the pangs of love too. Of course Papageno does not go through with hanging himself, and his costume's array of feathers and birds suggests the elements of fairy-tale comedy that his vocation of birdcatcher brings. He introduces himself by singing his famous, sprightly aria 'Der Vogelfänger bin ich ja' just after the prince has found himself rescued from the serpent, and he then accompanies him through many of the opera's ordeals and trials. But this does not just mean that the sombre story of initiation is broken up with a stream of goofy or mordant jokes. Few fairy-tale allegories can feature a central character who flunks his tests as wholeheartedly as Papageno proceeds to do, but his failures have none of the consequences that moral consistency would suggest. It is nicely unclear whether in the end he is united with his beloved Papagena because Sarastro has decided that the trials did not really matter, or as some odd reward for how charmingly and wholeheartedly he fell short. If he is in some ways Tamino's inconsistent double, the echoes between the characters are made even fuller and even more glitchy when the beautiful princess Pamina comes close to suicide too in the belief that the latter has rejected her. Suicide is both a joke and not a joke in this opera. But these two scenes are so uncanny because they press to the drama's surface the destructiveness and fragility that its cosmic imaginative flamboyance must be tied to. Goethe spent much of his life writing his rampantly cosmic version of the Faust story, maybe the most expansive treatment in modern culture of how close to destructiveness intense creativity comes. Maybe the kaleidoscopically free montages in *Die Zauberflöte* emboldened him. Mozart was long dead when he told a friend that he wished that the composer could write music for his great project.

The famous coloratura runs in the great second-act aria 'Der Hölle Rache' are all but violently dazzling as the Queen of the Night inveighs against Sarastro; the aria starts with a crash of orchestral playing that avidly reconquers the furthest reaches of the *Sturm und Drang* tendency. But the aria's splendour slides destructiveness and creativity together here too. All that she sings is both entirely humourless and luridly immoral, and the aria should be an antithesis of the drives within this most humorous and moralistic opera. Yet what she does with her voice, as she fuses an almost gaudy mellifluousness with stubborn and abrasive rhythms and crackling dynamic shifts, turns the aria into the fullest blazon of the opera's uncanny, prismatic vision. Perhaps this is just the opera's richest inconsistency. Mozart and Goethe both had to keep trying to get sheer creative largesse to outrun the feel for destructiveness that it may always be close to. *Die Zauberflöte* points deeply into but also far beyond the ferocious hopes and drives of the political world that was emerging around it. The aria has a celestial levity for all its bravura demands and fierce psychological bleakness.

Werther's illicit passion for Lotte is a double image for a sensibility that knows that it wants a new world but cannot work out how to make one. His is an imaginative freedom that victimizes itself by yearning for domestic norms that it also refuses. *Die Zauberflöte* is a wheeling vision of imaginative freedom as such in which all artistic conventions are thrown in the air and exuberantly rearranged, yet it is passionately devoted to ethical norms. The shattering of language in the regal villain's aria is answered by the gently extravagant assaults on the first syllable of his beloved Papagena's name that the tender and mainly jolly birdcatcher Papageno launches when he relinquishes his noose and is finally united with her. The opera constructs a version of modern culture that is deliriously inventive and tenaciously honest about loss and anger, but also solidly crafted and broadly based, and drastically pleasant. Goethe's later career as a sort of one-man cultural Olympus and the plenipotentiary of the Weimar court bewildered some who recalled how incandescent his emergence had seemed. But the opera that he evidently loved envisions identities in which inconsistency, jaggedness and reversal are the routes to wholeness. Early in October 1791 Mozart tried to tell his wife in a letter what it was like for him to witness opera-goers rapt at his creation; 'one can feel how this opera is rising and rising'. Its success is still succeeding in pleasing him some days later in the last letter that we have from him.

25

Indestructibility

Requiem

We sometimes become different versions of ourselves when we listen to music. In the moments before a concert begins, the audience can often be felt readying itself, as people shed parts of their characters that might get in the way. The same feeling of imminence can come to someone sitting alone, as the tray holding a disc slots into a machine or as the internet whirrs. Listening deeply can feel more like losing than gaining something. Maybe we seem as transient and strange to music as it seems to us.

Sometimes a piece uses this feeling of hush and imminence to achieve a particular dramatic impact, or gives it shape by interrupting or responding to it. Mozart's famous and uncanny K626 *Requiem* seems to absorb its listeners' states of expectancy into its own haltingly momentous unfolding as it begins. Its layers of richly scored, densely woven sound rise gradually out of the slight but oddly urgent accompanimental pulse with which the opening 'Introit' movement announces itself. The slow clamour with which the choir enters then draws into itself the quiet processional momentum of the strings and the floating harmonies of the winds. The music wants to generate itself out of the mood of flickering suspense in which listeners meet it, and the sweetly falling phrase that follows offers itself as a further interpretation of that mood or a further way of absorbing it. It tells us too how intimate the requiem will remain; the whole has a stark grandeur, but also directs itself with an almost clamorous tenderness into the inner reaches of whoever listens. Of course, in the eighteenth century requiems mostly expected their listeners to be grieving. But then in any audience there is normally plenty of grief to go round.

Mozart's requiem is sure that grieving means living, however; the work is overwhelmingly vivid. Partly this is because it engages such a complex array of styles and textures, moving among them with a speed that keeps our reactions flexible, vivacious. The writing for the four solo singers seldom gives any of them a sustained melodic sequence to unfold alone. Instead they weave among one another's lines, completing or revising one another's thoughts or harmonies as they go. Likewise, the solo passages generally switch and intersect very briskly with the choral sections, while the writing for the chorus shifts and veers so dramatically that it often feels highly soloistic itself. The requiem is filled with slippery, jagged momentum. Listening is both carried along by this motion and unsettled; the work keeps that feeling of suspense alive, rather than providing some tidy or fixed musical object. No one listening to this music feels at home in it.

The work came into the world already fragmented. A cultish pathos has long invested the artistic fragment in modern culture, and there is something paradoxically perfect about how it pervades a work here that concerns mourning and that is so associated with its composer's own death. The requiem's swarming styles and textures heighten its ragged sense of lost connections. But what meets us here is something whose fractures and jolts make it all the more whole and all the more itself. Fragments testify to indestructibility as well as to the workings of destruction, and the jumpiness of this music is driven by an aim of achieving wholeness, a desire for a newly comprehensive version of musical style. Music is always made of the ways in which time tears itself apart but also of the desire to hold time together; it is partly this that makes it resonate so richly within a period of rupture like the late eighteenth century. The weird symbiosis between its inner dramas and the circumstances of its creation has ended up making Mozart's requiem about as dense a meditation as can be imagined on wholeness and fragility and their shifting interrelations.

Let us deal with a few of the famous facts. Not all of the requiem's music was written by Mozart. The only section that he wrote out in a fully orchestrated score before his death was the 'Introit'. Its other sections all required at least some contributions from others. The story of how he came to undertake a requiem setting in the first place is indestructibly appealing, no matter how many times the basic and somewhat base facts behind the mysteriousness are explained. A messenger in dark clothing really does seem to have arrived in July 1791 to commission the piece from Mozart, and he probably really did refuse to name the source of the commission. Not much of this may have had anything like the significance that anecdote and myth have since bestowed, and it may have been pure pantomime, but this should not blind us to the power of the myths. A certain Franz von Walsegg turns out to have been behind it all. The Alps overlooked the castle ensconcing this odd Austrian count, who would commission music for his small court and then pass it off as his own. Whether this masquerade took many in seems less probable than commentators suggest. Because he wanted to keep a piece's real origin obscure, figuring out what happened here had to wait until the publication in the twentieth century of a manuscript that amply explains the farrago; it had been biding its time in a provincial archive. But Viennese musical culture was so sophisticated, gossipy and disillusioned that it must be unlikely that the truth about Walsegg was unknown. Imposture was rife in this world, but so was its unmasking.

The count's beloved wife had died in February and he wanted a mass to commemorate her, so the stakes were high for this job. Michael Puchberg was a close associate of both men, and very possibly the person who suggested that this special commission went Mozart's way, having been his long-standing creditor and confidant. It seems unlikely that he would have kept Mozart entirely in the dark about its weird origin. But there would have been plenty of other ways to find out. Walsegg was linked to Vienna's business world, and a likely object of gossipy curiosity. Composing such a score in ignorance of its destiny would have been largely alien to Mozart, and the staggering forcefulness of the music that he produced suggests instead that his imagination may have been fired precisely by the sheer strangeness of what he knew that he was embarked on. Mozart would hardly have failed to see the absurd side of writing music of such intensity for some silly ruling class specimen to blag about, and he knew how to find absurdity stimulating too. By this point, he knew his way around these aristocratic egos better than anyone.

Of course, the requiem has been inspiring cranky theories for centuries now, and this may be yet another. Mozart's fatal illness at the end of 1791 was sudden, rapid and confusing, and the weird circumstances surrounding the requiem became caught up in the atmosphere of distress and opacity around his death. He became seriously ill around the middle of November, as winter approached and the nights lengthened; early symptoms seem to have included terrible swellings in his feet and hands. He had probably been working on the requiem for several weeks on and off, and nothing about the piece suggests that it came easily. During much of October he had been without Constanze, who was having continued treatment in Baden, and the run of *Die Zauberflöte* preoccupied him. His letters to his wife were cheerful enough as the opera's popularity became clear, though he may be trying to bolster her with thoughts of hearty pleasures when he reports having 'just consumed a delicious piece of sturgeon'; he has just sent for another slice. But accounts which must have originated with her of the period later in the month after her return suggest that by then physical weakness and at least some psychic malaise had set in. Vienna was sunk in a stormy and oppressive autumn.

Perhaps Mozart really did never know anything about who wanted the requiem; perhaps there is some truth to the stories about some paranoia provoked in him by not knowing, as his health worsened and the days shortened. The requiem's fitful, nearly ragged multifariousness layers tumultuous episodes with bursts of calm or plangency as periods of wavering health can, and as an autumn of turbulent weather can too. Conjectures and speculations fill the houses of the seriously ill just as they have thronged our accounts of his last weeks and of the requiem ever since. In fact the music here is magnificently conjectural too, as the piece sends out its stylistic hypotheses about life and death and redemption. Years of scrambling travel and rushes of work had probably weakened Mozart's kidneys, and he seems to have been killed by some combination of fever with renal failure; the contemporary medical confidence in blood-letting may have been especially damaging for someone with his mixture of conditions. His sister-in-law Sophie helped to make him a special night-shirt once he became bedridden, because moving became so difficult that he needed something that could be put on from the front. A new quilted dressing gown was also supplied so that he had something comfortable for when he got up, and she says that 'he made it plain that he was greatly delighted'. But he probably never wore it.

After his death in the depths of a night during the first week in December, Constanze was left with fewer debts than she might have feared. But there was less money than the crammed and successful last couple of years might have led someone who did not know the couple well to expect; the successes were in fact rather scattergun, and their affairs were reliably diffuse. The fee for the requiem was not something that she was prepared to forego, so she decided not just that Walsegg should get a completed version, but that it should seem to be entirely of Mozart's own doing. She enlisted a little gang of the composer's close associates to help her with this intrigue, and we cannot know how far their extensive contributions were guided or not by instructions or drafts. Hints of weird comedy accompanied this most sonorous piece as it set out into the world, the situation echoing those eighteenth-century tales about tables being turned and deceivers deceived. The count who wanted to claim it as his own was himself hoodwinked as to vital aspects of its authorship. His countess would be delivered to eternity by shatteringly beautiful music that was laced with layers of imposture. Mozart's era never fused play and loss more bizarrely.

The largest part of the work on the requiem not securely attributable to Mozart was carried out by Franz Xaver Süssmayr, a pupil and assistant of the dead master's who had also become a good friend, and inevitably a butt of his jokes and teasing. Constanze seems to have only slowly conceded that he was the man for the job, and it is a fine question why this was so, if we consider what a plausible candidate he was. Süssmayr had been close to the composer during the period of the commission, had been widely immersed in his sensibility and working methods, and continued to be involved with the family after his death. Years later she claimed that she had been angry with Süssmayr over some issue that she did not or would not recall. A love affair between them has been suggested, unimaginatively.

A further mystery is just how cogent Mozart's requiem became and remains in this haphazard, mismanaged version. Two centuries and more of performance and speculation and alternative versions have only underlined how almost incredibly happily Süssmayr's involvement worked out. He was in no danger of turning into a master on a Mozartian scale. Considered in isolation from the whole, a passage like the 'Sanctus' can seem remote from the sorts of blazing poise that Mozart's style had become so casually capable of. But heard within the larger sequence, its blocky choral writing and its harmonic staunchness augment and play off the sharp shifts of texture surrounding it, and the anguished variousness of style throughout.

Of the other sections with no origin in Mozart's version of the score, the 'Benedictus' may be the most intriguing. It opens with interplay between the solo voices that is so delicate and suave that we can easily want Mozart to have been the origin. On the other hand the style here has struck many as too distinct from its surroundings to have been meant for them by Mozart, since its directness and its lightness of sound give it a feeling of the galant, cutting it away from the older church styles that thicken around the passage. The 'Tuba mirum' section comes directly from his hand though, and a stark stylistic swerve arrives there too, centring this time on soloistic passages for the trombone. The trombone writing is nimble and playfully brassy as well as powerfully expansive; it breaks loose from the thronging textures elsewhere in the requiem, but its almost skittish opulence adds to the general sense of a proliferating world of sound. It is the whole piece's ravenous drive towards stylistic inclusion and reinterpretation that such objections fail to grasp, and the likelihood must be that Mozart at least made the suggestion to his sometime pupil of what he had in mind for the

'Benedictus' section. Maybe the composer pointed him towards the exercise book in which its possible origin has been found, in a teaching example devised by himself. Constanze said later that she handed over to Süssmayr numerous musical jottings unexamined after her husband's death. The important thing here is how well the stylistic shift pushes forwards the layered, twisting drama of the whole sequence. Süssmayr is surely behind the wan, unpithy way in which the initial themes play out, and the garishly wrong-headed 'hosanna' passage that forms a sort of coda to the section. But again little of this detracts from the piece's momentous overall drive. We can even feel that all the bumps and scars and wobbles that cover the requiem heighten its impact; a wildly elusive formal freedom is working itself out, and it rewires these nice issues of craftsmanship and personal origin.

Frames of reference and historical phases crowd the requiem, yet it is trenchantly clear and swift. It is full of Mozart's characteristic desire to write music replete with all but desperate levels of invention, music charged with the newness of the moment from which it speaks. As the end of his life neared, he crammed as many different stylistic directions and forms of expressive potency as he could into a single musical edifice. Deepening illness was menacing his future, but creativity pulls the future hard towards itself, as artistic decisions quicken the present and fill it with intentness. But this is also a piece crammed with the past of music, one whose originality proceeds by way of an immersive attraction to the art's traditions. We seem to hear also the state of loss and confusion within Mozart's inner circle in the wake of his death, along with the murky process of wrestling with the meaning of his achievement. A lot needed to be organized and a lot mourned. The first phases of these responses were always going to be liable to be crude and glitchy.

It seems plausible on the whole to suppose that Mozart had far larger plans for the requiem than fulfilling the original commission, and that Süssmayr above all was party to those plans, and knew how the piece's drama was meant to gird itself together. At least this would make sense of how powerful his sections can be, of the ways in which their infelicities are so much less important than the twists that they give to the overall sense of excitement and variegation. Walsegg's commission provided the initial stimulus, and doubtless the fee remained a vivid motive. But some whirling together of factors must have taken hold in the dark first-floor apartment where Mozart worked on the requiem, bringing together everything that was both unsettled and expansive in his personal and artistic situations alike, in ways abetted by the massively ambitious scale on which he all but automatically thought as a composer.

Mozart may have decided for one thing that it was time to give a workout to his style as a church composer. Vienna was changing under the new emperor Leopold at a rate that was helped partly by the ways in which Joseph had already turned it into a city pledged to change, but partly also by the slumping atmosphere of the last patch of the latter's reign. The composer's associates spent 1791 being swept from their jobs one by one, but he was always inclined to be tenaciously flexible. He had already started to manoeuvre himself into a position to be able to take advantage of the high role that ambitious church music seemed likely to regain under Leopold, who did not share the anti-clericalism of his deceased brother. The requiem's craggy grandeur may have been part of some such strategy. It seems unlikely that Mozart would ever have let this music belong to the peculiar Walsegg in perpetuity, and he may well have contemplated specific audiences far beyond the count. If the piece were to become known as Mozart's during his lifetime, the ludicrous position of the count might have been in danger of exposure. England had been on Mozart's mind as an odd combination of spiritual homeland and lucrative market long before Lorenzo Da Ponte pointed to it as an escape chute from a changing Vienna; the debts to Handel that the requiem openly accrues may have been hopeful gestures towards an earlier Germanic composer whom London had enriched. After Mozart's death, Süssmayr's priority might have been to realize his mentor's musical intentions, while for Constanze the important thing was to push on with the immediate pragmatic aim of the commission. Maybe this was what brought the pair to disagree, and her reason for trying to bypass him. We need not ponder whether Constanze's later forgetfulness was disingenuous;

Mozart's wife deserves a fairer hearing on many issues than she has tended to get.

A requiem has to meditate on mysteries, and Mozart's requiem cannot be prised away from the speculations and mysteries that have surrounded it. The story of Walsegg's commission reprises the composer's tussling relationship with the old hierarchies of the aristocratic world. Within a couple of decades the requiem had shot away from that world, and been taken up as a wellspring of a new sort of musical culture, one obsessed with the prestige of composers generally and especially of this one. The lacerating directness of the requiem combines with its centrifugal variousness of style to make it uncannily open to that future, but the piece has spoken to any number of other cultural moments. Perhaps Mozart did not know exactly what he was doing or going to do with it. He may not have been much more at home with it than we are. Grimly familiar stories have him rehearsing the piece on his deathbed, and calling it a requiem that he was writing for himself. If he did say anything like it, he may only have meant that he was composing it finally for his own purposes. The likelihood is that he said no such thing, but evidentiary scruples are unlikely to affect the combinations of raw intimacy and tidal excess with which this music hits us. The stories that come down to us from the composer's circles about his last weeks and days are drenched with pathos. His life was being taken away by illness; maybe it was already being replaced with narrative too. Pathos is only one of the colours that the requiem strikes. Alongside it come a shimmering speed of thought and a flagrant dramatic chutzpah.

The work swivels among historical possibilities; it seems to contain one world in which music is briskly impersonal hackwork, and another in which it is inward spiritual striving. It also suggests that the classical style with all its strength and drama was edged with a certain labile frenzy. Mozart and Haydn especially had pieced it together with such heated fusions of historical logic and constructive energy that their achievements can seem as indisputable as mountains. But they had been able to do so because of the electrically intense fluidity and creativity of the musical scene that opened up across

Europe during the middle decades of the eighteenth century. Europe would soon hear in Beethoven how the very power of the stylistic models that they bequeathed him makes them splinter and founder. Something like this process whisperingly announces itself in the requiem already, as the work casts its ardent mind back into the musical past with all its variety and turbulence. The great link between the requiem and *Die Zauberflöte* is the almost brusque rapidity with which these two late masterpieces conjure and indeed fully develop such arrays of musical ideas and stylistic worlds. Moral density was already threaded into the opera's playful collage, but the later work's eclecticism is utterly frightening in what it shows of the tumult at the core of creativity. But pluralism can contain remedies for its own turbulence, and in the requiem they flow from how quickly the writing for the solo voices can become soaringly expansive. The solo parts are interwoven with one another with a richness that binds them into the large, nervous textures of the choral writing, but this also means that their flowerings into exuberance or tenderness are densely connected to the work's overall surges of tension.

Let us zoom in briefly on one moment to pinpoint how the requiem's dramatic force brings coherence and incoherence together. The text of the requiem mass is itself complex and erratic, and holds an odd place within liturgical tradition. So many composers have set it with such authority that we may forget what a wobbly institutional compromise it represents, as a survival of the kaleidoscopic eclecticism of the medieval church into the period of the Counter-Reformation and beyond. The upshot is a version of the mass adapted for the memorial occasion, but then also interpolated with the massive, searing medieval hymn text describing the Dies Irae, or day of judgement. Characteristically, Mozart lays maximum stress on the points of maximum uncertainty and strangeness that result. One crucial transition occurs near the beginning, between the second and third movements. The two movements belong to different strands of the textual whole, and Mozart opens his third-movement setting of the text about the day of wrath itself with a fierce emphasis on the alienness and starkness of the words, making them leap out and away from the exalted calls for divine mercy that comprise the second-movement 'Kyrie'. No instrumental introduction smooths this junction; the choir cannot wait to invoke righteous anger. The moment seems to turn staccato itself into a sort of structural principle, and the elegantly involuted version of fugal skill with which the 'Kyrie' ends gets chewed up by the charging momentum with which the new section sets off.

At the same time an uncanny consistency joins these movements, as if the same skin suddenly enfolded two very different bodies. The two movements end and begin sequentially with the same blazing unisonal texture; but the effect is to make consistency itself jarring. Since the heaving fugal exhaustiveness of the 'Kyrie' had made that texture feel like a hard-won climax, it is unnerving to find it replicated straightaway with structural implications that are very different, suggesting driving new forces instead. Two large bulks of sound end up abutting each other with an almost confrontational starkness. Stridently nervous accompanimental figures stalk particularly among the strings in both movements, and again the effect is double. The jittery phrases bind the two passages further together, but also inject both with more of the ongoing sonic restlessness that keeps the whole work spinning. The requiem casts its lines far down into the past of musical tradition and religious sensibility, but it also heightens the local impact of its every stylistic choice. It can feel as if holism and fragmentation had become allies; at the very end of his life Mozart found in the requiem text something both incoherent and fervent, something capable of opening itself to the most diverse stylistic choices and sponsoring the most extreme creative ardency. Comedic storytelling is often the source of the underlying dramatic concepts in Mozart's music, but in the requiem the drive towards reconciliation that normally comes from it is left behind, and whiplash speed and friskily teeming juxtapositions give the music its constant dramatic sharpness. Nothing very comic may result, but what does is flagrantly vibrant, multiple and faceted.

Was the work's magnificent casualness a gift that the composer's final illness brought him? It is certainly more than just the result of the fact that the illness killed him; he had been building up to a reckoning with the pluralism of his own artistry. During the 1780s the extravagance of his imagination was often ideally matched with a desire to create or to pursue normative visions, and the results were groups of works like his 'Haydn' quartets or the final three symphonies which can seem to offer themselves as templates even as they body forth the most extreme sorts of singularity. It is possible that the amounts of dance music that he was composing over the last few years of his life disrupted these equations for him, since the templates there were not ones that he had won or even really selected for himself. But the requiem is the culmination of what was one way or another a drive within several works during those very last years towards more extreme, exacerbated sorts of singularity or anomalousness. At the same time the requiem is a fulsome and pointed homage to musical history, and maybe this doubleness stems from Mozart's vision of his own position ten years on from his big move to Vienna. His definitive achievements across spheres from the concerto to comic opera had both exhausted the meaning of that move and established him as a giant with a reputation that went far beyond Viennese court appointments or the acclaim of this or that circle of grandees or connoisseurs. In a few of the works of the 1790s he composes with lacerating sorts of freedom and impulsiveness that suggest a new paradigm. No doubt they do not completely fulfil it. Maybe nothing could. Süssmayr claimed that he was following Mozart's own idea when he reused the fugal material from the 'Kyrie' for the work's final movement, and the effect is richly complex, as our ears recall at the very end what followed that music earlier. We half expect the whack of a Dies Irae passage that now does not arrive, except in a phantom echo that thus inflects the whole thing's final quietus.

Mozart's death was followed by entropy, but someone did organize a requiem service that was held a few days later in a church favoured by Vienna's artistic elite. Swieten had finally been sacked by Leopold II just as the awful news spread, and he set himself to help the composer's widow and circle. Mozart's actual burial was unceremonious in ways that have been much bewailed and much interpreted over the years. One of Joseph's reforms had been aimed at making funeral rites simpler and more egalitarian, and this is one reason why the composer's rather bare-bones interment does not have the implications of ill treatment or casualness that used to be imputed. But this gathering a few days afterwards did probably feature the first performance of at least some sections of the requiem. It is nice to imagine its fierce music now suddenly burning the air of the Viennese December. We can hope that Walsegg was thus pre-empted. But this music does not belong to any occasion, or to anyone. In fact it matches the austerity of Mozart's burial; large parts of the piece's power come from how ardently it chastens some of its century's musical styles. Its harshness and turbulence are partly driven by the desire to discover what would survive such a process. The requiem survived the fact that it was unfinished at Mozart's death partly because it was shot through from the start with such a dense will to test creativity to destruction.

Who was Mozart as he worked on the requiem? The enigmas of his own identity and of his professional future can seem the work's deepest subjects. His life ended in a state of suspense and ambiguity as he worked on it. Sometimes full recognition and vast success seemed around the corner; sometimes tricky rivalries, diffident audiences and financial woes seemed liable to stifle him. We know now how soon Europe would start waking up to what it had had in him. He may have guessed that it would; no one was more plugged into how musical culture moved than Mozart. His death accelerated the process, making it easier to recognize what he had been by dissolving the problem of who he actually was. No one, himself included, needed to worry any more about what he would do next or who should pay. The granularities of Vienna in late 1791 are all over the requiem, but it also stretches far across its culture and reaches deep inside it. Mozart had exhausted what someone in his culture could be, and the requiem mournfully marks that exhaustion, and creates a new and fraught freedom in the process. Its music combines loops of shattered introspection with an expansiveness that seems ready to eat up all obstacles and horizons. The piece does not know whether it believes in the future or not, or whether its gestures back to the generation of Handel and

Bach are homages or attempts to confront their imposing forms with a fissured cultural present. The image of Mozart at work on it on his deathbed has appealed for plenty of reasons, but one must be the almost violent glare of retrospection that the requiem gives off. Within it, vistas of musical history flash up just as someone's life is meant to do in its dying instants.

Drives to enshrine Mozart's status had been gathering pace among connoisseurs over his final few years, and knowledgeable listeners and even devotees could be found by the early 1790s in progressive cultural centres from Prague and Mainz and Weimar to London and Amsterdam. His requiem would transform church music over the following decades, and became a cult favourite within musical communities particularly, featuring in countless requiem services in honour of musicians early in the next century. Its harsh and opaque music was keenly embraced in the changed, shadowed version of Europe in which his reputation would rapidly blaze. The requiem came out of a strange period of glitchy hiatus in Mozart's epoch, as the revolution in France paused for thought about how far it wanted to go, and the great European monarchies tried to decide whether they should be pleased or horrified by the twilight of the Bourbons. Leopold had barely settled in as Habsburg emperor when he was confronted with the choice of whether he should exploit the weakness of the dynasty's inveterate western enemies, or seek to shore up the French monarchy in the interests of general conservatism and of the particular alignment that currently obtained by means of his sister Marie Antoinette. The decade would end up being dominated by the guillotine and Napoleon's ascent, and the vivid ardour of Mozart's requiem is built to survive on the darkening historical terrain that was coming. The sweet decorative glee of the eighteenth century has been purged almost wholly from the requiem, right at the same time as it drains from history. But the music does not pause to regret what it jettisons, because its commitment is to the passionate artistic adventurousness that it safeguards and extends even as it does so. The weather in Vienna late in 1791 was especially awful. As the nights lengthened around Mozart's dim apartment, he was composing something that would move beyond the ambiguities of his world and his situation precisely by grasping them so deeply. It would be finished by others just as his entire oeuvre was a bequest to others.

Something weirdly caustic can be heard in some passages of the requiem, as it tests the bare bones of the century's styles to see what remains. The 'Confutatis' features such trenchant shifts of rhythm and texture that even its passages of svelte beauty feel stark, as if all the culture's lyricism knew that it was being unhoused, and would need to sing henceforth with a new arduousness if it was going to stay resonant. The piece's basic phrase structures and its intimacy with formal norms are so secure that at times it can feel like the most typical product of its century's music. In the end this stylistic solidity is inseparable from the work's audacious swiftness. Musical impetuses that might have produced vast arches of structure in Sebastian Bach fifty years earlier, or might do so again in Berlioz or Bruckner decades later, are zoomed through here with startling hunger. In fact this meteoric speed may be something that the requiem has taken from the rococo. It is what allows the work to treat conventions with such strange mixtures of cursoriness and amplitude, as it meditates on its split historical world. At the same time it is part of the audacity whereby the requiem just outruns that world in the end. Great art swallows its world whole in order to outmanoeuvre it.

So let us move back a little to the great revolutionary year of 1789 before leaving the composer. The K574 gigue for solo keyboard may bring us close to hearing him improvise. It came out of Mozart's journey during that year in search of opportunities in northern Germany. Disorganization and frustration ended up pervading that quest, but Leipzig was where he seems to have found the most sympathetic audience, and he returned there in May, not long after first visiting. Leipzig was known for its connoisseurs, and the music scene there was less politically embattled than in Berlin. It had been the city of the great Sebastian Bach of course, and a cult of serious taste had formed around his memory. The final movement played during the ambitious concert that was the centrepiece of his second visit was the finale of the 'Jupiter' symphony, its deeply sprightly rethinking of fugal form doubtless reverberating sharply for listeners steeped in that tradition's grandeurs. During his earlier visit Mozart had sat at Bach's own organ to improvise. But this music is as much a teeming farewell to the past as a radiant and brusque renewal.

Mozart is likely to have based the gigue on something improvised, and the piece is full of the charms of transience. It is so brief that he could write it into the visitors' book of one of the most helpful of his Leipzig allies; the organist Carl Immanuel Engel had already conducted some of the earliest performances of *Don Giovanni* outside of the composer's purview. But real artistry feeds on transience as well as the eternal, using it precisely to stay fresh and strange. The gigue seems to owe everything to the great generation of Bach and the younger Scarlatti, and to the combinations of technical strenuousness with rapturous imaginative play that bound such figures. Its deep feel for the dances of the past gives it both a stunning garnish of freshness and a sense of enshrinement by tradition. At the same time its jabbing nimbleness ends up owing no one anything, and outdoing all examples by its sheer friskiness. It would be hard to dance to this jig, but if anything it has a surplus of dance energy, rather than a lack of it. Its rhythms shift and cross like light falling on rough water, as if all the levity of eighteenth-century dance finds itself faced with some suddenly choppy passages of the soul or of history, but then finds that it can traverse them without losing its kicks of tough pleasure. The music is bright and hard and soon finished. Vertigo is held here on a fingertip.

Europe would soon throw open the romantic period, and all the grace and happiness promised by the eighteenth century would come under as much devastating pressure in the arts as in politics and history. A new modern myth was already being assembled in the idea of the autonomous work of art; in this bargain artistic form would be allowed to revive these qualities, but at the price of a scission that would remove it from the world. Mozart moved right on the brink, driving into autonomy but still clasping the world. He kept creating. A piece like the little gigue is full of the muscular, skittish movements of his fingers upon the keyboard as they played; its feeling of fleshy animation gives it the toughness that it plays off against its brevity and giddiness. It is utterly anomalous and bizarre, and it is over before anyone can get a handle on it. But it is also just a delightful jig, whose brevity is a version of modesty. The piece is hectically minuscule, but it keeps loosely alluding to the vast spheres of the organ repertoire, as if the smallest possibilities could speak here for the largest vistas. A certain endless playfulness is what joins Mozart to permanence; listening to the gigue can throw us back with renewed clarity towards the requiem. The keyboard's sounds carry on dancing.

Sources

Mozart's ranging letters comprise the second most important source for coming to understand him, his musical work being of course the first by far. In their lively and suggestive translations by Robert Spaethling (*Mozart's Letters, Mozart's Life*, London: Faber & Faber, 2000) the attempt in this book to show the composer in motion found excellent assistance, and was much heartened by it too.

Other quotations come mainly from Eric Blom, Peter Branscombe and Jeremy Noble's translation of Otto Erich Deutsch's *Mozart: Die Dokumente seines Lebens* (1961), a titanic collation of documents and other materials relating to the composer (*Mozart: A Documentary Biography*, London: Simon & Schuster, 1990 [1965]).

Bringing Kant's essay 'An Answer to the Question: "What Is Enlightenment?"' into the book was greatly encouraged and skilfully aided by H. B. Nisbet's translation of it in Immanuel Kant, *Political Writings*, ed. Hans Reiss, 2nd edn, Cambridge: CUP, 1991 (1970).

Louis Crompton's *The Great Composers: Reviews and Bombardments by Bernard Shaw* (Berkeley, CA: University of California Press, 1978) collects some of George Bernard Shaw's music criticism, including that great gadfly and polymath's essay quoted in this book ('The Mozart Centenary', first published in *The Illustrated London News*, 12 December 1891).

Guy Debord's essential *Society of the Spectacle* is here in Donald Nicholson-Smith's fiercely crisp translation (New York: Zone Books, 1995).

H. C. Robbins Landon's *Mozart and Vienna: Including Selections from Johann Pezzl's 'Sketch of Vienna' 1786–1790* (London: Thames & Hudson, 1991) is the source for the treatment of Pezzl, and for the translations there by the author himself of selections from his writing.

Goethe's *Die Leiden des jungen Werther* has been gifted a forceful and lambent voice in English by Stanley Corngold (*The Sufferings of Young Werther*, New York: W. W. Norton & Co., 2012), on which this book's treatment of that amazing novel depends.

Scholarship of such terrific quality, and from so many directions, has fed whatever thinking this book can claim as its own that it is hard to know where or whether to begin listing them at all. But Michael Lorenz's website Musicological Trifles and Biographical Paralipomena (www.michaelorenz.blogspot.com) is such a singular resource, and the archival sleuthing that it records so revelatory, that it seems necessary to doff a special cap to him. Victoire Jenamy made her way into the book because of Lorenz, and the chapter on jokes owes much to him too.

In Cliff Eisen anglophone Mozart scholarship has a doyen who has made all sorts of fruitful marks on the field. Probably the single tome that has fed the most nutrition into this book, though, is his deftly updated edition of Hermann Abert's teemingly vast study of Mozart, which was originally published in Germany in 1923–24 (*W. A. Mozart*, trans. Stewart Spencer, New Haven, CT: Yale University Press, 2007). The result is a fusion of scholarly vistas that must be larger than ever, given the already high passion of mind and argument that suffuses Abert's book and has made it such a singular classic. Charles Rosen was working far later in the twentieth century when he wrote his once very famous study *The Classical Style: Haydn, Mozart, Beethoven* (London: Faber & Faber, 2005 [1971]); it may strike some readers as in dire need of updating, but my book owes it some defining debts. It remains a volume worth wrestling with, because it has both sweep and vim, and so at least tries to match up to what it is about.

Acknowledgements

So many years and so many odd turns have gone into the making of this book that it has been extravagantly reliant on its friends. An attempt to list them fully would be hard to conclude. The book has found more food in casual expressions of interest or encouragement than many may have realised; its subject must have often been the main reason, but we chew what we can. Certain names must be spelled out, however. In Adam Foulds the book had a friend whose own readers know him to have two of the best ears anywhere. Katherine Angel embodies the spirit of multifarious response to culture and much else that it has aspired to. In Rory Stewart it had a friend singularly able to remind it of the largest and most absurd strands of history. Winds of piquant support came from Lisa Appignanesi at a decisive moment. Above all the book found in Lara Feigel a tenacious advocate and an uplifting guide.

At Granta the book reached a team whose professionalism has been so careful, spirited and encompassing as to feel like friendship. In Bella Lacey it found an editor whose patience matched her scrupulousness and her richness of vision.

Index

A Note About the Author

Patrick Mackie is a poet whose work has appeared in *PN Review*, *The Poetry Review*, *The Paris Review*, and *The New Statesman*. A former visiting fellow at Harvard, he is the author of *The Further Adventures of the Lives of the Saints* and *Excerpts from the Memoirs of a Fool*.